普通高等学校少数民族预科教材

实用英语
语法与练习

主　编　付慧琳
编　者　何　杨　金海坤　李　俊　李智远
　　　　龙慧玲　托　娅　王丽丽　夏增艳
　　　　杨京鹏　杨　琴　张耀忠

北京邮电大学出版社
www.buptpress.com

内 容 简 介

《实用英语语法》全书共分23章,从语言学习的特点入手,首先介绍了英语语法所涉及的词法和句法。从第二章到第十三章为词法内容,以词性为主要脉络,用图表框架的形式对英语中名词、数词、形容词和副词、冠词、代词、介词、连词、动词、动词时态、被动语态、非谓语动词和构词法进行了全面系统的阐述。

本书结构清晰完整,内容丰富全面。每章节编排的配套练习和五套综合测试题均为百分制,涵盖了近年来语法的主要考试形式,练习采用填空、错误识别、单项选择、句型变化、完形填空和翻译等题型,便于学习和测试。

《实用英语语法》是专门为非英语国家的英语学习者编写的学习用书,也可以作为教师的教学参考书。

图书在版编目(CIP)数据

实用英语语法与练习/付慧琳主编. - - 北京:北京邮电大学出版社,2017.7(2022.1重印)
ISBN 978-7-5635-5134-7

Ⅰ.①实… Ⅱ.①付… Ⅲ.①英语-语法-高中-习题集-升学参考资料 Ⅳ.①G634.415

中国版本图书馆 CIP 数据核字(2017)第 156135 号

书　　　名：	实用英语语法与练习
著作责任者：	付慧琳　主编
责 任 编 辑：	徐振华　廖　娟
出 版 发 行：	北京邮电大学出版社
社　　　址：	北京市海淀区西土城路10号(邮编:100876)
发　行　部：	电话:010-62282185　传真:010-62283578
E-mail：	publish@bupt.edu.cn
经　　　销：	各地新华书店
印　　　刷：	北京九州迅驰传媒文化有限公司
开　　　本：	787 mm×1 092 mm　1/16
印　　　张：	15.25
字　　　数：	378 千字
版　　　次：	2017年7月第1版　2022年1月第3次印刷

ISBN 978-7-5635-5134-7　　　　　　　　　　　　　　　　　　　　定　价:32.00元
·如有印装质量问题,请与北京邮电大学出版社发行部联系·

前　言

语法是系统总结归纳出来的一系列语言规则,也是语言学习的必要基础和重要环节。通过掌握语法规则,形成英语逻辑思维能力,建立语法系统框架,从纷繁复杂的语言现象中领悟语言的基本规律,可以使语言学习达到事半功倍的结果。

为适应普通高等学校本科预科教学,满足学生需求,我们以教育部制定的《普通高等学校本科预科英语教学大纲》为依据,遵循语法教学的特点,组织了在普通高等学校本科预科教学中有多年教学经验的一线教师进行编写。本书贴近生活,注重实用性,既适用于教师教学,也可用于学生自主学习。

全书共分为 23 章,遵循语言从词到句的语法规则,分为词法篇和句法篇。词法篇共涉及从词性到构词法的 12 章内容;句法篇包括句式到直接引语和间接引语的 10 章内容。本书参照近年来的语法考试特点和变化情况,做到多层次、多角度、系统化的讲解,每章节中的例句均有译文,以便学生准确掌握。每章节后都有配套练习,练习涵盖了近年来语法的主要考试形式,采用填空、错误识别、单项选择、句型变化、完形填空和翻译等题型,让学生通过语言实践,将基本语法知识融会贯通,真正实现语法知识向语言能力的转化。

本书编排了五套综合性的测试题,用于复习和测试。配套练习和综合测试题均设为百分制,便于测试和掌握学习情况。

在全书的编写过程中,北京邮电大学民族教育学院的相关领导和北京邮电大学出版社的编辑及全体工作人员做了大量工作,在此向他们表示衷心感谢。本书编者编写过程中参阅了大量语法学习资料,结合自身在教学过程中积累的教学经验,认真完成了各个部分的编写。在此也对各位编者一并表示衷心的感谢。

限于编者水平和多种因素影响,难免有一些错误或疏漏,敬请广大读者在使用过程中提出宝贵意见,以待进一步改善和提高。

目　录

第一章　语法概论 ··· 1
　一、词法 ··· 1
　　（一）实词 ··· 1
　　（二）虚词 ··· 1
　二、句法 ··· 2
　　（一）句子的成分 ·· 2
　　（二）基本句型 ··· 3
　　（三）句子的种类 ·· 3

词　法

第二章　名词 ·· 5
　一、名词的句法功能 ·· 5
　二、名词的种类 ·· 5
　　（一）专有名词 ··· 6
　　（二）普通名词 ··· 6
　三、可数名词的复数 ·· 6
　　（一）可数名词复数的规则变化 ······························ 6
　　（二）可数名词复数的不规则变化 ··························· 7
　四、不可数名词 ·· 9
　　（一）物质名词 ··· 9
　　（二）抽象名词 ··· 10
　　（三）不可数名词的用法规则 ································ 10
　五、容易混淆的可数名词和不可数名词 ························ 10
　六、名词的所有格 ··· 10

第三章　数词 ·· 15
　一、数词的概述 ·· 15
　　（一）基数词和序数词 ·· 15
　　（二）基数词的表达法 ·· 16
　　（三）序数词的用法 ··· 17
　二、时间表达法 ·· 18

1

（一）具体时间的表达法 ………………………………………………………… 18
　　　（二）年、月、日的表达法 ……………………………………………………… 18
　三、小数和分数的表达法 …………………………………………………………… 19
　　　（一）小数表达法 ………………………………………………………………… 19
　　　（二）分数表达法 ………………………………………………………………… 19

第四章　形容词和副词 …………………………………………………………………… 23
　一、形容词和副词概述 ……………………………………………………………… 23
　二、形容词和副词的用法 …………………………………………………………… 23
　　　（一）形容词的用法 ……………………………………………………………… 23
　　　（二）副词的用法 ………………………………………………………………… 24
　三、形容词和副词的比较级和最高级构成 ………………………………………… 25
　　　（一）规则变化 …………………………………………………………………… 25
　　　（二）不规则变化 ………………………………………………………………… 25
　四、形容词和副词比较级的基本用法 ……………………………………………… 26
　五、比较状语从句 …………………………………………………………………… 26
　　　（一）同级比较句型 ……………………………………………………………… 26
　　　（二）比较级句型 ………………………………………………………………… 26
　　　（三）最高级句型 ………………………………………………………………… 26
　　　（四）其他句型 …………………………………………………………………… 27

第五章　冠词 ……………………………………………………………………………… 31
　一、冠词的基本概念 ………………………………………………………………… 31
　二、冠词的种类 ……………………………………………………………………… 31
　　　（一）定冠词 ……………………………………………………………………… 31
　　　（二）不定冠词 …………………………………………………………………… 32
　　　（三）零冠词 ……………………………………………………………………… 32

第六章　代词 ……………………………………………………………………………… 36
　一、代词概述 ………………………………………………………………………… 36
　二、代词的种类 ……………………………………………………………………… 36
　　　（一）指示代词 …………………………………………………………………… 36
　　　（二）人称代词 …………………………………………………………………… 36
　　　（三）物主代词 …………………………………………………………………… 37
　　　（四）反身代词 …………………………………………………………………… 38
　　　（五）不定代词 …………………………………………………………………… 38
　　　（六）疑问代词 …………………………………………………………………… 39
　　　（七）相互代词 …………………………………………………………………… 39

  （八）非人称代词 it ·· 39
  （九）关系代词 ·· 40

第七章　介词 ·· 44
 一、介词的概述 ·· 44
 二、介词的分类 ·· 44
  （一）词形上的分类 ·· 44
  （二）其他介词 ·· 45
 三、介词与形容词、分词连用 ··· 45
 四、动词和介词连用 ·· 45
 五、介词后的动名词 ·· 46
 六、既可作介词，又可作副词 ··· 46

第八章　连词 ·· 50
 一、连词概述 ·· 50
 二、连词种类 ·· 50
 三、并列连词 ·· 50
  （一）表示并列的连词 ·· 50
  （二）表示转折的连词 ·· 52
  （三）表示结果的连词 ·· 53
  （四）其他并列连词结构 ·· 53
 四、从属连词 ·· 54
  （一）名词性从句的从属连词 ···································· 54
  （二）状语从句的从属连词 ·· 54

第九章　动词 ·· 58
 一、动词概述 ·· 58
 二、动词的种类 ·· 58
  （一）实义动词 ·· 58
  （二）系动词 ·· 59
  （三）情态动词 ·· 60
  （四）助动词 ·· 62
 三、动词的基本形式 ·· 62
  （一）动词的过去式及过去分词的构成 ····················· 62
  （二）动词的现在分词的构成 ···································· 63
 四、动词的时态 ·· 63

第十章　动词时态 ·· 67
 一、时态概述 ·· 67

二、时态分类 ………………………………………………………… 67
　　(一)过去时间下的时态形式对比 ………………………………… 67
　　(二)现在时间下的时态形式对比 ………………………………… 69
　　(三)将来时间下的时态形式对比 ………………………………… 72
　　(四)过去将来时和过去将来完成时 ……………………………… 73
三、时态小结 ………………………………………………………… 74

第十一章　被动语态

一、被动语态的构成 ………………………………………………… 78
二、被动语态的时态 ………………………………………………… 78
三、被动语态的几种类型 …………………………………………… 79

第十二章　非谓语动词

一、非谓语动词 ……………………………………………………… 84
二、非谓语动词的分类 ……………………………………………… 84
　　(一)动词不定式 …………………………………………………… 84
　　(二)动名词 ………………………………………………………… 86
　　(三)分词 …………………………………………………………… 88

第十三章　构词法

一、构词法的概述 …………………………………………………… 94
二、构词法的种类 …………………………………………………… 94
　　(一)转化法 ………………………………………………………… 94
　　(二)派生法 ………………………………………………………… 95
　　(三)合成法 ………………………………………………………… 98
　　(四)混合法 ………………………………………………………… 99
　　(五)缩略法 ………………………………………………………… 100
　　(六)首尾字母缩略法 ……………………………………………… 100

句　法

第十四章　陈述句和感叹句

一、陈述句 …………………………………………………………… 104
　　(一)陈述句概述 …………………………………………………… 104
　　(二)陈述句的否定形式 …………………………………………… 104
二、感叹句 …………………………………………………………… 105
　　(一)感叹句概述 …………………………………………………… 105
　　(二)感叹句的形式 ………………………………………………… 105

第十五章　祈使句和疑问句 ··· 110
- 一、祈使句 ··· 110
- 二、疑问句 ··· 110
  - (一)一般疑问句 ··· 110
  - (二)特殊疑问句 ··· 111
  - (三)选择疑问句 ··· 111
  - (四)反义疑问句 ··· 112

第十六章　主谓一致 ··· 118
- 一、主谓一致的概述 ··· 118
- 二、主谓一致的种类 ··· 118
  - (一)语法一致 ··· 119
  - (二)意义一致 ··· 120
  - (三)就近一致 ··· 121

第十七章　名词性从句 ··· 126
- 一、名词性从句的概述 ··· 126
- 二、主语从句 ··· 126
  - (一)主语从句的引导词 ··· 126
  - (二)it 作形式主语的主语从句 ··· 127
  - (三)主语从句的数 ··· 128
- 三、宾语从句 ··· 129
  - (一)宾语从句的引导词 ··· 129
  - (二)宾语从句引导词的特殊用法 ··· 129
  - (三)宾语从句时态呼应 ··· 130
  - (四)it 作形式宾语的宾语从句 ··· 130
- 四、表语从句 ··· 130
- 五、同位语从句 ··· 131
  - (一)同位语概述 ··· 131
  - (二)同位语从句概述 ··· 132
  - (三)同位语从句和定语从句的区别 ··· 132
  - (四)同位语从句的特殊句型 ··· 133

第十八章　定语从句 ··· 136
- 一、定语从句概述 ··· 136
- 二、定语从句结构 ··· 136
- 三、定语从句常见关系词 ··· 137
  - (一)关系代词 who ··· 138

（二）关系代词 which ······ 138
　　（三）关系代词 that ······ 138
　　（四）关系副词 when ······ 138
　　（五）关系副词 where ······ 139
　　（六）关系副词 why ······ 139
　四、定语从句的种类 ······ 139
　　（一）限制性定语从句 ······ 139
　　（二）非限制性定语从句 ······ 139
　　（三）限制性定语从句与非限制性定语从句的区别 ······ 141
　五、"介词＋关系代词"引导的定语从句 ······ 141

第十九章　状语从句 ······ 146
　一、状语从句的概述 ······ 146
　二、状语从句的种类 ······ 146
　　（一）让步状语从句 ······ 146
　　（二）原因状语从句 ······ 148
　　（三）方式状语从句 ······ 149
　　（四）目的状语从句 ······ 149
　　（五）结果状语从句 ······ 150
　　（六）地点状语从句 ······ 150
　　（七）时间状语从句 ······ 151
　　（八）条件状语从句 ······ 152

第二十章　强调 ······ 156
　一、强调的定义 ······ 156
　二、强调的种类 ······ 156
　三、it 强调句 ······ 157
　四、词汇手段强调 ······ 158
　　（一）助动词强调 ······ 158
　　（二）"very"表强调 ······ 158
　　（三）"only"表强调 ······ 159
　五、倒装强调 ······ 159

第二十一章　虚拟语气 ······ 164
　一、语气的概述 ······ 164
　二、虚拟语气的应用 ······ 164
　　（一）虚拟语气在条件句中的应用 ······ 164
　　（二）虚拟语气在名词性从句中的应用 ······ 166

（三）情态动词和虚拟语气 ·· 168

第二十二章　倒装 ··· 172
　　一、倒装的概述 ·· 172
　　二、倒装的种类 ·· 172
　　（一）完全倒装 ·· 172
　　（二）部分倒装 ·· 173
　　（三）倒装特殊句型 ·· 175

第二十三章　直接引语与间接引语 ·· 179
　　一、直接引语与间接引语的定义 ·· 179
　　二、直接引语与间接引语之间的转变 ······································ 179
　　（一）人称变化 ·· 179
　　（二）动词变化 ·· 179
　　（三）时态变化 ·· 180
　　（四）时间状语、地点状语、指示代词和动词的变化 ·················· 181
　　（五）各种形式由直接引语变为间接引语的方法 ······················· 182

附件 ··· 188
　　Test 1 ·· 188
　　Test 2 ·· 192
　　Test 3 ·· 196
　　Test 4 ·· 200
　　Test 5 ·· 204

Appendix ·· 208

Reference Version ··· 214

目 录

第一章 语法概论

英语语法是针对英语语言进行研究后,归纳总结出来的一系列系统的语言规则。英语的语法是由词法和句法两个部分组成。词法包括各类词的形态、变化形式和用法规则。句法主要是句子的类型、句子的组成部分和结构规则。

一、词法

(一)实词

实词(Notional Word)有实在意义,在句子中能独立承担句子成分。实词按照意义和功能划分为名词、代词、数词、动词、形容词和副词。

<table>
<tr><th colspan="4">词类(Parts of Speech)</th></tr>
<tr><th></th><th>名称</th><th>定义</th><th>例词</th></tr>
<tr><td rowspan="6">实词</td><td>名词 n.
(noun)</td><td>表示人、事物或抽象概念的名称</td><td>effort 努力, stone 石头
policeman 警察, joy 快乐</td></tr>
<tr><td>代词 pron.
(pronoun)</td><td>代替名词、形容词或数词</td><td>another 另一个, those 那些
neither 两者都不, our 我们的</td></tr>
<tr><td>数词 num.
(numeral)</td><td>表示数量或顺序</td><td>one 一, thirty 三十
second 第二, fourth 第四</td></tr>
<tr><td>动词 v.
(verb)</td><td>表示动作或状态</td><td>hate 憎恨, dance 跳舞
need 需要, play 玩</td></tr>
<tr><td>形容词 adj.
(adjective)</td><td>表示名词(人或物)的特征</td><td>fresh 新鲜的, gentle 温和的
greedy 贪婪的, innocent 无辜的</td></tr>
<tr><td>副词 adv.
(adverb)</td><td>修饰动词、形容词、其他副词或全句,表示状态特征或行为</td><td>immediately 立刻, nearly 几乎
never 从未, carelessly 粗心大意地</td></tr>
</table>

(二)虚词

虚词(Form Word)没有实在意义,在句子中不能单独承担句子成分,包括冠词、介词、连词和感叹词。虚词有一个重要的特点:虚词没有词形的变化。

<table>
<tr><th colspan="4">词类（Parts of Speech）</th></tr>
<tr><th></th><th>名称</th><th>定义</th><th>分类</th></tr>
<tr><td rowspan="4">虚词</td><td>冠词 art.
（article）</td><td>用在名词前,说明名词所指的人或物</td><td>a 一个,the 指已提到的人或物</td></tr>
<tr><td>介词 prep.
（preposition）</td><td>用在名词、代词前,表示名词、代词与其他词的关系</td><td>in 在……里面,toward 向</td></tr>
<tr><td>连词 conj.
（conjunction）</td><td>用来连接词与词、短语与短语、句与句</td><td>but 但是,and 和</td></tr>
<tr><td>感叹词 interj.
（interjection）</td><td>表示说话时的感情或口气</td><td>ah 啊,hey 嘿
oh 噢,well 好吧</td></tr>
</table>

二、句法

英语句子是由词和词组构成的、能够表达完整意思的语言单位。

(一) 句子的成分

句子的成分是指构成句子的各组成部分,即词和短语在句子中的各种语法意义。具体地讲,主要有下列八种句子成分。

句法成分	定义	例句
主语 subject	句子所要说明的动作和状态的主体(人和物)	**We** must have a rest. 我们一定要休息一下。
谓语动词 predicate verb	说明主语的动作或状态	The students **discussed** the topic heatedly. 学生们激烈地讨论着这个话题。
表语 predicative	表语是放在连系动词（又称系动词）之后,表示主语的身份或特征	He is **my best friend**. 他是我最好的朋友。
宾语 object	宾语是及物动词动作的对象或介词后面的名词或代词,即动词或介词的宾语	He always helps **those people** in trouble. 他总是帮助那些身处困难中的人们。
定语 attribute	定语用于修饰、限定、说明名词或代词的品质与特征	Harvard University is a **famous American** university. 哈佛大学是一所著名的美国大学。
状语 adverbial	状语修饰动词、形容词、副词,表时间、地点、状态和程度等含义	The dentist often works **late at weekends**. 这位牙医经常在周末工作到很晚。
补语 complement	补语用来补充说明宾语或主语所处的状态或进行的动作	The story made everyone in the class **sleepy**. 这个故事让班里所有人都昏昏欲睡。
同位语 appositive	一个名词(或其他形式)跟在另一个名词或代词后并对其进行解释、说明或限定,这个名词(或其他形式)就是同位语	Beijing, **the capital of China**, is the center of politics, economics, education and culture. 北京,中国的首都,是政治、经济、教育和文化的中心。

(二) 基本句型

英语中只有五个基本句型,这五个基本句型可以演变出多种复杂的英语句子。换言之,绝大多数英语句子都是由这五个基本句型生成的。

序号	基本句式	定义	例句
1	主谓 S + Vi.	谓语动词是不及物动词,常带有状语	Time flies fast. 时光飞逝。
2	主谓宾 S + Vt. + O	谓语动词是及物动词,后面跟宾语	She likes playing the piano. 她喜欢弹钢琴。
3	主谓双宾 S + Vt. + IO + DO	谓语动词是带双宾语的及物动词。两个宾语中第一个为间接宾语,第二个为直接宾语	His son wrote him letters. 他的儿子给他写了信。
4	主谓宾补 S + Vt. + O + C	谓语动词除了一个直接宾语外,还要加上宾语补足语,句子才能完整;说明宾语所处的状态或进行的动作	We should keep our classroom clean and tidy. 我们应该保持教室干净整洁。
5	主系表 S + V + P	常用的系动词有 be, look, become, seem, taste, smell, sound, feel 和 keep 等	The cake tastes delicious. 蛋糕味道鲜美。

(三) 句子的种类

(1) 句子用途分类

句子按其用途可分为陈述句、疑问句、祈使句和感叹句四种。

句子种类 (Sentence Types)		
名称	定义	例句
陈述句	说明一个事实或陈述说话人的看法,分为肯定句和否定句	1) 肯定句 Anger is our natural response to some situations. 愤怒是我们对一些情况的自然反应。 2) 否定句 He will not give up his dreams. 他不会放弃梦想。
疑问句	提出问题,包括一般疑问句、特殊疑问句、选择疑问句和反义疑问句	1) 一般疑问句 Do you like playing football? 你喜欢踢足球吗? 2) 特殊疑问句 Which is your favorite book? 你喜欢哪本书? 3) 选择疑问句 Who runs faster in your class, Jack or John? 你们班谁跑得更快,杰克逊是约翰? 4) 反义疑问句 The problem made you worry, didn't it? 这个难题让你焦虑不安,是不是?

续表

句子种类（Sentence Types）		
名称	定义	例句
祈使句	表示请求、命令、劝告、建议等	Take a seat, please. 请坐。 Don't be late again! 不要再迟到！
感叹句	表示喜怒哀乐等强烈的情感	How nervous the little girl was! 这个小女孩好紧张呀！ What an emergency it is! 真是一个突发事件！

（2）句子结构分类

句子按其结构可以分为简单句、并列句和复合句三类。

句子种类（Sentence Types）		
名称	定义	例句
简单句	只有一个主语（或并列主语）和一个谓语动词（或并列谓语动词）的句子称为简单句	Successful learners are learners with purposes. 成功的学习者是有目的的学习者。
并列句	两个或者两个以上的简单句连在一起的句子，常用的连词包括 and、so、or 等（或用分号";"、冒号":"等连接两个或两个以上的简单句）	We should hurry, or we will miss the train. 我们要快点了，否则我们会误车。
复合句	复合句由一个主句和一个或一个以上从句所构成的句子结构，也叫主从复合句。从句由关联词引导，关联词将从句与主句联系在一起。根据其在复合句中的作用，从句可分为名词性从句、定语从句和状语从句	Where there is water, there is life. 有水的地方就有生命。

词 法

第二章 名 词

一、名词的句法功能

名词(Noun)是指表示人、事物、情感、地点等实体或抽象事物名称的词。名词可以在句中担任不同的成分。

句法成分	例句
主语	Technology is developing faster than we can imagine. 科技远比我们想象的发展得快。
宾语	She likes English so much that she wants to study abroad in the future. 她如此喜欢英语以至于她想将来出国留学。
表语	Computer science is his major. 计算机科技是他的专业。
定语	At the age of eight, he got his first birthday gift. 八岁的时候,他得到了第一件生日礼物。
同位语	This is Mr. Sun, our Chinese teacher. 这是孙先生,我们的中文教师。
补语	All of the students called the security guard Rain Man. 所有的学生都称这位保安为"雨人"。
状语	My best friend will be back Friday. 我最好的朋友将会周五回来。
连词	She called her mother the moment she arrived at the airport. 她一到机场就给自己的妈妈打了电话。

二、名词的种类

名词可以分为专有名词和普通名词两大类。名词有以下分类。

名词	专有名词(Proper Noun)		不可数名词 Uncountable Nouns
	普通名词	物质名词(Material Noun)	
		抽象名词(Abstract Noun)	
		个体名词(Individual Noun)	可数名词 Countable Nouns
		集体名词(Collective Noun)	

(一)专有名词

名词可以分为专有名词和普通名词。专有名词是某个(些)人、地方、组织、机构等专有的名称,多为独一无二的事物,通常前面不加冠词,没有复数形式;专有名词的首字母要大写,如 Shanghai 和 America 等。

专有名词	地名	Africa 非洲,London 伦敦 Japan 日本,Australia 澳大利亚
	某些抽象事物的名称	Buddhism 佛教,Christianity 基督教
	月份、星期及节日名称	September 九月,Sunday 星期日 Christmas 圣诞节,Spring Festival 春节
	书名、电影名及诗歌名	*Gone with the Wind*《飘》,*Titanic*《泰坦尼克号》
	对家人的称呼	Mum 妈妈,Daddy 爸爸

(二)普通名词

普通名词是一类人或事物所通用的名称,或是一个抽象概念的名词,如:car 和 happiness 等。普通名词又可分为以下四类。

1)个体名词:可以单个独立存在的人、动植物和团体的名称。个体名词通常是可数名词,有单复数之分。如:book,worker,horse 和 person 等。

2)集体名词:表示若干个个体组成的集合体,也表示一群人或一类事物的名称。如:family 和 class 等。

3)物质名词:表示有具体的存在,但不具备确定形状和大小的物质,或者表示无法分为个体的事物,如:air,rice 和 water 等。

4)抽象名词:表示动作、状态、品质和感情等抽象概念的名词,如:work,health 和 friendship 等。

个体名词和集体名词可以用数目来计算,称为可数名词(Countable Nouns);物质名词和抽象名词一般无法用数目计算,称为不可数名词(Uncountable Nouns),请参看以下表格。

普通名词	类别		意义	例词
	可数名词	个体名词	表示个别的人或事物的名称	test 考试,table 桌子
		集体名词	表示一类人或事物的集合体	audience 观众,police 警察
	不可数名词	物质名词	表示物质或材料的名称	glass 玻璃,iron 铁
		抽象名词	表示性质行为状态或情感等抽象概念的名称	sadness 悲伤,honesty 诚实

三、可数名词的复数

(一)可数名词复数的规则变化

可数名词复数形式遵循一定的规则进行变化,具体规则变化如下。

分类	构成方法	读音	例词
一般情况	加-s	1.清辅音后读 /s/； 2.浊辅音和元音后读 /z/	phone-phones 电话 book-books 书 bed-beds 床
以 s,sh,ch,x 等结尾的词	加-es	读 /iz/	box-boxes 盒子 match-matches 火柴；比赛
ce,se,ze,(d)ge 等结尾的词	加-s	读 /iz/	disease-diseases 疾病 bridge-bridges 桥
以辅音字母 + y 结尾的词	变 y 为 i,再加 es	读 /z/	story-stories 故事
元音字母 + y 结尾的名词	加-s	读 /s/ 读 /z/	monkey-monkeys 猴子 day-days 天
以 o 结尾的名词	加-s	读 /s/	zoo-zoos 动物园 radio-radios 收音机
	加-es	"黑人""英雄"读 /s/ "番茄""土豆"读 /z/	Negro-Negroes 黑人 hero-heroes 英雄 tomato-tomatoes 番茄 potato-potatoes 土豆；马铃薯
以 f 或 fe 结尾的名词	加-s	读 /s/	roof- roofs 屋顶 proof-proofs 证明 cliff-cliffs 悬崖 belief-beliefs 信仰
	把 f 或 fe 改为 v,加 es	读 /z/	wife-wives 妻子 knife-knives 刀 life-lives 生活；生命 leaf-leaves 叶子
	两者均可	读 /s/ 或 /z/	handkerchief-handkerchiefs/ handkerchieves 手帕 scarf-scarfs/scarves 围巾

(二)可数名词复数的不规则变化

可数名词复数的不规则变化如下。
(1)元音发生变化

序号	名词单数	发音	名词复数	发音	汉语
1	foot	[fut]	feet	[fi:t]	脚,英尺
2	man	[mæn]	men	[men]	男人
3	mouse	[maus]	mice	[mais]	老鼠
4	woman	['wumən]	women	['wimin]	女人
5	goose	[gu:s]	geese	[gi:s]	鹅
6	tooth	[tu:θ]	teeth	[ti:θ]	牙

(2) 单复数形式不变

序号	名词单数	发音	名词复数	发音	汉语
1	deer	[diə]	deer	[diə]	鹿
2	fish	[fiʃ]	fish	[fiʃ]	鱼
3	sheep	[ʃi:p]	sheep	[ʃi:p]	绵羊
4	Chinese	[ˈtʃaiˈni:z]	Chinese	[ˈtʃaiˈni:z]	中国人
5	Japanese	[ˌdʒæpəˈni:z]	Japanese	[ˌdʒæpəˈni:z]	日本人
6	Swiss	[swis]	Swiss	[swis]	瑞典人

注意:
1) 当 fish 用作可数名词指"鱼的条数"时单数和复数形式相同(three fish 三条鱼)。当 fish 指"鱼的种类"时复数形式才为 fishes(three fishes 三种鱼);fish 用作"鱼肉"则为不可数名词而且无复数形式。
2) 以 -ese 结尾的表示国籍的名词,单数、复数一样;其他表示国籍的名词都按正常规划变化,如 Americans 和 Canadians。而表示"某国人"的时候,以 man 结尾的名词有两种情况:German 和 Roman 直接加 -s 变为 Germans 和 Romans;其他以 man 结尾的词改为 men,如 Englishmen 和 Frenchmen 等。

(3) 词尾发生变化

序号	名词单数	发音	名词复数	发音	汉语
1	child	[tʃaild]	children	[ˈtʃildrən]	孩子
2	ox	[ɔks]	oxen	[ˈɔksn]	牛,公牛

(4) 只有复数形式的名词

序号	名词单数	发音	名词复数	发音	汉语
1	clothes	[kləuðz]	clothes	[kləuðz]	衣服
2	compasses	[ˈkɔmpəsiz]	compasses	[ˈkɔmpəsiz]	圆规
3	glasses	[ˈglɑ:siz]	glasses	[ˈglɑ:siz]	眼镜
4	pants	[pænts]	pants	[pænts]	长裤
5	scissors	[ˈsizəz]	scissors	[ˈsizəz]	剪子
6	trousers	[ˈtrauzəz]	trousers	[ˈtrauzəz]	裤子
7	shorts	[ʃɔ:ts]	shorts	[ʃɔ:ts]	短裤
8	series	[ˈsiəri:z]	series	[ˈsiəri:z]	系列
9	species	[ˈspi:ʃiz]	species	[ˈspi:ʃiz]	物种;种类
10	means	[mi:nz]	means	[mi:nz]	手段;方法

注意:学科或疾病名词为不可数名词,虽然以 s 结尾,仍为单数的名词,如:politics 和 physics 等。

（5）合成名词变成复数时，复数加在核心词的后面

序号	合成名词单数	合成名词复数	汉语
1	girl friend	girl friends	女朋友
2	boy friend	boy friends	男朋友
3	go-between	go-betweens	中间人
4	highway	highways	公路
5	passer-by	passers-by	过路人
6	looker-on	lookers-on	观看者，旁观者
7	son-in-law	sons-in-law	女婿
8	daughter-in-law	daughters-in-law	儿媳
9	brother-in-law	brothers-in-law	姐夫，妹夫
10	sister-in-law	sisters-in-law	嫂子，弟媳
11	father-in-law	fathers-in-law	岳父，公公
12	mother-in-law	mothers-in-law	岳母，婆婆

（6）以 man 和 woman 与其他名词构成的合成名词变成复数时，这两个名词都要变为复数

序号	合成名词单数	合成名词复数	汉语
1	man teacher	men teachers	男老师
2	woman teacher	women teachers	女老师
3	man driver	men drivers	男司机
4	woman driver	women drivers	女司机

四、不可数名词

不可以用数目来计算的名词称为不可数名词。通常物质名词和抽象名词一般无法用数目计算，一般不能加不定冠词，也没有复数形式。

（一）物质名词

物质名词是指有具体的存在，表示无法分为个体的实物，如气体、液体、粉状或细粒状物体、材料、块状或片状物体等。

序号	物质名词存在形式	例词
1	气体	air 空气，smoke 烟，oxygen 氧，steam 蒸汽
2	液体	water 水，oil 油，milk 牛奶，beer 啤酒，coffee 咖啡
3	粉状或细粒状物体	salt 盐，sugar 糖，rice 米，flour 面粉
4	块状或片状物体	meat 肉，paper 纸，money 钱，gold 黄金，glass 玻璃

(二)抽象名词

抽象名词主要指一些抽象概念的名称,包括表示性质、状态、动作的名词。常用的抽象名词如下。

loneliness 孤独	courage 勇气	work 工作	health 健康
anger 愤怒	death 死亡	music 音乐	technology 技术
homework 家庭作业	power 力量;权力	truth 真理;真相	wealth 财富
housework 家务劳动	importance 重要性	wisdom 智慧	freedom 自由
practice 练习	furniture 家具	advice 建议	bravery 勇敢

(三)不可数名词的用法规则

学习不可数名词时,应注意以下几点。

①不可数名词没有复数形式。如:some water 或 some money,不可说 some waters 或 some moneys。

②不可数名词不能用不定冠词 a 和 an 及数词修饰,但可用 some, any, much, a lot of 或 a little 等直接修饰。如:不可以说 a bread 和 two gold,但可以用 some bread 和 much gold。

③不可数名词前通常用量词来表示具体的数,如:a glass of beer 和 six pieces of paper。

④不可数名词作主语时,谓语动词用单数形式。如:

Water <u>covers</u> most parts of the earth. 地球上大多数地方被水覆盖。

⑤若不可数名词前有复数数量词修饰时,谓语动词用复数形式。例如:

There <u>are</u> five pieces of paper on the desk. 桌上有五张纸。

试比较:There <u>is</u> some paper on the desk. 桌上有一些纸。

五、容易混淆的可数名词和不可数名词

可数名词	不可数名词	可数名词	不可数名词
a room 一个房间	room 空间	woods 树林	wood 木材
a glass 一个玻璃杯	glass 玻璃	glasses 眼镜	glass 玻璃
a chicken 一只小鸡	chicken 鸡肉	fishes 多种种类的鱼	fish 鱼肉
a paper 一篇论文	paper 纸张	works 工厂;著作	work 工作
an orange 一个橙子	orange 橙色	times 次数;时代	time 时间

注意:对比可数名词,不可数名词多为抽象概念或物质概念。

六、名词的所有格

在英语中,名词所有格表示所属关系,有些名词可以加 's 或 s' 来表示所有关系相当于物主代词,带这种词尾的名词形式称为该名词的所有格,如:today's newspaper 和 boys' toys。

名词所有格的规则

所有格形式	使用范围	例词
's 或 s'	表示人或其他有生命的东西的名词常在词尾加 's	my father's bike 我父亲的自行车 Teachers' Day 教师节
	用于表示时间、距离、价格、重量、国家、世界、城市等无生命的名词后面	ten minutes' walk 十分钟的步行时间 China's economy 中国的经济
	表示店铺或某人的家时,常在名词所有格后省去 shop 或 house 等名词	the tailor's (store) 裁缝店 go to the doctor's (office) 去看医生
of 所有格	无论表示有生命还是无生命的名词,一般均可用介词 of 短语来表示所有关系。一般而言,如果 of 后面是有生命的名词,表示其所有者,就要用双重格式"of + 名词所有格/名词性物主代词"或 's 属格,如 a friend of my father's (我父亲的一个朋友)或 my father's friend	a map of Italy 一张意大利地图 a painting of Jane 简的一幅画(画上的人物) a painting of Jane's 简所拥有的一幅画(画的拥有者)

Grammar Exercises
语法训练

I. Fill in the blanks with what you have learnt. 用所学知识填空。(5%)

名词	1. ( )		4. ( )
	2. ( )	物质名词	
		3. ( )	
		集体名词	5. ( )
		个体名词	

II. Fill in the blanks with the noun's syntactic function. 填写名词的句法功能。(10%)

1. My friends often give me *a lot of advice*. ( )
2. In Olympic Games, *each player* follows the rules of "being swifter, higher and stronger". ( )
3. This is not *a game*, while we are killing time in this way. ( )
4. Although Mr. Smith, *my neighbor*, is too young for the job, he still believes that he can do it. ( )
5. We will look into the matter *each time* the machine is out of order. ( )
6. All of the students in the class elected him *the monitor*. ( )
7. He does not want to change his job since he has been working in the *car* factory for a long time. ( )
8. Would you like to visit the national museum *this Sunday*? ( )
9. Mr. Brown is such *a great man* that he may help anyone in need. ( )
10. They've missed the last bus. I'm afraid they have *no choice* but to take a taxi. ( )

Ⅲ．Error identification. 错误辨识。（20%）

1. （A）The hospital （B）announced that （C）three woman doctors would be sent to the battle field （D）in a week.

2. （A）As a matter of fact, （B）those goes-between were （C）curious about （D）what had happened there.

3. （A）The number of （B）deers, lions and wolves （C）will not change much if we do not （D）destroy their living environment.

4. （A）What a fun （B）it is to celebrate （C）a special Christmas （D）with your family!

5. （A）It is reported that （B）a large number of （C）Germen will visit （D）the national museum next week.

6. （A）Many countries are （B）increasing their （C）use of natural gas, wind and （D）other form of energy.

7. （A）Whatever he does, （B）once he sets up （C）goal, he would start pursuing it （D）without hesitation.

8. Jack （A）took the newspapers （B）off the little table （C）to make rooms （D）for the TV set.

9. （A）Because there are （B）ten shoes shops （C）in the street, you may find （D）what you like at last.

10. （A）Sometimes, （B）looker-ons have （C）a better view of the game than （D）its participants.

Ⅳ．Multiple choice. 单项选择。（30%）

1. Mrs. Jones got her _____ by printing _____ of famous writers.
   A. wealths; works　　　　　　　　　B. wealth; work
   C. wealth; works　　　　　　　　　D. wealths; work

2. During their summer holiday, they may enjoy themselves much, because they do not have _____ to do.
   A. many homeworks　　　　　　　　B. much homeworks
   C. many homework　　　　　　　　D. much homework

3. All of a sudden, the waiter broke a _____ while he was serving.
   A. glass water　　　　　　　　　　B. water glass
   C. glass of water　　　　　　　　　D. water's glass

4. _____ terrible news we've been having these days!
   A. What a　　B. What　　C. How a　　D. How

5. —How many _____ are there on the farm? —About ten.
   A. chicken　　B. deers　　C. cow　　D. sheep

6. In the busy street, _____ were attracted by the music played by the little boy.
   A. passers-by　　　　　　　　　　B. passer-bys
   C. passers-bys　　　　　　　　　　D. passer-by

7. After a day's work, those _____ like to have a gathering at the coffee bar.
   A. man driver　　B. man drivers　　C. men drivers　　D. men driver

8. Mr. Stone is such a nice person that he always gives us _____ on how to study English well.
   A. some advice			B. some advices
   C. a advice			D. an advice
9. The town is so far away from the school and it is a _____ walk.
   A. six hour		B. six hour's		C. six-hours		D. six hours'
10. It was in the car accident that Laura hurt one of her _____ a few days ago.
    A. arm		B. ear		C. feet		D. hand
11. From various media, they prefer to get much _____ from books.
    A. stories		B. information		C. message		D. ideas
12. Since the chair is made of _____, many visitors want to see it in their own eyes.
    A. gold		B. golds		C. many gold		D. much golds
13. Look, two _____ are singing while a group of _____ are dancing.
    A. Frenchmans; Germen			B. Germans; Frenchmans
    C. Frenchmen; Germans			D. Germen; Frenchmen
14. It is June 1st today, which is _____ Day. Don't forget to buy your son a gift.
    A. Child		B. Child's		C. Childrens'		D. Children's
15. Physics _____ to matter and motion.
    A. is related		B. are connected		C. connect		D. relate
16. In autumn, when it turns cold, the tree _____ begin to fall down from trees.
    A. leaf		B. leave		C. leafs		D. leaves
17. Last week my wife went to the nearest market and bought a lot of _____.
    A. vegetable		B. potatos		C. tomatoes		D. meats
18. In the small supermarket, there is some _____ for you to choose.
    A. fish		B. cakes		C. pears		D. peaches
19. The mother found that her little baby had four _____.
    A. tooth		B. teeth		C. tooths		D. teeths
20. —Would you like _____ to drink? —No, thanks. I have drunk two _____.
    A. any; bottles of apple juices			B. some; bottles of apple juice
    C. many; bottles of apples juice			D. few; bottle of apples juice

V. Fill in the blanks with the correct forms of nouns in the following passage. 填写名词的正确形式。(20%)

O. Henry was a pen (1) _____ (name) used by an American writer of short (2) _____ (story). His real name was William Sydney Porter. He was born in North (3) _____ (carolina) in 1862. As a young boy he lived an exciting (4) _____ (life). He did not go to school for very long, but he managed to teach himself everything he needed to know. When he was about 20 (5) _____ (year) old, O. Henry went to Texas, where he tried different (6) _____ (job). He first worked on a newspaper, and then had a job in a bank. When some (7) _____ (money) went missing from the bank, O. Henry was believed to have stolen it. Because of that, he was sent to prison. During the three years in (8)_____ (prison), he learned to write short stories. After he got out of prison, he went to (9)_____ (new york) and continued writing. He wrote mostly about New York and the life of the poor there. People liked his stories, because simple as the tales were, they would finish with a sudden change at the end, to the (10)_____ (reader) surprise.

VI. Translate the following sentences into English. 将下列句子译成英语。(15%)

1. 为了学中文和这个国家的文化,许多人来到中国。
2. 只有读小学的学生们庆祝六月一日,儿童节。
3. 现在主要的问题是如何找到他丢失的羊。
4. 因为家里没有钱,他不得不借了一些钱。
5. ——两杯咖啡多少钱?
   ——大概五美元。

第三章 数 词

一、数词的概述

数词分为基数词和序数词。用来表示数量的是基数词(Cardinal Number),用来表示顺序的是序数词(Ordinal Number)。

(一)基数词和序数词

序数词一般是在与之相应的基数词后加"th"构成,但有些词有特殊变化,见下表。

基数词变序数词特殊变化口诀	例 词
一二三,特殊记	one-first 第一,two-second 第二,three-third 第三
八去 t,九去 e	eight-eighth 第八,nine-ninth 第九
ty 变成 tie	twenty-twentieth 第二十
ve 用 f 来代替	five-fifth 第五,twelve-twelfth 第十二
遇到数字几十几,只将个位基数变序数	twenty-one—twenty-first 第二十一

数字	基 数 词		序 数 词
1	one [wʌn]	1st	first
2	two [tu:]	2nd	second
3	three [θri:]	3rd	third
4	four [fɔ:]	4th	fourth
5	five [faiv]	5th	fifth
6	six [siks]	6th	sixth
7	seven ['sevən]	7th	seventh
8	eight [eit]	8th	eighth
9	nine [nain]	9th	ninth
10	ten [ten]	10th	tenth
11	eleven [i'levən]	11th	eleventh
12	twelve [twelv]	12th	twelfth
13	thirteen ['θə:'ti:n]	13th	thirteenth

续表

基 数 词		序 数 词	
14	fourteen ['fɔː'tiːn]	14th	fourteenth
15	fifteen ['fif'tiːn]	15th	fifteenth
16	sixteen ['siks'tiːn]	16th	sixteenth
17	seventeen ['sevən'tiːn]	17th	seventeenth
18	eighteen ['ei'tiːn]	18th	eighteenth
19	nineteen ['nain'tiːn]	19th	nineteenth
20	twenty ['twenti]	20th	twentieth
21	twenty-one	21st	twenty-first
22	twenty-two	22nd	twenty-second
23	twenty-three	23rd	twenty-third
24	twenty-four	24th	twenty-fourth
30	thirty ['θəti]	30th	thirtieth
40	forty ['fɔːti]	40th	fortieth
50	fifty ['fifti]	50th	fiftieth
60	sixty ['siksti]	60th	sixtieth
70	seventy ['sevənti]	70th	seventieth
80	eighty ['eiti]	80th	eightieth
90	ninety ['nainti]	90th	ninetieth
100	one hundred ['hʌndrəd]	100th	one hundredth
101	one hundred and one	101st	one hundred and first
1000	one thousand ['θauzənd]	1000th	one thousandth

(二) 基数词的表达法

①13~19 的基数词，由个位数加上后缀-teen 构成，并有两个重音，如：nineteen ['nain'tiːn]。

②20~90 整十位数的基数词都以-ty 结尾，重音在第一音节，如：ninety ['nainti]。

③21~99 之间的基数词由整十位数加上个位数合成，中间加连字符"-"，如：twenty-four。

④101~999 的基数词由 hundred 加上 and，再加上后面两位数（或末位数）构成，hundred 不加 s，如：376 读成 three hundred and seventy-six。

⑤1000 以上的数字，从后往前数，每三位数加"，"；第一个"，"号前为 thousand（千）；第二个"，"号前为 million（百万）；第三个"，"为 billion（十亿）。英语没有"万"的名称，一万是"ten thousand"（十千）；具体数字后的 thousand 也不加 s，如：

1 001　　one thousand and one

35 006　thirty-five thousand and six
3 658 473　three million six hundred and fifty-eight thousand four hundred and seventy-three
100 000　one hundred thousand
1 000 000　one million['mɪljən]
1 000 000 000　one billion['bɪljən]

注意：

a. hundred,thousand,million 等词在具体的数字或 several 后一般都不加复数词尾-s,如：several **hundred** trees,two **hundred** teachers,several **thousand** workers,six **thousand** books 和 seven **million** people。

b. 如果 hundred,thousand,million 等词后面跟 of,则要用复数形式,如：**hundreds of** workers（成百上千的工人）和 **thousands of** trees（成千上万的树）。

(三)序数词的用法

①序数词前面一般加定冠词(the)或物主代词,在句子中主要作定语、表语和宾语。如：

This is **my first** visit to China. 这是我第一次来中国。（定语）
Today is **my eighteenth** birthday. 今天是我的十八岁生日。（定语）
My room is on **the second** floor. 我的房间在二楼。（定语）
I am **the first**. 我是第一个。（表语）
Please pass me **the third**. 请递给我第三个。（宾语）

②序数词的前面可以加上不定冠词 a/an,用来表示"再一"或"又一"的意思。如：

In addition to English,we have to study **a second** foreign language.
除英语外,我们还要学第二外语。

③日期的表达要用序数词,读时前面要用定冠词 the,介词用 on,但在年份和月份前用 in。如：

六月一日 June **1st** 读作 June (**the**) **first**
I was born **on** May **4th**, 1995. 我出生于 1995 年 5 月 4 日。
Thousands of trees are planted on Tree Planting Day **in March**.
在三月的植树节会种植成千上万棵树。

④世纪前也要用序数词,因为是第几个世纪,而不是多少个世纪。如：

The name of the book is *China's Population and Development in* **the 21st Century**.
这本书的名字是《二十一世纪中国的人口与发展》。

⑤凡编了号的东西,除了可以用序数词表达外,还可以用基数词表示顺序。如：

"第一单元"除了可以说成 **the first** unit,也可说成 Unit **One**。
"第二课"除了可以说成 **the second** lesson,也可说成 Lesson **Two**。
通常门牌号、房间号、电话号码、邮政编码、车牌号码等数字按照基数词的方法读,如：

Page **6**　　　　第 6 页　　　　Room **211**　　　　211 房间
Bus No. **22**　　22 路公共汽车　Class **One** Grade **Two**　二年一班

二、时间表达法

(一)具体时间的表达法

	类 别	读 法	说 明
时间表述法	小时;分钟	7:15 seven fifteen 9:25 nine twenty-five	时间前用介词 at
	分钟 + past + 该小时	7:15 a quarter **past** seven 9:30 half **past** nine	quarter 读为 [ˈkwɔːtə] quarter 即四分之一,一刻钟是一个小时的四分之一,所以前面用 a 少于 30 分钟用 past 表示几点过几分钟
	分钟 + to + 下一小时	8:45 a quarter **to** nine 9:55 five **to** ten	多于 30 分钟的用 to 表示几点差几分,to 后的小时为 $n+1$
	整点	6:00 six o'clock	整点时间后的"o'clock"可省略,说成 at six

(二)年、月、日的表达法

(1)年份表达法

读年份时,一般分成两个单位来读,前两个数为一个单位,后两个数为一个单位。如果是三位数,先读第一位,再把后两个数合起来读。

年	英语表达法
1982 年	nineteen eighty-two
1909 年	nineteen o[əu] nine
2008 年	(the year) two thousand and eight
1900 年	nineteen hundred
公元 2000 年	the year two thousand (A.D.)
公元 984 年	nine eighty-four
公元前 451 年	four five one B.C. (或 four hundred and fifty-one B.C.)

(2)"年月日"的表达法

读年月日时可按照国际惯例的"日月年"的顺序读,也可按照美国通用的"月日年"的顺序读。

年 月 日	英 语 表 达 法
6月22日	June 22nd 读作 June (the) twenty-second 22nd June 读作 the twenty-second of June
2007年3月21日	March 21st, 2007 读作 March (the) twenty-first, two thousand and seven the 21 of March, 2007 读作 the twenty-first of March, two thousand and seven

三、小数和分数的表达法

(一)小数表达法

小数	英语表达法	说明
5.76	five **point** seven six	小数点读成"point"
0.15	**nought**(or **zero**) point one five	零可用"nought"或"zero"表达
18.308	eighteen point three o eight	小数点后的数字依次读成基数词

(二)分数表达法

分数	英语表达法	说明
1/2	one half/a half	二分之一也可以用 one second 表达
1/3	one-third/a third	分子用基数词,分母用序数词,两者用"-"连接
1/4	one-fourth/a quarter	分子等于1,分母用单数
5/7	five-sevenths	分子大于1,分母用复数

Grammar Exercises
语法训练

Ⅰ. Write the corresponding Ordinal Numbers for the following Cardinal Numbers in English. 用英语写出下列基数词相应的序数词。(5%)

基数词	序数词	基数词	序数词
one		thirty	
two		forty-one	
three		five	
eight		twelve	
nine		twenty-six	

Ⅱ. Write the following time expressions in English. 用英语表达下列时间。(10%)

1. 5:30 _____
2. 7:15 _____
3. 8:25 _____
4. 9:50 _____
5. 10:45 _____
6. 7:20 _____
7. 12:10 _____
8. 11:35 _____
9. 5:55 _____
10. 6:00 _____

Ⅲ. Error identification. 错误辨识。(20%)

1. (A) There are (B) two hundreds (C) and seventy students D) in our school.
2. 2 568 459 can be read as (A) two billion (B) five hundred and sixty-eight thousand (C) four hundred(D) and fifty-nine
3. (A) I saw (B) thousand of birds (C) in the forest park (D) at that weekend.
4. (A) The Greens had (B) a big party to celebrate (C) their daughter's (D) twenty-two birthday yesterday.
5. (A) Teachers' Day (B) is on (C) the ten of (D) September.
6. (A) September (B) is (C) the nineth month (D) of the year.
7. (A) Our classroom (B) is on the one floor (C) and theirs is (D) on the ground floor.
8. (A) Two-third of the land (B) in this area (C) is covered (D) with snow.
9. (A) Please turn to (B) Page twentieth and (C) we will learn (D) Unit Three.
10. Paul's daughter (A) is a pupil and (B) studies in (C) Class Third, Great Four (D) of the school.

Ⅳ. Multiple choice. 单项选择。(30%)

1. Today is my mother's _____ birthday. I'll cook something delicious for her.
   A. fourteen   B. fourtieth   C. forty   D. fortieth
2. There are _____ books in our reading-room.
   A. hundred of
   B. hundreds of
   C. several hundred of
   D. several hundreds
3. Father's Day is on _____ Sunday of June.
   A. the second   B. third   C. the third   D. second
4. —How many English books are there on the table?
   —There is only _____ English book on it.
   A. a   B. an   C. one   D. the
5. Mr. Smith lives in _____ on _____.
   A. Room 403; the second floor
   B. the Room 403; second floor
   C. the 403 room; two floor
   D. the 403 room; the floor two
6. Another way of saying Lesson 12 is _____.
   A. Lesson Twelveth
   B. Lesson Twelfth
   C. the twelfth lesson
   D. twelfth lesson
7. December the _____ is Christmas.
   A. twenty-five
   B. twenty-fifth
   C. twentieth-five
   D. twenty-fiveth
8. My parents have three children. My brother is older than I and my sister is younger than I. So I am the _____ child of my parents.
   A. third   B. second   C. two   D. first
9. My elder brother graduated from Beijing University _____ 2013.
   A. at   B. in   C. of   D. on

10. Nearly _____ of the earth _____ covered by sea.
    A. three fourth; is
    B. three fourths; is
    C. three fourth; are
    D. three fourths; are
11. _____ of the students in our class are from Xinjiang.
    A. One third   B. One three   C. One threes   D. One thirds
12. The _____ century was a century that began on January 1st, 1901 and ended on December 31st, 2000.
    A. 21st   B. 20th   C. 19th   D. 18th
13. 39 208 should be read as _____.
    A. thirty-nine thousands two hundreds and eight
    B. thirty-nine thousands two hundred and eight
    C. thirty-nine thousand two hundreds and eight
    D. thirty-nine thousand two hundred and eight
14. —What date is it today?
    —It's the _____ of April.
    A. twenty-eight
    B. twenty-eighth
    C. twentieth-eight
    D. twentieth-eighth
15. Thirty-nine minus(减) six is _____.
    A. the thirty-three
    B. the thirty-third
    C. thirty-three
    D. thirty-third
16. —What time is it now?
    —It is _____.
    A. eleven and thirty
    B. eleven thirty
    C. thirty eleven
    D. eleven thirties
17. In our university _____ of the students _____ boys.
    A. three-fifth; are   B. three-fifth; is   C. three-fifths; are   D. three-fifths; is
18. My parents bought me a beautiful bike on my _____ birthday.
    A. nine   B. ninth   C. the nine   D. the ninth
19. Although I failed three times, my teacher encouraged me to have a _____ try.
    A. third   B. fourth   C. fifth   D. sixth
20. —There is a wrong word on Page _____.
    —Where?
    —On the _____ page.
    A. Two; two   B. Two; second   C. second; Two   D. second; Second

Ⅴ. Fill in the blanks with the correct forms of words. 填写词的正确形式。(20%)

Mr. Wang was an excellent teacher. He spoke __1__ languages. Chinese was his mother tongue. English was his second language and French was his __2__ language. He taught English in a middle school and he loved his work deeply.

There were six classes in a school day at Mr. Wang's middle school. Mr. Wang taught five of these __3__ classes. In his "free" hour from two to __4__ o'clock in the afternoon, Mr. Wang had to meet with students' parents, check students' homework and deal with many other things. Mr. Wang worked hard from the moment he got to school early in the morning __5__ he left for home late in the afternoon, so his "free" hour was not free at all.

It was the last day of a year. He wanted to teach his students something special. So in his __6__ class in the afternoon, Mr. Wang taught his students a poem. After reading and interpreting the poem, he encouraged his students to talk about it. They enjoyed the poem so much that __7__ one wanted to stop when the bell rang at __8__.

On his way home, Mr. Wang thought about the fifth class. He was __9__ about what he did as a teacher. __10__ was indeed a meaningful and unforgettable day for him.

1. A. three B. third C. two D. second
2. A. three B. third C. thirteen D. thirty
3. A. three B. six C. five D. two
4. A. ten B. eight C. nine D. three
5. A. until B. when C. while D. as soon as
6. A. five B. fifth C. two D. second
7. A. not B. no C. any D. none
8. A. half past five B. half to six C. thirty before six D. five thirtieth
9. A. happy B. sad C. embarrassed D. angry
10. A. January 1st B. December 31th C. December 31st D. January 1th

VI. Translate the following sentences into English. 将下列句子译成英语。(15%)
1. 这是我第一次来美国。
2. 他们在辩论赛中得了三等奖。
3. 五分之四的工作已经被做完了。
4. 第二十九届奥运会开幕式于2008年8月8日在北京举行。
5. 我们六点五十在电影院见面吧？

第四章 形容词和副词

一、形容词和副词概述

形容词(Adjective)是用来描写或修饰名词的一类词。在句子中,形容词可用作定语、表语和宾语补足语等,通常位于它所修饰的名词前。

副词(Adverb)是用来修饰动词、形容词、其他副词以及全句的词,表示时间、地点、程度、方式等概念。副词的位置比较灵活,可放在句首、句中或句末的任一位置。

英语中,在表示"比较……""最……"的概念时,要用其特有的形式来表达。大多数形容词和副词都有比较级和最高级的变化,即原级(Positive Degree)、比较级(Comparative Degree)和最高级(Superlative Degree),用来表示事物的等级差别。原级即形容词和副词的原形,比较级和最高级的形式变化分为两种,即规则变化和不规则变化。

二、形容词和副词的用法

(一)形容词的用法

①直接说明事物的性质或特征的形容词是性质形容词,它有级的变化,可以用程度副词修饰,在句中可作定语、表语和宾语补足语。如:

句法成分	例句
定语	He is a very **happy** boy. 他是一个非常快乐的男孩。
表语	The life here is **convenient** and **comfortable**. 这里的生活方便和舒适。
宾语补足语	We will make our country **properous**. 我们要使我们的国家富裕。

叙述形容词只能作表语,所以又称为表语形容词。这类形容词没有级的变化,也不可用程度副词修饰。大多数以 a- 开头的形容词都属于这一类。如:

The girl is **afraid**. (正确)女孩有点害怕。

She is an **afraid** girl. (错误)

The old man is **asleep** now.（正确）现在老人睡着了。

He is an **asleep** man.（错误）

注意：这类词还有 alike、alive、alone、awake、faint、ill、well 和 unwell 等。

②形容词作定语修饰名词时，常放在它所修饰的名词之前。但是当形容词修饰复合不定代词时，要放在这些词之后。如：

There is something **wrong** with my cell phone. 我的手机坏了。

③用形容词表示类别和整体。某些形容词加上定冠词可以泛指一类人，与谓语动词的复数连接。如：

If it is possible, **the rich** may help **the poor**. 如果有可能的话，富人可以帮助穷人。

The hungry are losing hope in that area. 在这个地区，饥饿的人们感到绝望。

④有关国家和民族的形容词前加上定冠词，指这个民族的整体，与动词的复数连用。如：

The Chinese are proud of their four great inventions. 中国人以四大发明而自豪。

The English have a wonderful sense of humor. 英国人有幽默感。

⑤多个形容词修饰名词时，其顺序为限定词——数词——描绘性形容词（大小、长短、形状、新旧、颜色）——国别——材料性质——类别——名词。如：

a **small round** table 一张小圆桌子

a **tall gray** building 一栋高大的灰色建筑

a **dirty old brown** shirt 一件脏的旧棕色衬衫

a **famous German medical** school 一所著名的德国医学院

an **expensive Japanese sports** car 一辆昂贵的日本跑车

（二）副词的用法

副词可用于动词之前、be 动词或助动词之后；若有多个助动词时，副词一般放在第一个助动词后。

1）修饰形容词时，须放在被修饰词前。如：

The room is small but **very** quiet. 这房间虽小，可是很安静。

2）修饰副词时，须放在被修饰词前。如：

He played this old man **very** well. 他演这位老人演得很好。

3）修饰动词时，通常位于句子基本结构之后。如：

She appeared at the party but left **quickly**. 她在聚会上露面，但很快就离开了。

4）修饰整个句子时，通常位于句子基本结构之前。如：

Fortunately, you have the power to change all that.

幸运的是，你还有能力去改变所有那一切。

三、形容词和副词的比较级和最高级构成

(一)规则变化

<table>
<tr><th colspan="2">情　况</th><th>词尾变化方式</th><th>例子(原级-比较级-最高级)</th></tr>
<tr><td rowspan="6">单音节词和少数双音节词</td><td>多数单音节词</td><td>加-er/-est</td><td>loud - louder - loudest
slow - slower - slowest</td></tr>
<tr><td>以不发音 -e 结尾单音节词和少数双音节词</td><td>加-r/-st</td><td>nice - nicer - nicest
large - larger - largest</td></tr>
<tr><td>重读闭音节结尾的单音节词,如词尾只有一个辅音字母</td><td>把最后的辅音字母双写,再加-er/-est</td><td>big - bigger - biggest
fat - fatter - fattest
hot - hotter - hottest</td></tr>
<tr><td>少数以辅音字母加-y 结尾的双音节词</td><td>变 y 为-i,再加-er/-est</td><td>busy - busier - busiest
crazy - crazier - craziest</td></tr>
<tr><td>少数以-er 或-ow 结尾的双音节词</td><td>加-er/-est</td><td>clever- cleverer - cleverest
narrow-narrower - narrowest</td></tr>
<tr><td>少数以-ble 结尾的双音节词</td><td>加-r/-st</td><td>able - abler - ablest
noble - nobler - noblest</td></tr>
<tr><td colspan="2">多音节词和部分双音节词</td><td>在该词前加 more/the most</td><td>useful - more useful - the most useful
important - more important - the most important
happily - more happily - the most happily</td></tr>
</table>

(二)不规则变化

少数形容词和副词的比较级和最高级有特殊变化,如下表。

原　级	比　较　级	最　高　级
good well	better	best
bad badly ill 不好的;有病的	worse	worst
many much	more	most
little	less	least
far	farther 距离较远 further 程度进一步	farthest furthest
old	older 年纪较大 elder 长幼关系	oldest eldest

四、形容词和副词比较级的基本用法

	形容词	副词
原级	Kate is **young**. 凯特很年轻。	Bob studies **hard**. 鲍勃学习很努力。
比较级	Kate is **younger** than Laura. 凯特比劳拉年轻。	Bob studies **harder** than Tom. 鲍勃比汤姆学习更努力。
最高级	Kate is **the youngest** in our class. 我们班里凯特年龄最小。	Bob studies (**the**) **hardest** in our class. 鲍勃在我们班学习最努力。

五、比较状语从句

比较状语从句是对人或物的特征、性质和数量等进行比较的句型。常见的比较状语从句如下。

(一)同级比较句型

①同级比较:A + 动词 + as + 形容词或副词原级 + as + B,表示"A 和 B 一样……"。如:

Mary is **as beautiful as** her friend. 玛丽和她朋友一样漂亮。(形容词)

He can speak French **as fluently as** a Frenchman.

他法语说得像法国人一样流利。(副词)

②同级比较的否定形式为:A + 动词 + not so/as + 形容词或副词原级 + as + B,表示"A 不如 B 那样……"或"A 不如 B……"。如:

Jim doesn't study **so/as hard as** Kate. 吉姆不如凯特学习努力。

I didn't do **so/as well as** I should. 我并没有做得如我应该做的那么好。

(二)比较级句型

①比较级 + than...,表示"……比……一些"。如:

This skirt is **cheaper than** that one. 这件衬衫比那件衬衫便宜。

The suggestions you made is **more practicable than** the one he made.

你给的建议比他给的更有可行性。

②the + 比较级 + of...,表示"两个中……的一个"。如:

He is **the younger of** the two brothers. 他是哥俩中较年轻的那个。

Of the two cities, Suzhou is **the more comfortable** for people to live in.

两个城市中,苏州是让人生活过得更舒适的那座城市。

(三)最高级句型

①主要用法为:A + 动词 + the + 形容词或副词最高级 + (比较范围),表示"A(在

某范围里)最……"(副词前的 the 可省略)。如：

This apple is **the smallest** one in the box. 这是盒子里最小的一个苹果。
Autumn is **the best** season in Beijing. 秋天是北京最好的季节。
Of all my friends, she studies (**the**) **most carefully**. 在我所有朋友中,她学习得最认真。
②最高级也可单独使用,后面不跟表示比较范围的修饰语。如：
My **eldest son** is twelve years old. 我的大儿子十二岁。

(四)其他句型

①比较级 + 比较级,表示"越来越……"。如：
Our country is getting **stronger and stronger**. 我们国家正变得越来越强大。
②The + 比较级,the + 比较级,表示"越……,就越……"。如：
The more books we read, **the wiser** we will be. 读书越多,我们就会越智慧。
The more money you make, **the more** you spend. 钱你赚得越多,花得越多。
The sooner, **the better**. 越快越好。
③可修饰比较级的词汇：a bit、a great deal、a little、a lot、any、by far、even、far、much、rather 和 still 等。如：
He is **much younger** than his wife. 他比妻子小得多。
④可修饰最高级的词汇：almost、by far、mostly 和 nearly 等。如：
This coat is **almost/nearly the biggest**. 这件衣服几乎是最大的。
⑤在含有 or 的选择疑问句中,如果有两者供选择,前面的形容词要用比较级形式。如：
Who is **taller**, Tim or Tom? 谁更高,提姆还是汤姆？
⑥表示倍数的比较级用法：

倍数	例句
A is … times the size/height/length/width of B	The new building is **three times the height of** the old one. 这座新楼比那座旧楼高三倍。(新楼是旧楼的四倍高)
A is … times as big/high/long/wide/large as B	Asia is **four times as large as** Europe. 亚洲是欧洲的四倍大。(亚洲比欧洲大三倍)
A is twice/ … times larger/higher/longer/wider than B	Our school is **twice/two times bigger than** yours. 我们学校比你们学校大两倍。

⑦"否定词语 + 比较级,""否定词语 + so … as"结构表示最高级含义。如：
Nothing is **so easy as** this. = Nothing is **easier** than this. = This is the **easiest** thing. 这是最容易的事。
⑧比较级与最高级的转换。如：
Mike is **the most intelligent** in his class. 迈克是班里最聪明的。
Mike is **more intelligent than any other** student in his class.

注意：any other + 名词，表示其他任何之一，所以名词要用单数。

⑨特殊结构

特殊结构	例句
no more than 表示"两者都不……"	This bedroom is **no bigger than** that one. 这个卧室与那个都不大。
not more than 表示"不多于"	This bedroom is **not bigger than** that one. 这个卧室不比那个大。 （没有"两个卧室都有不大或都不小"的含义）

Grammar Exercises
语法训练

Ⅰ．**Write the comparative and superlative forms of the words.** 写出下列词的比较级和最高级。(5%)

原级	比较级	最高级
happy		
wild		
long		
short		
big		

Ⅱ．**Fill in the blanks with proper forms of the given words.** 用所给词的适当形式填空。(10%)

1. Your classroom is _____ (wide) and _____ (bright) than ours.
2. There are _____ (few) hours of sunlight a day in winter than in summer.
3. Which do you like _____ (well), Maths or Chemistry?
4. This is the _____ (good) film I have ever seen.
5. Africa is the second _____ (large) continent in the world.
6. What he said made his mother much _____ (angry).
7. I'm not as _____ (careful) as he.
8. We've got as _____ (many) books as we need.
9. Practice as _____ (much) as you can.
10. They have done _____ (much) work with _____ (little) money than most of their colleagues.

Ⅲ．**Error identification.** 错误辨识。(20%)

1. He (A) is (B) as (C) taller as I (D) am.
2. She (A) is (B) getting (C) thin (D) every day.

3. (A) In fact, Bob is (B) heavier than (C) any boys (D) in the class.
4. (A) The girls study (B) the better (C) than (D) the boys.
5. It (A) is one of (B) the most interesting (C) book (D) that I have ever read.
6. He (A) says Mary is (B) most friendliest (C) person in (D) her family.
7. Which (A) city is (B) most (C) beautiful, (D) Beijing or Guangzhou?
8. Jack (A) works (B) hard, while Mike works (C) very harder (D) than Jack.
9. London is (A) the (B) bigger (C) city (D) in Britain.
10. Bob (A) plays football (B) terribly, but Fred plays football (C) much (D) bad than Bob.

IV. Multiple choice. 单项选择。（30%）

1. Which does Jimmy like _____, Chinese or Art?
   A. well   B. best   C. better   D. much
2. The Yangtze River is one of _____ in the world.
   A. the longest river   B. longest rivers
   C. the longest rivers   D. longer rivers
3. The box is _____ than I wanted.
   A. biger   B. the bigger   C. bigger   D. more bigger
4. My moon cake is much nicer _____ his.
   A. like   B. with   C. for   D. than
5. You are fatter than _____.
   A. he   B. his   C. him   D. himself
6. He did a better job than _____ student in his class.
   A. any   B. more   C. any other   D. any more
7. My hair is longer than _____.
   A. she   B. her   C. hers   D. she's
8. There is _____ paper here. Please bring some.
   A. little   B. less   C. fewer   D. a little
9. The pen is _____ than that one.
   A. more cheap   B. cheap
   C. much cheaper   D. quite cheaper
10. Tom speaks Chinese _____ better than Jimmy.
    A. more   B. very   C. a lot of   D. much
11. There are _____ girls in Class Two than in Class Four.
    A. more   B. nicest   C. most   D. best
12. It's too _____ for you to do that.
    A. easy   B. more dangerous C. harder   D. the easiest
13. Who has _____ apples now, Jim, Lily or Lucy?
    A. much   B. biggest   C. better   D. the most
14. I do not feel very _____ today.
    A. well   B. nice   C. better   D. good

15. Alice is _____ than Mary, but Mary is _____ than Alice.
    A. tall; stronger   B. taller; strongest
    C. tallest; strong   D. taller; stronger

16. Mother is _____ in my family.
    A. busy   B. busier   C. the busiest   D. more busy

17. There are _____ in the park on Sunday.
    A. much of children   B. a lot of people
    C. more of men   D. many of people

18. —This blue sweater is too big for me.
    —Will you please show me a _____ one?
    A. small   B. smaller   C. the smallest   D. smallest

19. No one is _____ Mary in the class.
    A. so tallest as   B. as taller as   C. so high as   D. so tall as

20. This bike is _____ than that one.
    A. twenty yuan cheap   B. twenty yuan cheaper
    C. cheap twenty yuan   D. cheaper twenty yuan

V. Fill in the blanks with the correct forms of adjectives and adverbs. 填写形容词和副词的正确形式。(20%)

I have studied in three schools — a kindergarten, a primary school and Huanggang Middle school. Let me tell you something about them.

My kindergarten is near my home. My primary school is (1) _____ (far) than kindergarten and the middle school is the (2) _____ (far), so I can't go home every day.

My primary school is very (3) _____ (small), but is as (4) _____ (beautiful) as my kindergarten. My middle school is the (5) _____ (large) and the (6) _____ (beautiful) of the three. There are many trees and sweet flowers. I like them very much. In my middle school, there is a lot of homework every day, so I am the (7) _____ (busy). There is (8) _____ (more) homework than that in primary schools and kindergartens. After class, I can play with my friends without thinking about the homework. Although I am busy in the middle school, I feel (9) _____ (happy) every day. I think my school life will be (10) _____ (good) and better.

VI. Translate the following sentences into English. 将下列句子译成英语。(15%)

1. 这件衬衫比那件衬衫便宜很多。
2. 这首歌不久后变得越来越流行了。
3. 你读书越多,就会变得越聪明。
4. 吉姆是我们学校最优秀的学生之一。
5. 我的词典比他的厚。

第五章 冠 词

一、冠词的基本概念

冠词(Article)属于虚词,是一种限定词,不可单独使用,用来表示名词的某种特性,特指专门修饰的人或物,或者泛指同一类的人或物。

二、冠词的种类

冠词分为定冠词(the)、不定冠词(a, an)和零冠词三种。

(一)定冠词

定冠词主要用于表示特指和类指,具体用法如下。

序号	表示含义	例词或例句
1	用于可数或者不可数名词前,表示特指或者已知的人或物	Tom worked in **the** college last year. 汤姆去年在那所大学上班。 He bought a house. **The** house is very large. 他买了一栋房子。那个房子非常大。
2	用于单数可数名词前,表示类指此类人或者物	**The** bird can fly in the sky. 鸟能在天上飞。 **The** cat eats the mice and **the** rabbit eats grass. 猫吃老鼠,兔吃草。
3	用于某些形容词或者分词前表示某一类人或者事情	We should respect **the** old and care for **the** young. 我们应该尊老爱幼。 **The** wounded are being treated by the doctors. 伤员正在被医生治疗。
4	用在表示独一无二的事物的名词前	**The** earth travels around **the** sun. 地球绕着太阳转。 We can see stars in **the** sky at night. 晚上我们能看见天上的星星。
5	用于序数词和形容词最高级前	Spring is **the** best season in my hometown. 春季是我家乡最好的季节。 She can never forget **the** first day in the university. 她永远也忘不了在大学里的第一天。
6	用于普通名词构成的专有名词前	She once worked in **the** United Nations. 她曾经在联合国工作过。 I have never been to **the** Great Wall. 我从未去过长城。
7	用于表示乐器的名词前,中国民族乐器除外	His younger sister likes playing **the** flute. 他妹妹喜欢吹笛子。 She always **plays erhu** in the evening. 她总是在晚上拉二胡。

续表

序号	表示含义	例词或例句
8	用于江、河、湖、海等地理名词前	The Nile is the longest river in the world. 尼罗河是世界上最长的河流。 The West Lake is really famous in China. 西湖在中国真的很有名。
9	用于一些固定词组或者搭配	in the morning 在早上　　at the moment 当时 by the way 顺便说一下　　out of the question 毫无可能

(二)不定冠词

不定冠词(a, an)表示"一个"的意思,只能在单数可数名词前面使用,表示这个人或事物是泛指的不确定的一个。其中 a 用在辅音音素开头的单词前,如 a desk;an 用在元音音素开头的单词前,如 an orange。其具体用法如下。

序号	表示含义	例词或例句
1	用于单数可数名词前,泛指一类人或物	A panda is an animal. 熊猫是一种动物。 A house is a place for people to live in. 房子是人们住的地方。
2	用于单数可数名词前,表示首次提到的人或物	A stranger came to see her yesterday. 昨天一个陌生人来找她。 This is an interesting film. 这是一部有趣的电影。
3	用于单数可数名词前,表示单一的概念	I want to buy her a gift. 我想给她买件礼物。 There is a cup on the table. 桌子上有一个杯子。
4	用在表示时间或者度量衡的名词前,表示"每一、每个"	I watch a film once a month. 我一个月看一次电影。 These apples are ten yuan a kilogram. 这些苹果每公斤十元。
5	用于一些固定词组或者搭配	have a good time 玩得开心　　in a word 简言之 in a way 某种程度上　　have a good command of 精通

(三)零冠词

零冠词,即不使用冠词,主要与不可数名词和复数名词搭配,表示特指、类指等意义。具体用法如下。

序号	用法	例词或例句
1	物质名词、抽象名词和专有名词前不用任何冠词	Water is really important to human beings. 水对人类真的很重要。 Do you like music? 你喜欢音乐吗? Cambridge University is famous all over the world. 剑桥大学全球闻名。
2	在季节、月份、假日、节日、日期、星期等表示时间的名词前不加冠词	Christmas is on December 25th. 圣诞节是在十二月二十五日。 We are always busy on Friday. 周五我们总是很忙。 If winter comes, can spring be far away? 冬天来了,春天还会远吗?
3	在三餐和球类运动的名词前不加冠词	My son has breakfast at school every day. 每天我儿子在学校吃早饭。 He enjoys playing badminton. 他喜欢打羽毛球。

续表

序号	用法	例词或例句
4	用在大部分疾病名称前	She got SARS in 2003. 2003年她得了非典。 His father is in hospital with lung cancer. 他父亲因肺癌而住院。
5	用于一些固定词组或者搭配	day after day 日复一日　heart and soul 全心全意 by bus 坐公交车　out of question 毫无疑问

Grammar Exercises
语法训练

Ⅰ. Fill in the blanks with "a" or "an". 用 a 或者 an 填空。(5%)

1. ＿＿＿ person　2. ＿＿＿ hill　3. ＿＿＿ inch　4. ＿＿＿ job　5. ＿＿＿ F
6. ＿＿＿ university　7. ＿＿＿ uncle　8. ＿＿＿ game　9. ＿＿＿ class　10. ＿＿＿ K

Ⅱ. Fill in the blanks with "a" "an" or "the". 用 a, an 或者 the 填空。(10%)

1. There are ＿＿＿ lot of birds in ＿＿＿ tree.
2. I want ＿＿＿ piece of paper.
3. He found ＿＿＿ part-time job and was paid eight dollars ＿＿＿ hour.
4. They found ＿＿＿ river to swim in.
5. She is such ＿＿＿ honest girl that she will be given ＿＿＿ Person of the Year Reward.
6. ＿＿＿ rich should help ＿＿＿ poor.
7. The little boy likes to watch ＿＿＿ stars in ＿＿＿ sky in the evening.
8. The story has ＿＿＿ unexpected ending.
9. He is always ＿＿＿ last to hand in his homework.
10. The students had finished ＿＿＿ assignment their teacher gave, so they left.

Ⅲ. Error identification. 错误辨识。(20%)

1. (A) The children usually (B) go to school (C) at an age of six (D) in China.
2. There is (A) a table by (B) the door. (C) On a table there is (D) an English book.
3. She (A) is going to (B) play guitar (C) at the concert (D) in the evening.
4. Beijing (A) is (B) one of (C) the most beautiful cities (D) in a world.
5. (A) What a pity (B) that they couldn't be there to receive (C) the prize (D) on the yesterday afternoon!
6. I (A) don't understand what (B) a boss meant, but I've got (C) a general idea of (D) the project plan.
7. We went (A) right round to (B) the west coast (C) by sea instead of driving across (D) a continent.
8. In (A) the United States, there is always (B) the flow of people to (C) the areas of (D) the

· 33 ·

country where more jobs can be found.

9. (A) The biggest whale is (B) the blue whale, which grows to be about 29 meters long, (C) the height of (D) the 9-storey building.

10. (A) The washing machines made by (B) the China have drawn (C) a worldwide attention and Haier has become (D) a popular name.

Ⅳ. Multiple choice. 单项选择。(30%)

1. In many places in China, _____ bicycle is still _____ popular means of transportation.
    A. /; a   B. the; a   C. a; the   D. the; the

2. People should make _____ room in their day for exercise.
    A. /   B. a   C. the   D. one

3. Let's go to _____ cinema—that'll help you relax for _____ while.
    A. the; the   B. the; a   C. a; the   D. a; a

4. My friend asked me to go for _____ walk, but I don't think I've got _____ energy.
    A. a; /   B. the; the   C. /; the   D. a; the

5. She wanted to catch _____ early flight, but couldn't get _____ ride to the airport.
    A. an; the   B. the; the   C. an; /   D. the; a

6. If people sit near _____ front of the bus, they can have _____ better view.
    A. the; the   B. the; a   C. /; /   D. /; a

7. The travelers here are greatly impressed because _____ people from all walks of life are working hard for _____ new Beijing.
    A. /; a   B. /; the   C. the; a   D. the; the

8. Many lifestyles do such _____ great harm to health that they actually speed up _____ weakening of the human body.
    A. a; /   B. /; the   C. a; the   D. /; /

9. There are over 60 000 satellites in _____ space, about 1 000 of which could fall down onto _____ earth.
    A. the; the   B. /; the   C. the; /   D. a; the

10. First impressions are very important. After all, you never get _____ second chance to make _____ first impression.
    A. a; the   B. the; the   C. a; a   D. the; a

11. Everything comes with _____ price; there is no such _____ thing as a free lunch in the world.
    A. a; /   B. the; a   C. the; /   D. a; a

12. In _____ most countries, a university degree can give you _____ good start in life.
    A. the; a   B. the; /   C. /; /   D. /; a

13. Jack didn't work very hard this year. As _____ result, he has made _____ little progress.
    A. a; /   B. a; the   C. /; the   D. /; /

14. —What should I do if I lose my wallet at _____ midnight on my way home?
    —You can ask _____ police for help.
    A. /; the   B. /; a   C. the; the   D. the; a

15. —_____ Internet has completely changed _____ way in which people communicate with one another.
    —Right. People rarely write letters now.
    A. /; a   B. The; the   C. An; the   D. The; a

16. She ate _____ hamburger while she was waiting for _____ 19:30 flight.
    A. the; a   B. the; the   C. a; the   D. a; a

17. Jack wanted to be _____ college student, but he failed in _____ entrance examination.
    A. a; an   B. the; the   C. the; an   D. a; the

18. —Does your father have _____ sweet tooth?
    —He used to, but now he is on _____ diet.
    A. a; /   B. /; /   C. /; a   D. a; a

19. According to the radio news, as a result of _____ heavy fog, _____ expressway has been closed up for now.
    A. a; the   B. the; /   C. /; an   D. the; the

20. I looked under _____ desk and found _____ pen I lost last week.
    A. the; a   B. the; the   C. /; the   D. the; /

V. Fill in the blanks with the proper articles. 用适当的冠词填空。(20%)

(1)_____ expensive car speeding down the main street of (2)_____ small town was soon caught up with by (3)_____ young motorcycle policeman. As he started to make out the ticket, (4)_____ woman behind the wheel said proudly, "Before you go any further, young man, I think you should know that (5)_____ mayor of this city is (6)_____ good friend of mine." (7)_____ officer did not say (8)_____ word, but kept writing. "I am also a friend of chief of police Barens," continued the woman, getting angrier each moment. Still he kept on writing. "Young man," she persisted, "I know Judge Lawson and State Senator (参议员) Patton." Handing (9)_____ ticket to the woman, the officer asked pleasantly, "Tell me, do you know Bill Bronson."

"Why? No." she answered.

"Well, that is (10)_____ man you should have known," he said, heading back to his motorcycle, "I am Bill Bronson."

VI. Translate the following sentences into English. 将下列句子译成英语。(15%)

1. 这里有家商店。我想在这个店里买一支笔。
2. 那是世界上最好看的电影。
3. 我们在夜晚看不到太阳。
4. 请把桌子上的橡皮递给我。
5. 她精通好几门外语。

第六章 代　　词

一、代词概述

代词(Pronoun)是用来代替名词的词类。英语中的代词使用频率很高,当第二次提到一些名词时,往往用代词代替。代词在句中可以作不同的成分。

序号	句法成分	例句
1	主语	**He** is a teacher. 他是位老师。
2	宾语	Have a talk with **me**. 跟我聊聊吧。
3	表语	What I want is **this**. 这就是我想要的。
4	定语	Mike wants **those** books. 迈克想要那些书。
5	同位语	Tom **himself** opened the door. 汤姆亲自开门。

二、代词的种类

英语的代词可分为:指示代词、人称代词、物主代词、反身代词、不定代词、疑问代词、相互代词,非人称代词 it,以及关系代词。关系代词将会在定语从句的章节中重点讲述,本章主要介绍前八类。

(一) 指示代词

指示代词是用来指示人或物的代词,主要有 this,that,these,those 等。

指示代词	用法	例句
this/these	指时间或地点上离说话人较近的人或物	**This** is an apple. 这是个苹果。 **These** are apples. 这些是苹果。
that/those	指时间或地点上离说话人较远的人或物	**That** is a watermelon. 那是个西瓜。 **Those** are watermelons. 那些是西瓜。

(二) 人称代词

人称代词指的是表示"你""我""他""她""它""你们""我们""它们"等词。人称代词有人称、格和数的变化。

(1) 人称代词的分类

人称代词	单数		复数	
	主格	宾格	主格	宾格
第一人称	I	me	we	us
第二人称	you	you	you	you
第三人称	he	him	they	them
	she	her		
	it	it		

(2) 人称代词的基本用法

序号	用法	例句
1	作主语	**I** like music. 我喜欢音乐。
2	作表语	—Who is there? ——是谁啊？—It's **me**. ——是我。
3	作宾语	Do you know **her**? 你认识她吗？

(三) 物主代词

表示所有关系的代词叫作物主代词,可分为两种:形容词性物主代词和名词性物主代词。

(1) 物主代词的分类

物主代词	单数			复数		
	第一人称	第二人称	第三人称	第一人称	第二人称	第三人称
形容词性物主代词	my	your	his/her/its	our	your	their
名词性物主代词	mine	yours	his/hers/its	ours	yours	theirs

(2) 物主代词的基本用法

种类	基本用法	例句
形容词性物主代词	只可用在名词前作定语,起到形容词的作用	I like **his** pencil-case. 我喜欢他的铅笔盒。
名词性物主代词	1. 作主语	Our car is here, and **theirs** is there. 我们的车在这里,他们的在那里。
	2. 作宾语	I can't find my pen. Can you lend me **yours**? 我找不到我的笔了,能把你的借给我吗?
	3. 作表语	—Whose house is that? 那是谁的房子? —It's **ours**. 那是我们的。

(四)反身代词

反身代词表示动作行为反射到动作执行者本身。

(1)反身代词的分类

人称 数	第一人称	第二人称	第三人称
单数	myself	yourself	himself/herself/itself
复数	ourselves	yourselves	themselves

(2)反身代词的用法

序号	用法	例句
1	作表语	I am not **myself** today. 我今天不舒服。
2	作宾语	She can take care of **herself** now. 她现在可以照顾自己。
3	作同位语	He can finish the task **himself**. 他自己可以完成任务。

(五)不定代词

常见的不定代词有 each,every,both,all,some,any,many,much,one,ones,other,another,neither,no,none 以及含有 some-,any-,no-等的合成词。

①all 表示三者或三者以上的人或物,或不可数的事物,如:

All of us love music. 我们都喜欢音乐。

②both 意为"两者都……",表示肯定。both 要与可数名词连用,如:

Both of the two men are doctors. 他们两个都是医生。

③none 表示三者或三者以上的否定;neither 指两者的全部否定;either 指两者中任一个,如:

None of us can speak French. 我们都不会说法语。

I like **neither** of them. 他们两个我都不喜欢。

He doesn't like **either** of the movies. 这两个电影他都不喜欢。

④each 意为"单个",侧重于个体,可作主语、定语、同位语;every 意为"每个",强调全体和共性,只能作定语,如:

He has three sons. **Each** of them has his own hobby.

他有三个儿子,每个儿子都有自己的爱好。(主语)

He has apples on **each** hand. 他的两手都有苹果。(定语)

We **each** voiced our opinion. 我们每个人都说出了自己的想法。(同位语)

There are people on **every** side of the square. 广场四周都是人。(定语)

⑤复合不定代词是由 some,any,no,every 和 body,thing,one 构成的词。

复合不定代词分类	body	thing	one
some 表示"某",一般用于肯定句	somebody	something	someone
any 表示"任何,某",常用于否定句或疑问句	anybody	anything	anyone
no 表示"没有",常用于肯定句表示否定意义	nobody	nothing	no one
every 表示"每一",常用于肯定句或疑问句	everybody	everything	everyone

注意：

a. 复合不定代词作主语时，其谓语为单数；当陈述部分的主语是 everybody、everyone 和 nobody 等，反义疑问句中的主语通常用 they。如：

Someone gives me a movie ticket. 有人给我张电影票。

Everybody likes Tom, don't **they**? 所有人都喜欢汤姆，不是吗？

Everyone has got the new book, haven't **they**? 每个人都有那本新书，不是吗？

Nobody was hurt, were **they**? 没人受伤，对吧？

b. 当陈述部分的主语是 everything、nothing、anything 和 something 时，反义疑问句中的主语一般用 it，如：

Everything seems to go right, doesn't **it**? 每一件事似乎进行得都很顺利，不是吗？

Nothing is impossible, is **it**? 没有不可能，对吗？

(六)疑问代词

常见的疑问代词见下表。

序号	疑问代词	例句
1	what 什么	**What** is this? 这是什么？
2	which 哪个,哪些	**Which** of you is the eldest? 你们中谁最大？
3	who 谁	**Who** can give me a hand? 谁能帮帮我？
4	whom 谁	**Whom** did you meet yesterday? 你昨天见了谁？
5	whose 谁的	**Whose** books are these? 这些是谁的书？

(七)相互代词

在英语中，相互代词 each other 指两者，one another 指三者或三者以上的人或物，意思为"相互,彼此"。如：

They help **each other**. 他们互相帮助。

Don't talk to **one another** in class. 课上不要互相说话。

注意： each other 和 one another 都不可以用作句子主语。

(八)非人称代词 it

①非人称代词 it 一般表示人以外的东西，是单数名词的代词，译为"它"，如：

—Where is your bike? 你的自行车在哪里？

—**It** is over there. 它在那边。

②在英语中,it 还可以用来表示时间、季节、天气和距离等。在这样的句子中,it 作为句子的主语,但不可译为"它",如:

It is eight o'clock in the morning. 现在是早上八点钟。

It is spring now. 现在是春天。

It often rains in this city. 这个城市经常下雨。

③由于主语或宾语过长,it 可以代替真正的主语或宾语成为形式主语或形式宾语,这样的句型如下:

	句型	例句
it 作形式主语	It be + 形容词 + 主语从句	It is important that we study in school. 在学校学习很重要。
	It be + 名词词组 + 主语从句	It is a pity that you missed the match. 真可惜你错过了比赛。
	It be + 过去分词 + 主语从句	It is said that 5 people dies in the accident. 据说,5 人在事故中死亡。
	It + 不及物动词 + 主语从句	It seems that he doesn't tell the truth. 似乎他没有说实话。
	It + be + 形容词 + 动词不定式	It is hard to make a good friend. 很难交到一个好朋友。
	It be + 名词词组 + 动词不定义	It is a bad habit to stay up late. 熬夜是不好的习惯。
	It be + 名词/形容词 + 动名词	It is a waste of time arguing with her. 和她争论真是浪费时间。
	It takes(sb.) + 时间/金钱 + 动词不定式	It takes them a day to reach the city. 花了他们一天时间才到达那座城市。
it 作形式复语	make、think 等及物动词 + it + 动词不定式	We think it best to get along well with others. 我们认为最好要与人好好相处。

(九)关系代词

关系代词用来引导定语从句,它代表先行词,同时在从句中可以作一定的成分。关系代词的详细句法功能和具体用法请参考定语从句这一章,本章只概述关系代词的分类。

	指人	指物	指人或指物
主格	who	which	that
宾格	whom	that	that
属格	whose	whose/of which	whose/of which

如:

She is the girl **who** comes from Beijing. 她就是那个来自北京的女孩。

Tony came back for the book **which** he had forgotten. 托尼回来取他落下的书。

This is the book **whose cover**/**the cover of which** is torn. 这就是那本封面撕破了的书。

Grammar Exercises
语法训练

I. Fill in the blanks with what you have learnt. 用所学知识填空。(5%)

人称代词	单数		复数	
	主格	宾格	主格	宾格
第一人称	I	me	we	5. _____
第二人称	you	2. _____	you	you
第三人称	1. _____	him	4. _____	them
	she	3. _____		
	it	it		

II. Fill in the blanks with the pronoun's syntactic function. 填写代词的句法功能。(10%)

1. The teacher often gives <u>me</u> a lot of help. (   )
2. In <u>our</u> class, we often have discussions about English culture. (   )
3. <u>This</u> is not a watermelon. (   )
4. —Who is there? —It is <u>me</u>, Kate. (   )
5. We will help <u>each other</u> whenever it is necessary. (   )
6. <u>All</u> of the students are late for the English lecture. (   )
7. He is not quite <u>himself</u> today. (   )
8. Which pencil is <u>yours</u>, this one or that one? (   )
9. Bob is so kind that he may help <u>anyone</u> in need. (   )
10. We <u>all</u> like to have some snacks. (   )

III. Error identification. 错误辨识。(20%)

1. If only (A) <u>your</u> (B) <u>had listened to</u> (C) <u>my advice</u> (D) <u>in the first place</u>!
2. (A) <u>Boys and girls</u> (B) <u>of mine class</u> (C) <u>were playing</u> (D) <u>in the park</u>.
3. I (A) <u>am</u> afraid I (B) <u>will miss</u> (C) <u>you birthday party</u> (D) <u>tomorrow night</u>.
4. Those (A) <u>plant</u> (B) <u>haven't been</u> (C) <u>watered</u> for (D) <u>a month</u>.
5. (A) <u>Him family</u> (B) <u>has already returned</u> (C) <u>the sports car</u> (D) <u>to you</u>.
6. (A) <u>Ten minutes earlier</u>, we (B) <u>could have spoken to</u> (C) <u>us teacher</u> (D) <u>before she left</u>.
7. (A) <u>Without</u> modern tools, (B) <u>they are</u> very hard (C) <u>to build</u> (D) <u>the Great Wall</u>.
8. He (A) <u>was</u> (B) <u>sleeping</u> (C) <u>when I</u> (D) <u>called to him</u>.
9. It's (A) <u>the second time</u> (B) <u>that he</u> (C) <u>have read</u> (D) <u>this book</u>.
10. (A) <u>After</u> (B) <u>being interviewed</u> (C) <u>for the job</u>, both of them (D) <u>takes a language test</u>.

IV. Multiple choice. 单项选择。(30%)

1. Do you remember the day _____ he was wounded?

A. that　　　　　　B. while　　　　　　C. in which　　　　　D. when
2. Is _____ necessary to knock at the door before we are allowed to come in?
   A. everyone　　　　B. this　　　　　　C. her　　　　　　　D. it
3. Her parents wouldn't let her marry anyone _____ family was poor.
   A. of whom　　　　B. whom　　　　　　C. of whose　　　　　D. whose
4. _____ leaves the room last ought to turn off the light and lock the door.
   A. Anyone　　　　　B. The person　　　　C. Whoever　　　　　D. Who
5. _____ writer is more famous in your country, Shakespeare or Mark Twain?
   A. Which　　　　　B. What　　　　　　C. Either　　　　　　D. Whether
6. —Have you seen Jack and Jane?
   —No, I haven't seen _____ of them.
   A. neither　　　　　B. any　　　　　　　C. either　　　　　　D. all
7. All _____ is needed is your help.
   A. the thing　　　　B. that　　　　　　　C. what　　　　　　D. which
8. My phone is more expensive than _____.
   A. hers　　　　　　B. her　　　　　　　C. she　　　　　　　D. he
9. I don't think _____ possible to finish the work in such a short period of time.
   A. this　　　　　　B. that　　　　　　　C. its　　　　　　　D. it
10. _____ of them knew about the plan because it was kept in a secret.
    A. Each　　　　　B. Any　　　　　　　C. No one　　　　　　D. None
11. She paid the boy 15 dollars for washing ten windows, most of _____ hadn't been cleaned for at least a year.
    A. these　　　　　B. those　　　　　　C. that　　　　　　　D. which
12. Tom and his brother went to holiday with a friend of _____.
    A. their　　　　　B. theirs　　　　　　C. hers　　　　　　　D. him
13. My sister invited John and Linda to dinner, but _____ of them came.
    A. neither　　　　B. both　　　　　　　C. either　　　　　　D. none
14. The project needs their cooperation. _____ will be achieved if we do not work well together.
    A. Anything　　　B. Nothing　　　　　C. Everything　　　　D. Something
15. Lisa and Tony have known _____ for years.
    A. each another　　B. one another　　　C. one other　　　　D. one each
16. Does _____ matter if he can't attend the meeting?
    A. this　　　　　　B. that　　　　　　　C. he　　　　　　　　D. it
17. Mr. Zhao gave the textbooks to all the pupils except _____ who had already taken them.
    A. the ones　　　　　　　　　　　　　B. ones
    C. some　　　　　　　　　　　　　　D. the others
18. There are so many kinds of computers on sale that I can't make up my mind _____ to buy.
    A. what　　　　　B. which　　　　　　C. how　　　　　　　D. where

19. Although she is very poor, she spends _____ on clothes.
   A. much		B. many		C. any		D. little
20. At our school, there are a few computers similar to _____ described in the book.
   A. ones		B. them		C. these		D. those

Ⅴ. **Fill in the blanks with the correct forms of pronouns.** 填写代词的正确形式。(20%)

Look! Here come two people, a boy and a girl. That boy is my brother. (1)_____ (he) name is Jack. (2)_____ (he) is nineteen years old. These stamps are (3)_____ (he). But those stamps are (4)_____ (I). The stamps that he has and the stamps that I own are quite different. (5)_____ (he) are quite classic while (6)_____ (I) are much more modern.

The girl next to Jack is Lisa. She is Jack's girlfriend. Look at (7)_____ (she) big smile! Isn't she lovely? Jack loves (8)_____ (she) very much. She is (9)_____ (I) schoolmate. (10)_____ (we) school is right around the corner. I can give you a tour if you want.

Ⅵ. **Translate the following sentences into English.** 将下列句子译成英语。(15%)
1. 上周来看我的那个女孩是我姐姐。
2. 他花了四个小时才找到钥匙。
3. ——是谁的狗在那边？
   ——那是我的狗。
4. 你们中谁是班长？
5. 由于正在下雨,没人愿意去做这项工作。

第七章 介　　词

一、介词的概述

介词(Preposition)是一种虚词,它不能单独担任句子成分,必须与名词、代词或相当于名词的其他词类、短语或从句构成介词短语,才能作句子成分。介词短语可以在句中担任不同的成分:

序号	句法成分	例句
1	定语	A lady **in red** is coming to the front door. 一个穿红衣服的女士正朝前门走来。
2	状语	She gets up **at six** every morning in order to catch the first bus. 为了赶上第一班公共汽车她每天早上六点起床。
3	表语	The two boys are **of the same age**. 这两个男孩子同龄。
4	宾语补足语	We helped her **out of danger**. 我们使她脱离了危险。

二、介词的分类

(一) 词形上的分类

介词由词形上可分为以下两种,即简单介词和短语介词。简单介词只有一个单词,如:in,on 和 after 等。短语介词是由两个以上单词集合而成,如:out of,in front of,because of 和 instead of 等。

表示时间的介词	(1) 表示年、月、日、时刻:in, on, at (2) 表示时间的前后:before, after (3) 表示期限:by, until, till (4) 表示期间:for, during, through (5) 表示时间的起点:from, since (6) 表示时间的经过:in, within
表示场所、方向的介词	(1) 表示场所:at, in, on, under, by, near, between, around, opposite (2) 表示方向:into, out of, along, across, through, up, past, down

续表

表示进行	表示正在"进行"的动作:at, on, under
表示原因	表示原因:for
表示数量	表示数量:about (around), over
介词短语	(1) 动词 + 介词 如:look at (2) 动词 + 形容词 + 介词 如:take pride in (3) 介词 + 名词 如:in silence

(二)其他介词

其他介词	(1) 表示手段和材料:with, in, by (2) 表示(属于)……的,……的数量或种类,来自(某地、某人),以……起始(时间或地点):of, from (3) 表示没有,像……一样,作为:without, like, as (4) 表示反对,靠着,关于,各处,身旁,询问某人或某物的情况或提出建议:against, about

三、介词与形容词、分词连用

某些形容词和用作形容词的过去分词的后面可以跟介词,介词后面加名词或动名词。通常特定的形容词和分词要求跟特定的介词,如 about, at, for, in, of, on, to, with 与某些形容词和分词连用,如:

absorbed in 专心于…… according to 按照 due to 由于
accustomed to 习惯于…… ashamed of 耻于…… bad for 有害于
involved in 参与 used to 习惯于…… liable for/to 对……有责任
fit for 适合 good at 擅长 capable of 有……能力
keen on 热衷于…… exposed of 暴露 nervous of 紧张
pleased with 对……感到高兴 responsible for 为……负责 prepared for 准备
scared of 害怕 successful in 成功做…… terrified of 对……恐慌
suspicious of 怀疑 afraid of 害怕 tired of 厌烦

如:

That little girl is **absorbed in** her novel. 那个小女孩在聚精会神地读小说。

I'm **sorry about/for** the delay. 关于延迟的事,我很抱歉。

Most boys are **keen on** basketballs. 大多数男孩子都很喜欢篮球。

Parents should be **responsible for** their children's growth.
父母应该对孩子们的成长负责任。

Walking is **good for** the health of the senior. 散步对老年人的身体好。

四、动词和介词连用

动词 + 介词可以组成复合结构,如:

accuse of 指责,控告
charge sb. with 控告
conform to 符合
dream of 梦想
insist on 坚决要求
persist in 坚持某事

long for 渴望
beware of 谨防
deal in 从事于
break into 闯入
object to 反对
abide by 遵守

apologize for 为……道歉
compare sth. with 和……相比较
depend on 依靠
hope for 希望
occur to 想起
approve of 批准

He was **charged with** theft. 他被指控偷窃。

It never **occurred to** me to insure the apartment. 我从来没有想到给公寓投保。

Such a big family **depends on** the father's little income.
那么一个大家庭都依靠父亲的微薄收入。

注意:feel like + 名词/代词,意指"觉得想吃(喝)某东西或做某事",如:

Do you **feel like** Fish and Chips? 你想吃点炸鱼薯条么?

I don't **feel like** feeding such a young kid. 我不想独立带那么小的孩子。

五、介词后的动名词

紧挨在介词后的动词必须用动名词形式,如:

That man left the restaurant **without paying** for his bill.
那个男的没有付账就离开了饭店。

Before signing the contract, please read the terms carefully.
在签署合同之前,请认真阅读条款。

注意:一些名词 + 介词 + 动名词结构,如:

I am in **favor of offering** women teachers and female students one day off on Women's Day.
我赞同三八妇女节给女老师和女学生放一天假。

Is there any **chance of her changing** her mind? 你认为她有可能改变主意吗?

六、既可作介词,又可作副词

既可作介词又可作副词的词有:above,about,across,along,before,behind,below,besides,by,down,in,near,off,on,over,past,round,since,through,under 和 up 等。如:

These things are parked **behind** the truck. (介词)这些东西被放在了卡车后面。

If you don't work hard, you will fall **behind**. (副词)如果你不努力工作,你就落后了。

Grammar Exercises
语法训练

I. Fill in the blanks with prepositions. 用介词填空。(10%)

1. China is famous _____ silk and tea.
2. She has been absent _____ school for two weeks because of illness.
3. I am really disappointed _____ the new generation of teachers who think of everything in terms of money.
4. He was curious _____ the local wedding ceremony.

5. The teacher is standing next _____ the blackboard.
6. What is the weather _____ today?
7. Classroom testing most certainly acts _____ a stimulus (刺激) to study and real learning.
8. The police broke _____ the house and arrested the criminals.
9. She knows how to deal _____ such people.
10. These two buildings were named _____ an educator who made large contributions to the university.

Ⅱ. Fill in the blanks with the prepositional phrases' syntactic function. 填写介词短语的句法功能。(5%)
1. My friends bought a house *of five rooms*. (   )
2. The post office is not far *from the shopping mall*. (   )
3. Make yourself *at home*. (   )
4. *To my surprise*, she passed all of the exams. (   )
5. We are *for you* all the time. (   )

Ⅲ. Error identification. 错误辨识。(20%)
1. (A) Stick your dream, and (B) go for it; (C) you will achieve it (D) in time.
2. (A) On the one hand they'd love to have kids, but (B) in the other hand, (C) they don't want to (D) give up their freedom.
3. (A) Nobody knows (B) what (C) happened to her (D) in the morning of March 3rd.
4. (A) He looked me (B) in surprise and asked me (C) why I was (D) in such a hurry.
5. (A) He stood (B) against the wall, (C) waiting for the children (D) to come on.
6. (A) In front of the theatre, there is (B) a large statue (C) in George Washington (D) riding on a horse.
7. (A) On (B) arriving in the shore, the girl (C) struggled up the hill (D) towards the light she had seen.
8. (A) In spring and summer all the flowers (B) in the garden (C) are (D) on bloom.
9. The school bus comes to (A) pick up him (B) on 8:30 in the morning and sends him back (C) at 3:30 in the afternoon (D) on school days.
10. (A) After rush hours, he will go home (B) to have a rest (C) during four (D) in the afternoon.

Ⅳ. Multiple choice. 单项选择。(30%)
1. There is a house _____ the post office.
   A. next to   B. next   C. close   D. close by
2. That woman will quarrel _____ everybody _____ everything.
   A. about; about
   C. with; about
   B. about; with
   D. with; with
3. The old man was knocked over by a running car when he went _____ the street.
   A. cross   B. with   C. through   D. across
4. Fish cannot live _____ water.
   A. before   B. in   C. without   D. with

5. We know that a new bridge is being built _____ the river.
   A. along   B. in   C. on   D. above
6. Jonny will have finished the work _____ the end of tomorrow.
   A. by   B. at   C. in   D. on
7. Look! The building is _____ construction.
   A. on   B. under   C. at   D. in
8. Have you any objection _____ changing your working hours?
   A. at   B. with   C. on   D. to
9. She insisted _____ paying for herself.
   A. on   B. in   C. from   D. with
10. The well-known reporter asked _____ an interview with the President.
    A. at   B. in   C. for   D. to
11. We can sit _____ the trees when we have a rest.
    A. from   B. between   C. to   D. in
12. I am not familiar _____ his novels and not very keen _____ reading them.
    A. with; in   B. with; on   C. to; on   D. to; in
13. All of us agreed to abide _____ rules of the game.
    A. by   B. to   C. in   D. with
14. You should not laugh _____ your younger brother for giving the incorrect answer to the question.
    A. in   B. to   C. /   D. at
15. The great scientist is worthy _____ the Nobel Prize.
    A. to   B. /   C. of   D. with
16. —Which colour do you like?
    —I prefer blue _____ red.
    A. than   B. to   C. as   D. with
17. Instead of calling _____ his uncle, he called _____ my new house with his wife that day.
    A. by; at   B. on; at   C. on; on   D. at; by
18. —Do you have any difficulty working out the problem?
    —Yes. It is _____ me.
    A. for   B. within   C. beyond   D. within
19. Mr. Green was driving fast to take his wife to a nearby hospital because their baby is _____ .
    A. on its way   B. in the way   C. by the way   D. out of the way
20. Food prices increased _____ 10% in less than a year.
    A. at   B. on   C. by   D. for

V. Fill in the blanks with the correct prepositions. 填写正确的介词。(20%)

Father's Day occurs on the 3rd Sunday in June. The idea for creating a day (1) _____ children to honor their fathers began in Spokane, Washington. A woman (2) _____ the name of Sonora Smart Dodd thought (3)_____ the idea for Father's Day while listening to a Mother's Day sermon(布道) (4)_____ 1909. Having been raised (5)_____ her father, Henry Jackson Smart, after her mother died, Sonora wanted her father to know how special he was (6)_____ her. It was her father that made all the parental sacrifices and was, (7)_____ the eyes of his daughter, a courageous, selfless, and loving man. Sonora's father was born in June, so she chose to hold the first Father's Day celebration (8)_____ Spokane, Washington (9)_____ the 19th of June, 1910. In 1924 President Calvin Coolidge announced the third Sunday in June (10)_____ Father's Day. Roses are the Father's Day flowers.

Ⅵ. Translate the following sentences into English. 将下列句子译成英语。(15%)
1. 地球绕着太阳转。
2. 那个小姑娘独自穿过森林。
3. 你不该害怕犯错误。
4. 同学之间相处得非常好。
5. 这些玩具飞机是竹子做成的。

第八章 连　　词

一、连词概述

连词(Conjunction)是虚词,不能在句中担任成分。它的作用是用来连接词语与词语、短语与短语以及分句与分句,如:

I want to buy some apples **and** bananas. 我想买一些苹果和香蕉。

Is our sports meet going to be held this week **or** next week?
我们的运动会是这周开还是下周开?

She was taking a bath **when** the telephone rang. 她正在洗澡,这时电话铃响了。

二、连词种类

连词种类	定义	例词
并列连词 Coordinating Conjunction	主要连接并列关系的成分和分句	and,but,or,so
从属连词 Subordinating Conjunction	主要引导状语从句和名词性从句	when, where, because, if, although, as, that,whether

三、并列连词

(一) 表示并列的连词

(1) and

a. and 连接三个以上的并列的语言单位(单词、词组、分句)时,只在最后两个并列成分之间用 and,如:

I like having fruits such as apples, pears, bananas **and** oranges.
我喜欢吃水果,如苹果、梨、香蕉以及橘子。

He was tall **and** handsome. 他又高又英俊。

Sit down **and** tell me all about it. 坐下来,告诉我发生了什么。

b. 如果每两个并列成分之间都使用 and 则表示强调,如:

Men in such a state are badly in need of food **and** water **and** care.
这种状态下的人急需食物、水和关照。

c. both 与 and 连用,表示"两个都;既……又……",如:

Both Tom **and** Jane are late. 汤姆和简都迟到了。

All of the people **both** sang **and** danced at the party. 所有的人在聚会上都又唱又跳。

(2) or

a. 用在选择疑问句中连接被选择的对象,意为"或者,还是",如:

What would you like to drink, coffee **or** tea? 你想喝点什么,咖啡还是茶?

b. 在肯定句里,并列成分用 and 连接,在否定句里,并列成分用 or 连接,如:

I like running **and** swimming. 我喜欢跑步和游泳。

I don't like running **or** swimming. 我不喜欢跑步和游泳。

c. or 也有"否则"的意思,如:

He must be at home, **or** his car wouldn't be here.
他一定在家里,否则他的汽车不可能停在这里。

d. either 与 or 连用,构成"either...or..."结构表示"或者……或者……"或"要么……要么……",可用来连接两个并列的成分,如:

When he is happy, he **either** sings **or** dances. 当他高兴的时候,要么唱歌要么跳舞。

I go to school **either** on foot **or** by bike. 我不是步行上学,就是骑车上学。

注意:"either...or..."在连接两个主语时,谓语应遵循就近一致原则。

Either you **or** your husband has to go. 或者你或者你的丈夫,必须要去一趟。

I guess that **either** the cakes **or** the juice is free of charge.
我猜或者是蛋糕或者是果汁是免费的。

I guess that **either** the juice **or** the cakes are free of charge.
我猜或者是果汁或者是蛋糕是免费的。

另外,either 作副词单独使用时,意为"也(不)",用于否定句的句末。如:

If you don't go there, I won't, **either**. 如果你不去那里,我也不去。

(3) nor

a. 用来连接否定的并列成分,放在 not、no、never 等否定词后,表示"也不",如:

You should not be too proud **nor** too humble. 你不要太骄傲,也不要太谦卑。

b. 用于否定句后引出另外一个否定句,引出的否定句要用部分倒装,如:

I don't have money, **nor do I** want to earn it. 我没有钱,我也不想去赚钱。

It is not your fault, **nor** mine. 这既不是你的错,也不是我的错。

I didn't pass the English exam **and nor** did Xiaoming.
我没有通过英语考试,小明也没通过。

c. 与 neither 连用,构成 neither...nor...结构表示"既不……也不……",可用来连接并列的成分,如:

George **neither** drinks **nor** smokes. 乔治既不喝酒也不吸烟。

They work **neither** for fame **nor** for money. 他们工作既不为名也不为利。

注意:"neither...nor..."在连接两个主语时,谓语应遵循就近一致原则。

Neither the teacher **nor** his students like listening to the speech.
这名老师和他的学生们都不喜欢听这个演讲。
Neither the students **nor** their teacher likes listening to the speech.
这些学生们和他们的老师都不喜欢听这个演讲。

(4) otherwise

otherwise 意为"否则;不然",相当于 or 或 if not,如:
Put the cap back on the bottle, **otherwise** the juice will spill.
把瓶盖儿盖好,否则果汁就洒出来了。
You have to go now, **otherwise** you'll miss the bus.
你现在必须出发了,否则你就赶不上公交车了。

(二)表示转折的连词

(1) but

but 可以连接两个并列成分或两个并列分句,意为"而是,但是,然而",如:
I did this not for you **but** for your parents. 我这么做,不是为了你,而是为了你的父母。
He rushed to the station **but** he was too late to catch the last subway.
他冲向车站,但还是太晚了,没有赶上末班地铁。
注意:but 不能与 though/although 连用。

(2) yet

yet 作为连词,表示"然而,但是",用法和 but 相同,如:
The tongue is not steel, **yet** (= but) it cuts. 舌头不是铁做的,但却能伤人。
The matter sounds strange, **yet** (= but) it is true. 此事听起来奇怪,但却是事实。
注意:but 表示对照或对立时,一般都比较轻松自然;yet 在表示对照或对立时,则往往比较强烈,时常出人意料。此外,but 是并列连词,而 yet 则可作并列连词或副词,可以说 and yet,但不可说 and but,如:
She does not speak our language **and yet** (= but) she seems to understand what we say.
她不会说我们的语言,但似乎她理解我们说的话。

(3) however

however 既有连词的词性又有副词的词性,所以它的用法更灵活一些,放在句子中的位置也更为灵活,如:
She felt ill, **however**, she still went on working. 她生病了,但是她仍然坚持工作。
I was angry. I kept patient and listened to her, **however**.
我很生气,但是我还是保持耐心,听她讲话。
注意:however 与 but 两者都有"但是,然而"之意,都引出并列句。从语义上讲,but 所表示的是非常明显的对比和转折的意味,比 however 转折意义要强。在语序上,but 总是位于所引出的分句之首,而 however 却可位于句首、句中和句末。从标点符号上对比,but 之后一般不使用逗号,而 however 无论在句首、句中和句末则必须用逗号与句子其他部分分开。如:
It was bad weather, **however**, we still enjoyed our holiday.
It was bad weather. We, **however**, still enjoyed our holiday.

It was bad weather. We enjoyed our holiday, **however**.
天气虽然不好,但是我们仍然度假愉快。

(三)表示结果的连词

(1) so

用作连词时,so 可独立引导并列分句(分句前可用逗号或不用),如:

I was feeling hungry **so** I made myself a sandwich. 我很饿,所以我做了一个三明治。

There are no buses, **so** you'll have to walk. 没有公交了,因此你必须得走路了。

(2) therefore

therefore 是连接性副词,用法比较灵活,放在句子中的位置也比较灵活,可放于句首和句中,前后用逗号隔开。如:

I think, **therefore** I am. 我思故我在。

It rained heavily; **therefore**, the game was called off.

It rained heavily; the game, **therefore**, was called off. 雨下得很大,因此比赛被取消了。

注意:therefore 前一般有分号(或破折号)隔开或与 and 连用,才能引导并列分句。如:

He was ill, **and therefore** he could not come. 他生病了,所以不能来。

(四)其他并列连词结构

并列连词	例句	注释
not only... but also...	His rude words made **not only** me **but also** my parents very angry. 他粗鲁的话不仅令我生气,也令我的父母很生气。 He **not only** turned up late **but also** forgot to take his books. 他不仅来晚了,而且还忘记带书了。	not only...but also...常用来连接两个对等的成分,但连接两个主语时,谓语动词要遵循"就近原则"。如: **Not only** Jack **but also** his parents are fond of watching football matches. 不但杰克,而且他的父母都喜欢看足球比赛。 如果 not only...but also 连接两个句子并放在句首时,前一个分句常用倒装来表示强调,而 but(also)后的分句仍用陈述语序。如: **Not only** did he turn up late **but he also** forgot to take his books. 他不仅来晚了,而且还忘记带书了。
as well as	She likes reading **as well as** talking in her spare time. 在业余时间,她喜欢阅读,也喜欢交谈。 It is important for you **as well as** for me. 这对你我来说都很重要。 A lot of modern women can do professional jobs **as well as** take good care of their families. 很多当代女性都有自己的职业而且还能照顾好家庭。	as well as 只能连接并列的词和词组,不能连接两个分句,例如下面的句子就是错误的: I can play the piano **as well as** he can play the violin. 另外,as well as 连接两个主语时,谓语要与第一个主语保持一致,如: The teacher **as well as** some of his students is going to attend the meeting. 这个老师以及他的一些学生会参加这个会议。

四、从属连词

从属连词用于引导从句以形成句子的一部分或修饰句子的构成要素,从属连词是连词的一种,用来引导名词性从句和状语从句。

(一)名词性从句的从属连词

分类	例句
that 引导的名词性从句	The fact is **that** we have to prepare for that project. 事实是我们要为那个项目做准备。
wh-引导的名词性从句	The production is decided by **what** customers need. 顾客的需求决定生产。
if 或 whether 引导的名词从句	His parents worried about **whether** he could pass through the crisis of his illness. 他的父母担心他是否能度过疾病的危险期。

(二)状语从句的从属连词

分类	例词	例句
引导时间状语从句的从属连词	when, while, before	Turn the lights off **before** you leave. 离开前请关灯。
引导条件状语从句的从属连词	if, unless, as long as	You will fail **unless** you work hard. 你若不努力就会失败。
引导目的状语从句的从属连词	in order that, so that	We traveled by air **in order that** we might save time. 我们坐飞机旅行是为了节约时间。
引导结果状语从句的从属连词	so...that, such...that	He is **so** careless **that** he has been fired several times. 他特别粗心以至于被多次解雇。
引导原因状语从句的从属连词	because, as, since	**Because** she had a cold, she went to see a doctor. 由于感冒,她去看了病。
引导让步状语从句的从属连词	although, though, even if	**Although** he is poor, he is satisfied. 他虽穷却能知足常乐。
引导方式状语从句的从属连词	as, like, as if, as though	Her husband behaved **as if** nothing had happened. 她的丈夫装作若无其事的样子。
引导地点状语从句的从属连词	where, wherever	Sit **wherever** you like, please. 请随便坐。
引导比较状语从句的从属连词	than, as...as	It was more difficult **than** I thought. 这比我想象的要难。

Grammar Exercises
语法训练

Ⅰ. Combine the two sentences with the conjuctions in the brackets. 用括号内连词连接句子。(5%)

1. She cooked on Saturday. She cooked on Sunday. (both…and…)
_____

2. She didn't do her homework. She didn't watch TV. (neither…nor…)
_____

3. You may leave at once. You may also wait till tomorrow. (either…or…)
_____

4. I don't care who did this. I don't want to know what happened. (neither…nor…)
_____

5. You apologize to me face to face. Or you do it by writing a letter. (either…or…)
_____

Ⅱ. Match the two parts of the sentences. 连线。(10%)

A.

1. Focus on your work
2. I've tried my best to persuade him
3. These goods are very expensive
4. The wonder boy can not only write good essays
5. She should be honest next time

A. or I won't trust her.
B. but also speak five foreign languages.
C. but he won't listen.
D. so please be careful with them.
E. and you can finish it on time.

B.

6. He didn't understand the question
7. They own three apartments in the city
8. Do as I've told you,
9. It was really cold outside,
10. He is rich, honest and handsome,

A. otherwise you can't work out the problem.
B. as well as a house in the country.
C. and nor did I.
D. therefore, a lot of girls like him.
E. however, we still went jogging.

Ⅲ. Error identification. 错误辨识。(20%)

1. Little Ben (A) practised not only (B) playing the piano (C) but also (D) swim this summer.

2. The young mother (A) as well as her (B) two children often (C) buy a lot (D) in the supermarket.

3. (A) Although I said (B) sorry to him, but he (C) didn't (D) forgive me.

4. Jack is a good boy (A) who (B) neither drinks (C) nor (D) smoke.
5. (A) Which one (B) would you like (C) to have, hamburger (D) and pie?
6. (A) I am afraid (B) of it is a huge (C) challenge; nobody, (D) therefore, wants to take it.
7. (A) Neither (B) the drinks nor the food (C) are cheap in (D) this restaurant.
8. I (A) have to say either your mother (B) nor your father (C) has to (D) pay for this.
9. We (A) wonder (B) if there has been life (C) on other planets or not (D) when looking at the sky.
10. (A) Last night Martha (B) had to study (C) for a test; she, (D) otherwise, went to the library.

IV. Multiple choice. 单项选择。(30%)

1. The colours in that picture are red, gold, black, _____ green.
   A. and   B. but   C. or   D. so
2. My car is rather old _____ comfortable. So I continue to drive it.
   A. and   B. but   C. or   D. so
3. We don't usually go shopping _____ go hiking. We just like staying at home and doing nothing.
   A. and   B. but   C. or   D. so
4. He was very tired last night, _____ he went to bed early.
   A. however   B. but   C. or   D. so
5. What he said seemed very rude and cruel _____ it was true.
   A. yet   B. as well as   C. or   D. nor
6. I didn't write to him and _____ did I phone him.
   A. yet   B. as well as   C. or   D. nor
7. Alice is kind _____ honest and we all like her.
   A. yet   B. as well as   C. or   D. nor
8. Jake, we have to go shopping after work _____ we have nothing to cook.
   A. yet   B. as well as   C. or   D. nor
9. Helen Keller couldn't hear and she couldn't speak, _____.
   A. therefore   B. otherwise   C. however   D. either
10. Adam got injured in the game and _____ he had to give it up.
    A. therefore   B. otherwise   C. however   D. either
11. The price of the houses has been rising; a lot of people, _____, still continue to buy them.
    A. therefore   B. otherwise   C. however   D. either
12. We were delayed at the airport, _____ we would have been here by lunch time.
    A. therefore   B. otherwise   C. however   D. either
13. —Do you want tea or coffee?
    —_____. I really don't mind.
    A. Both   B. Either   C. Neither   D. As well

14. —What day is it today, the 5th or the 6th?
    —_____. It's 7th.
    A. Both   B. Either   C. Neither   D. As well

15. —Where did you go for your holidays, Urumchi or Karamay?
    —_____. A week in Urumchi and a week in Karamay.
    A. Both   B. Either   C. Neither   D. As well

16. She sings beautifully and plays the piano _____.
    A. both   B. either   C. neither   D. as well

17. Neither my parents nor I _____ going to buy a car because we think it is useless.
    A. are   B. am   C. is   D. will

18. The CD player as well as the CDs _____ popular with young people some years ago.
    A. is   B. was   C. are   D. were

19. I don't know what has happened between them and probably _____ do they themselves.
    A. only   B. both   C. either   D. neither

20. Why the fire occurred was _____ a worker forgot to turn off the machine.
    A. due to   B. owning to   C. that   D. because of

Ⅴ. **Fill in the blanks with proper conjunctions. 用恰当的连词填空。**(20%)

I always have rich breakfast in the morning. On weekdays, I have milk (1)_____ cereal (麦片), and toast (面包) as well as jam. After that I drink (2)_____ a cup of tea or a cup of coffee. You may say it's a big breakfast, (3)_____ you should see what I eat on Saturdays and Sundays. I (4)_____ have bacon but also sausages (香肠) and eggs. I drink (5)_____ fruit juice and tea, and I eat some fruits as well. Sometimes I have some Chinese fried rice (6)_____ Japanese sushi (寿司). Either of them has to be prepared well the night before; (7)_____, I don't have enough time to do it in the morning.

From my breakfast you can know I love food. Actually, I love cooking more (8)_____ I love food. I buy ingredients (材料) in the market (9)_____ I cook them at home. To be honest, if I don't enjoy cooking, (10)_____ will I enjoy eating.

Ⅵ. **Translate the following sentences into English. 将下列句子译成英语。**(15%)
1. 穿上你的衣服,否则你会着凉的。
2. 一家好的公司不仅应该为员工提供好的薪水还应该关心员工的健康。
3. 这个计划听起来几乎不可能,但是他决定试一试。
4. 这个暑假我或者留在学校学习或者出去打工。
5. 比赛结果既不是特别好也不是特别差。

第九章 动 词

一、动词概述

动词(Verb)是用来表示动作或状态的词类。在英语中,每个句子都需有一个动词来担当谓语。一般来说,没有动词不成句,动词是英语句子的重心,表示句子的主语"是什么"或者"做什么"。本章将综述动词的种类、基本形式和时态等内容。

二、动词的种类

按词义和功能可分为实义动词、系动词、情态动词和助动词。见下表:

动词		例词
实义动词	及物动词	love 爱, like 喜欢, buy 买
	不及物动词	rise 升起, work 工作, go 去
系动词		be, feel 感觉, get 得到
情态动词		can 能, must 必须, may 可以
助动词		do, have, does

注意: 只有实义动词担当谓语成分,系动词后为表语,要使用主系表结构。如:
We **love** the idea of sharing. 我们喜欢分享这个概念。(谓语)
My parents **go** to work together every day. 我父母每天一起上班。(谓语)
He **is** very tall. 他很高。(系动词)
You **must** feel really proud of your daughter for getting into Harward.
你女儿考上哈佛,你肯定很自豪了。(情态动词)
They **have** been living overseas since 2000.
他们从2000年开始就侨居海外了。(助动词)

(一)实义动词

实义动词又称行为动词,它的词汇意义完整,可以单独作谓语。按照是否能够跟宾语,实义动词又分为及物动词和不及物动词。

(1)及物动词
①及物动词的用法
及物动词的后面需要跟名词或代词作它的宾语,如:

I **have** fruits every day. 我每天吃水果。

He really **loves** his wife. 他很爱他的妻子。

②及物动词的句式有主谓宾、主谓双宾和主谓宾补,如:

We often **play** basketball after class. 我们经常课后打篮球。(主谓宾)

Tony has **bought** me a book. 托尼给我买了本书。(主谓双宾)

We **made** Jerry our monitor. 我们选杰瑞当我们的班长。(主谓宾补)

③及物动词的被动语态

英语里面只有后面可以直接跟宾语的动词,也就是及物动词才有被动语态。被动语态是由原主动句的宾语变成被动句的主语。如:

We **sold** the car yesterday. 我们昨天卖了这辆车。(主动)

The car **was sold** yesterday. 这辆车昨天卖了。(被动)

(2)不及物动词

①不及物动词的用法

不及物动词不能直接跟宾语,但可以有"不及物动词 + 介词 + 宾语"的结构。如:

He is **looking** at the photo. 他在看照片。

Tom and Mary always **laugh** at each other. 汤姆和玛丽总是互相嘲笑。

注意:英语中的许多动词既可以作及物动词,又可以作不及物动词,如:

Let's **begin**. 咱们开始吧。(不及物动词)

Let's **begin** our class. 咱们开始上课吧。(及物动词)

②常见的不及物动词,如:walk,listen,look,run,go,swim,stand 和 sleep 等

(二)系动词

"He <u>is</u> very tall."用中文可以说,"他很高"。在汉语中,"高"可以直接作谓语,但是英语中,tall 不能作谓语,需要在前面加上系动词 is,变成了"He <u>is</u> very tall."主系表结构,而系动词又叫作连系动词。因为在汉语语法中没有系动词的概念,所以大家在学习和运用系动词时会感到困难。最常见的系动词是 be,在句中有时可以翻译为"是",有时不用翻译出来。它不能单独成谓语,它必须要和它后面的表语一起构成合成谓语。它后面的表语可以是形容词、名词、动名词、副词、不定式和介词短语。

另外有一些词既可以作为实义动词,又可以作为系动词,表示"变成某种状态""保持某种状态"或"某种感受",如:come,feel,taste,get,look,smell 和 seem 等。

常见系动词	例 句
be	I **am** the only child in my family. 我是家里的独生子女。
look	This girl **looks** so sad. 这姑娘看上去如此悲伤。
get	When did you **get** married? 你们什么时候结婚的?
come	All my dreams will **come** true. 我所有的梦想都将成真。
seem	That child **seems** lost. 那孩子看上去似乎迷路了。
smell	The dish **smells** so good. 那道菜闻起来太香了。
feel	I **felt** terrible for telling her the bad news. 告诉她这个坏消息,我感觉糟透了。

(三)情态动词

情态动词表示说话人对某一动作或状态的态度,如"应当""可能"等。情态动词虽然本身具有意义,但是不能单独作谓语。情态动词必须和实义动词的原形连用,一起构成谓语。情态动词是没有人称和数的变化的,如:

I **can** swim. 我会游泳。
You **can** swim. 你会游泳。
She **can** swim. 她会游泳。

在上面三个例句中,情态动词没有人称的变化。即使主语是第三人称单数,can 这个情态动词也依旧要用原形,不能加"s"。

注意:情态动词和助动词相同的是,它们都不能单独作谓语。但是,情态动词和助动词不同的是:助动词没有实际词义,而情态动词却是具有实际词义的。常见的情态动词见下表:

序号	原形	词义	否定形式	过去式	否定形式
1	can	能够	cannot 或 can't	could	could not 或 couldn't
2	may	可以,或许	may not	might	might not 或 mightn't
3	must	必须	must not 或 mustn't	must	must not 或 mustn't
4	will	愿意	will not 或 won't	would	would not 或 wouldn't
5	shall	应该	shall not 或 shan't	should	should not 或 shouldn't
6	need	需要	need not 或 needn't	need	need not 或 needn't
7	dare	敢于	dare not 或 daren't	dare	dare not 或 daren't
8	had better	最好	had better not	had better	had better not
9	ought to	应该	ought not to	ought to	ought not to
10	have to	必须	don't/doesn't have to	had to	didn't have to

接下来,介绍一下最常见的情态动词的用法:

①can 表示能力或可能性。can 的否定式是 cannot,或者可以缩写为 can't。如:
I **can** speak English. 我会说英语。→否定句:I **cannot** speak English. 我不会说英语。
Tom **can** be right. 汤姆有可能是对的。→否定句:Tom **can't** be right. 汤姆不可能是对的。

②may 表示"可以",用在问句中表示征求对方的许可,在肯定回答时一般不用它。如:
—**May** I come in? 我能进来吗?
—Yes, you **can**. 可以,请进。

③must 表示"必须",如:
You **must** do your homework today. 你必须今天做作业。
We **must** speak English in class. 我们课上必须讲英语。

注意:在回答以 must 引导的问句时,否定回答要用 needn't(不必),如:
— **Must** I hand in my homework today? 我今天必须要交作业吗?

—No, you **needn't**. 不,不必。

另外,mustn't 表示的意思是"禁止""不准",如:

You **mustn't** take the book out of the library. 禁止把书带出图书馆。

④can,could,may,might 和 must 表推测

这五个情态动词都可以用于对存在或发生的事情的推测。其中,推测语气最弱的是 can 和 could,意为"或许";may 和 might 居中,意为"可能";而推测语气最强的是 must,意为"断定,肯定"。

另外,在肯定句中,can 表示比较一般的可能性;而 may 则表示实际上正在发生或即将发生的可能性,如:

The bad news **could** be true. 那个坏消息或许是真的。

—Where is Amy? 艾米在哪儿?

—She **may/might** be in her room. 她可能在她房间。

My sister isn't answering the telephone. She **must** be out.

我姐姐没接电话。她肯定出去了。

Your brother **can't** be in New York. I saw him just now.

你哥哥不可能在纽约。我刚刚还看到他。

⑤had better 表示建议,没有词形变化,用于一切人称,后面接不带 to 的不定式,意思为"最好",如:

We **had better** go over the notes again. 我们最好把笔记再复习一遍。

You **had better** not tell him the news. 你最好别告诉他这个消息。

⑥need 用作情态动词时,表示"需要做某事",need 后直接跟动词原型,而且 need 没有人称、数的变化(第三人称单数不加 s),其对应否定形式为 need not do 或 needn't do。如:

⎰He **need** think about this before he makes the final decision.
⎱在做最后决定之前,他需要想一想。
⎰He **need not think** about this before he makes the final decision.
⎱在做最后决定之前,他不需要想一想。
⎰You **need** discuss with your tutor when writing your paper.
⎱写论文的时候,你需要和导师商量一下。
⎰You **needn't** discuss with your tutor when writing your paper.
⎱写论文的时候,你不需要和导师商量一下。

注意:need 还可以作实意动词使用时,need 有人称、数和时态的变化,用法如下:

a. need + something 需要某物→否定形式 <u>do/does</u> not need anything 不需要某物

She **needs** some water to drink. 她需要喝水。

She **does not need** any water to drink. 她不需要喝水。

b. need to do something 需要做某事→否定形式 <u>do/does</u> not need to do anything 不需要做某事

He **needs to have** his bike repaired right away. 他需要马上修车。

He **does not need to have** his bike repaired right away. 他不用马上修车。

c. need somebody to do something 需要某人做某事→否定形式 <u>do/does</u> not need somebody to do anything 不需要做某事

We **need** volunteers **to clean** up the hall. 我们需要志愿者打扫礼堂。

We **do not need** volunteers **to clean** up the hall. 我们不需要志愿者打扫礼堂。

d. need doing = need to be done 被需要……

The room **needs cleaning** = The room **needs to be cleaned**. 房间需要打扫了。

(四)助动词

助动词本身没有意义,它必须和实义动词一起构成谓语。主要有 be,have,do,shall,will 与实义动词一起,构成各种时态、语态、否定和疑问。如:

He **doesn't** like Japanese food. 他不喜欢日本菜。

Do you have anything important to tell them? 你有没有重要的事情要告诉他们?

Will you buy the dictionary from the book store? 你会从书店里买那本字典吗?

三、动词的基本形式

英语中动词有四种基本形式,分别是动词原形、过去式、过去分词和现在分词。

(一)动词的过去式及过去分词的构成

(1)规则动词的变化

序号	构成法	例词
1	一般加 -ed	work,worked,worked
2	以 e 结尾的词加 -d	live,lived,lived
3	以"辅音字母 + y"结尾的词,改 y 为 i,再加 -ed	study,studied,studied
4	以"元音字母 + y"结尾的词,直接加 -ed	play,played,played
5	以重读闭音节或 r 音节结尾,末尾只有一个辅音字母的词,要双写这个辅音字母,再加 -ed	stop,stopped,stopped prefer,preferred,preferred

(2)英语常用不规则动词的形式

动词不规则变化形式	动词原形	过去式	过去分词
AAA 动词	cost 花费	cost	cost
	cut 割,切	cut	cut
	hurt 受伤	hurt	hurt
AAB 动词	beat 打败	beat	beaten
ABA 动词	come 来	came	come
	become 变	became	become
	run 跑	ran	run

续表

动词不规则变化形式	动词原形	过去式	过去分词
ABB 动词	burn 燃烧	burnt	burnt
	deal 解决	dealt	dealt
	spend 花费	spent	spent
ABC 动词	blow 吹	blew	blown
	drive 驾驶	drove	driven
	draw 画画	drew	drawn

具体情况,可参考本书附录或英语字典中的不规则动词表。

(二)动词的现在分词的构成

序号	构成法	例词
1	一般加-ing	work, working
2	以 e 结尾的词去 e 加-ing	live, living
3	以重读闭音节或 r 音节结尾,末尾只有一个辅音字母的词,双写这个辅音字母,再加-ing	stop, stopping prefer, preferring
4	以 ie 结尾的重读开音节的词,改 ie 为 y,再加-ing	die, dying

四、动词的时态

作谓语的动词用来表示动作发生时间的各种形式叫作时态。在英语中,一般利用动词本身的词形变化或加助动词来表示动作发生的时间,即动词的时态。这一点与汉语是大不相同的,因为汉语动词本身没有时态形式的变化。在中文里,动词不是用词形的变化来体现时态,而是借助特定的词语,如:了、正、将等,来体现动作发生的时间,到底是过去、现在还是将来。

动词时态的具体定义、内容和用法将在下一章当中详述,本章只概述英语中动词时态的种类。一般来讲,英语动词有十六种时态,分四大类:过去、现在、将来、过去将来。每一类又含有四种形式:一般、进行、完成、完成进行,共计十六个时态形式。以 work 为例,详见下表。

时间 \ 形式	一般时	进行时	完成时	完成进行时
过去	worked	was/were working	had worked	had been working
现在	works/work	is/am/are working	has/have worked	has/have been working
将来	shall/will work	shall/will be working	shall/will have worked	shall/will have been working
过去将来	would work	would be working	would have worked	would have been working

Grammar Exercises
语法训练

I. Fill in the blanks with what you have learnt. 用所学知识填空。(5%)

原形	过去式	词义
can	1. _____	能够
may	2. _____	可以,或许
must	3. _____	必须
4. _____	would	愿意
5. _____	should	应该

II. Fill in the blanks with the verb category. 填写动词种类。(10%)

1. Who <u>can</u> tell the difference between those twins? (　　)
2. They often <u>have</u> debates about various hot issues. (　　)
3. That boy <u>seemed</u> extremely confused about the current situation. (　　)
4. He <u>doesn't</u> know the sad news yet. (　　)
5. Friends <u>should</u> help each other whenever and wherever they are. (　　)
6. People usually <u>get</u> excited on holidays. (　　)
7. His entire family <u>live</u> in Hong Kong right now. (　　)
8. <u>May</u> I borrow your history textbook? (　　)
9. You <u>had better</u> tell her the truth before it is too late. (　　)
10. They <u>have</u> been studying since yesterday morning. (　　)

III. Error identification. 错误辨识。(20%)

1. (A) <u>Last week</u> (B) <u>they</u> came to Beijing and (C) <u>visit</u> (D) <u>the Great Wall</u>.
2. (A) <u>I have ever</u> (B) <u>work</u> in that bank (C) <u>in England</u> (D) <u>where</u> my family stayed with me.
3. (A) <u>His boss</u> (B) <u>made</u> (C) <u>him</u> (D) <u>did the job</u> alone.
4. (A) <u>The lady</u> just now (B) <u>steals</u> (C) <u>from me</u> (D) <u>in the No.5 subway line</u>.
5. (A) <u>My father</u> (B) <u>leaves</u> (C) <u>the key</u> (D) <u>on the table</u> the day before yesterday.
6. Those bridges (A) <u>were</u> (B) <u>build</u> many years (C) <u>ago</u>, but they (D) <u>are</u> still standing.
7. (A) <u>This are</u> (B) <u>the book</u> (C) <u>that</u> I (D) <u>talked about</u>.
8. My aunt (A) <u>have</u> (B) <u>a friend</u> working (C) <u>in the army</u> (D) <u>of that country</u>.
9. (A) <u>Friendship</u> is important (B) <u>to us</u> and (C) <u>everyone</u> (D) <u>need</u> friendship.
10. The more he (A) <u>will know</u>, the more he (B) <u>will realize</u> (C) <u>how wrong you</u> (D) <u>are</u>.

IV. Multiple choice. 单项选择。(30%)

1. —Mary, _____ you play the piano?
   —Yes, only a little.

A. may　　　　　B. can　　　　　C. need　　　　　D. must
2. When traffic lights turn red, we _____ stop and wait.
　　A. can　　　　　B. must　　　　C. may　　　　　D. need
3. Schools _____ allow students at least one hour a day for sports.
　　A. would　　　　B. could　　　　C. should　　　　D. might
4. You _____ be tired after working for eight hours without a rest.
　　A. must　　　　B. can　　　　　C. may　　　　　D. should
5. —Are you going to Beijing by plane?
　　—It's fast but expensive. So I am not sure. I _____ take a train.
　　A. will　　　　　B. should　　　　C. must　　　　　D. may
6. —Look at the boy running on the ground. Is it Davis?
　　—It _____ be him. I saw him go to the teacher's office just now.
　　A. won't　　　　B. mayn't　　　　C. mustn't　　　　D. can't
7. John, you needn't do your work today. If you are busy, you _____ do it tomorrow.
　　A. can　　　　　B. must　　　　C. need　　　　　D. ought to
8. —Can you clean the blackboard now, Dick?
　　—Sorry, my hands are full but John _____.
　　A. may　　　　　B. should　　　　C. can　　　　　D. shall
9. —_____ Tom be here tomorrow?
　　—Probably. I am not sure.
　　A. Will　　　　　B. Would　　　　C. Does　　　　　D. Are
10. —Must I stay at home, Mum?
　　—No, you _____.
　　A. can't　　　　B. needn't　　　　C. mustn't　　　　D. shouldn't
11. We regret to inform you that you _____ the exam.
　　A. fail　　　　　B. have failed　　C. failing　　　　D. will fail
12. By the end of the year all people _____.
　　A. have left　　　　　　　　　　B. will leave
　　C. will be leaving　　　　　　　　D. will have left
13. Look! Your jacket is so dirty. It _____.
　　A. need wash　　　　　　　　　B. need to wash
　　C. need washing　　　　　　　　D. needs washing
14. I regret that I left him. I _____ stupid.
　　A. am just　　　　B. will be　　　C. was being　　　D. would be
15. I'm rather bored; I _____ since this morning.
　　A. am doing homework　　　　　B. did homework
　　C. was doing homework　　　　　D. have been doing homework
16. It has been about 7 years since they _____.
　　A. got marry　　　B. got married　　C. get marry　　　D. get married

17. The teacher worked late into the night, and _____ a long speech.
    A. to prepare   B. preparing   C. prepared   D. was prepared
18. Will you come and join us when we _____ a birthday party?
    A. will give   B. gave   C. give   D. have given
19. —Have you had dinner?
    —Not yet. The meal _____.
    A. are being cooked   B. is being cooked
    C. is cooked   D. are cooked
20. —Has Jim finished his homework?
    —He _____ it this morning.
    A. did   B. does   C. has done   D. had done

Ⅴ. Fill in the blanks with the correct forms of verbs. 填写动词的正确形式。(20%)

Villages in (1) _____ (develop) countries often (2) _____ (lack) experts. Many villages have no doctors, engineers or scientists.

There (3) _____ (be) a way to (4) _____ (solve) these problems. In the past few years, computer scientists around the world have (5) _____ (develop) expert systems. An expert system is a special kind of computer program. In some situations, it can (6) _____ (take) the place of a human expert. For example, a medical computer program can help care for a sick person. A question (7) _____ (appear) on the computer screen, "Is the person hot?" You tell the computer either yes or no. The computer (8) _____ (continue) to ask questions until it (9) _____ (have) enough information to make a decision. Then it tells what medicine or other treatment is (10) _____ (need).

Ⅵ. Translate the following sentences into English. 将下列句子译成英语。(15%)。
1. 在某种程度上,我认为你是不对的。
2. 我们都知道这个消息不可能是真的。
3. 自从毕业以来,你当老师多久了?
4. 如果你爱我,你愿意嫁给我吗?
5. 李先生每天踢足球,而他的妻子每天拉小提琴。

第十章 动词时态

一、时态概述

英语中的谓语动词所表示的各种不同时间处于不同状态下的形式叫作时态(Tense)。从时间上可以分为四种:过去、现在、将来和过去将来;从动作所处的形式也可分为四种:一般式、进行式、完成式和完成进行式。四种时间和四种形式结合共有16种时态,列表如下。

形式 时间	一般式 (Simple)	进行式 (Continuous)	完成式 (Perfect)	完成进行式 (Perfect Continuous)
过去	一般过去时 Past Simple	过去进行时 Past Continuous	过去完成时 Past Perfect Simple	过去完成进行时 Past Perfect Continuous
现在	一般现在时 Present simple	现在进行时 Present Continuous	现在完成时 Present Perfect Simple	现在完成进行时 Present Perfect Continuous
将来	一般将来时 Future Simple	将来进行时 Future Continuous	将来完成时 Future Perfect Simple	将来完成进行时 Future Perfect Continuous
过去将来	过去将来时 Past Future	过去将来进行时 Past Future Continuous	过去将来完成时 Past Future Perfect	过去将来完成进行时 Past Future Perfect Continuous

二、时态分类

(一)过去时间下的时态形式对比

(1)一般过去时和过去进行时

时态	一般过去时	过去进行时
形式	did	was/were doing
定义	过去某个时间里发生的动作或状态;过去习惯性、经常性的动作或行为	表示过去某一时间正在进行的动作,常与表示过去的时间状语连用
常用状语	last week, yesterday, …ago	过去具体的某个时间点,when/while/as引导的过去时间状语

续表

相似	都是表示过去发生的动作或状态	
区别	在确定的过去时间里所发生的动作或存在的状态。一般过去时表示的动作或状态都已成为过去，现已不复存在。 He **left** his hometown for Sichuan ten years ago. 十年前他离开家乡到了四川。	描述过去时间正在发生的动作。 He **was playing** table tennis at five yesterday afternoon. 他昨天下午五点正在打网球。

注意：过去进行时的特殊用法。

分类	例句
表示过去某一时间正在进行的动作，常与表示过去的时间状语连用	He **was playing** football at six yesterday morning. 他昨天早上六点正在踢足球。 We **were having** supper when he called me up. 他给我打电话时我们正在吃晚饭。
描述故事的背景，以此引出一般过去时表示的新动作	It **was getting** late. The little girl had to go home. 天色渐晚，小女孩得回家了。
与 always、constantly、continually 和 forever 等连用，表示过去反复出现的动作，常带有不满、厌烦、抱怨或称赞等感情色彩	She **was** always **changing** her mind. 她总是改变主意。 My mother **was** constantly **praising** my younger brother. 我妈总是不断的夸奖我弟弟。
表示按计划安排过去将要发生的动作，常用于 go、come、leave、arrive、stay 和 start 等动词	He told her he **was leaving** soon. 他告诉她他就要离开了。 Five of them **were coming** for the meeting. 他们中的五个人正在赶来开会。

(2) 过去完成时和过去完成进行时

时态	过去完成时	过去完成进行时
形式	had done	had been doing
定义	表示过去某一时刻或某一动作之前已经完成的动作或发生的情况，强调"过去的过去"	相对过去的某个时刻来说已经对现在有直接影响并且还在进行的动作
常用状语	already, just	for, before
例句	Joan **had already prepared** the dinner before her mother came home. 在母亲回家前，琼已做好了饭。 On the way to work, I suddenly remembered that I **had not locked** the door. 在上班的路上，我突然想起没锁门。	She said that she **had been watching** TV before I came in. 她说在我进来前她一直在看电视。 They were sweating all over because they **had been playing** basketball. 他们浑身是汗，因为他们一直在打篮球。

注意:常用过去完成时的句型结构。

过去完成时常用句型	例句
It/This/That was the first ... + time + (that) + 过去完成时	It was the first time I **had rode** a horse. 这是我第一次骑马。
It/This/That was...years since + 过去完成时	It was three years since I **had left** my hometown. 那时我已离家三年。
no sooner...than + 过去时	No sooner **had I gone** to bed than the telephone rang. 我刚要睡觉,电话就响了。(部分倒装)
hardly/scarcely...when + 过去时	He **had hardly got** on the train when the train started out. 他刚一上火车,火车就开动了。

(二)现在时间下的时态形式对比

(1)一般现在时和现在进行时

时态	一般现在时	现在进行时
形式	do/does	is/am/are doing
定义	表达现在重复发生的习惯性动作和经常存在的状况,或表示普遍真理、客观存在等	表示说话时或现阶段正在发生的动作;也可用于表示一个按计划将要发生的动作
常用状语	often, always, usually, sometimes, never, normally, generally, rarely, everyday...	at the moment, currently, now, this weekend/month/year...
例句	The first bus to our main campus **leaves** at 6 every morning. 到主校区的第一班车每天早晨6点发车。 Metal **expands** when heated. 金属加热会膨胀。	All the students **are attending** the lecture now. 现在所有的学生都在听讲座。 My father **is living** in Thailand at the moment. 我的父亲现在居住在泰国。
区别	经常性动作 The computer **works** perfectly. 计算机运转良好。	暂时性动作 The computer **is working** perfectly. 计算机正良好运行着。
	短暂性动作 The bus **stops**. 公共汽车停了。	持续性动作 The bus **is stopping**. 公共汽车渐渐地停下来。
	永久性动作 The city **lies** at the foot of the hill. 这个城市位于山脚下。	短暂性动作 People **are lying** on the beach. 人们正躺在海滩上。
	不带感情色彩 He always **looks** for faults. 他总是找缺点。	带有感情色彩 He **is** always **looking** for faults. 他是在找茬。

注意：

1) 某些具有"出发，到达"等含义的动词，如 arrive、be、begin、go、leave、start 和 stay 等，其一般现在时表示按计划即将发生的动作。如：

The delegation **arrives** in Beijing this afternoon. 代表团今天下午到北京。

2) 有些动词通常不能用于进行时态。

不能用于进行时态的情况	例句
某些实义动词用在表示事实状态时，如：have, belong, possess, cost, owe, exist, include, contain, matter, weigh, measure 和 continue 等	The dress **costs** $19. 那条裙子19美元。 This house **belongs** to my younger brother. 这个房子属于我弟弟。
某些表示心理状态的动词，如 know, realize, interest, believe, suppose, imagine, agree, want, recognize, remember, need, forget, prefer, mean, understand, love 和 hate 等	I **need** your help. 我需要你的帮助。 She **loves** her baby more than anything in the world. 她对她宝宝的爱胜过世上其他任何事物。
瞬间动词，如 accept, receive, complete, end, finish, give, allow, admit, permit, decide, determine, refuse 和 deny 等	I **accept** your advice. 我接受你的建议。 The teacher **allows** her students to finish the test in an hour. 老师让学生一小时内完成考试。
系动词，如 seem, remain, lie, hear, smell, feel, taste, get, become 和 turn 等	She **seems** a little unhappy. 她似乎有点不高兴。 Leaves **turn** green in spring. 在春季树叶变绿。

（2）现在完成时和现在完成进行时

时态	现在完成时	现在完成进行时
形式	has/have done	has/have been doing
定义	表示过去发生的动作，但动作的影响持续到现在；也可以用来表示从过去某一时间开始一直持续到现在的动作	表示动作从某一时间开始，一直持续到现在，或者刚刚终止，或者可能仍然要继续下去
常用状语	since, for, already, yet, just, recently	since, for
例句	He **has worked** for ten hours. 他已经工作十个小时了。 (侧重于这个动作所造成的结果和影响)	He **has been working** for ten hours. 他一直工作了十个小时。 (强调的是持续性的过程，即一直在工作)

注意：

1) 现在完成时中如果用瞬间动词，一般其后不跟表示时间段的时间状语。常用瞬间动词如：begin, start, end, die, lose, find, fall, go, come, join, knock, strike, hit, arrive, reach 和 leave 等。

{ The dog has died for several days. （错误）
{ The dog **has been dead** for several days. （正确）这条狗已经死了几天了。
{ The dog **died** several days ago. （正确）几天前这条狗死了。

其中需要对比记忆 have/has gone 和 have/has been，如：

{ —Where is your husband? 你丈夫在哪里？
{ —He **has gone to** Shanghai on business. 他去上海出差了。（人不在当场，还在上海。）

{ —Have you ever been to Xinjiang? 你曾经去过新疆吗?
{ —I **have never been** there. 我从来没有到过那里。(人在当场,叙述经历。)

2)完成时的固定句型

完成时句型	例句
It/This is the only + 名词 + (that) + 现在完成时	This is the only skirt that she **has** ever **worn**. 这是她穿过的唯一的一条裙子。
It/This is the first /second/last time + 名词 + (that) + 现在完成时	It is the second time that we **have met** each other. 这是我们第二次见面了。
It/This is one of + 形容词最高级+名词 + (that) + 现在完成时	This is one of the most interesting novels that he **has** ever **written**. 这是他所写的最有趣的小说之一。

注意:

①现在完成时和现在完成进行时的相似

a. 都可以表示从过去某一时刻开始一直延续到现在的动作。如:

I **have worked** in this factory since 2013. → I **have been working** in this factory since 2013.

自从2013年,我一直在这个工厂工作。

b. 都可以表示一段时间内进行的动作,如:

Lily **has taught** English for 30 years. → Lily **has been teaching** English for 30 years.

莉莉已经教英语三十年了。

②现在完成时和现在完成进行时的区别

现在完成时	现在完成进行时
表示已经完成的动作或者状态,常常与already(已经)或ever(曾经)连用	表示从过去某一时刻开始一直延续到现在,有可能还要进行下去的动作,一般不与already或ever等连用
现在完成时强调的是动作的结果 We **have lived** here for ten years. 我们已经在这里住十年了。	现在完成进行时强调的则是动作的过程,更强调动作的延续性 We **have been living** here for ten years. 我们一直这里住十年了。(现在还在这里住)
不用时间状语时,表示动作已经结束 I **have read** the novel. 我读过那小说。	表示动作仍在进行,还将继续 I **have been reading** the novel. 我一直在读那部小说。
现在完成时感情色彩不浓,只陈述事实 They **have known** each other for several years. 我们互相认识多年。	现在完成进行时带有较为强烈的感情色彩 You **have been talking** too much and doing too little. 你一直说得太多做得太少。
现在完成时态可以谈某个动作的具体次数或几件事情 My mother **has drunk** two cups of coffee. 我妈妈已经喝了两杯咖啡。	现在完成进行时态不能用来表示某个动作的具体次数或几件事情 My mother has been drinking two cups of coffee.(错误)

(三)将来时间下的时态形式对比

(1)一般将来时和将来进行时

时态	一般将来时	将来进行时
形式	shall/will do	shall/will be doing
定义	表示将来的动作或状态	表示将来某一时间正在进行的动作,常表示安排好之事,给人一种期待之感
常用状语	tomorrow, next year next week/weekend/month/summer	tomorrow, then 或将来具体的时间点
例句	She **will graduate** next year. 明年她将毕业。 I **shall/will be** twenty years old next month. 下个月我将二十岁了。	I **shall be walking** on the beach of the sea this time tomorrow. 明天这时候我正在海滩散步。 Don't call me at 4:00 this afternoon. I **shall/will be having** a meeting then. 今天下午四点不要给我打电话,我那时正在开会。

注意:其他表示将来时的形式及用法。

形式	用法	例句
be going to + 动词原形	表示近期的打算或即将发生的事	**Are you going to go** downtown for shopping? 你要去市中心购物吗? It **is going** to rain. 要下雨了。
be about to + 动词原形	表示正要做的事或将发生的事,比"be going to do"表示更近的将来	Don't go out. We **are about to have** dinner. 不要外出了,我们将要吃晚饭了。 The conference **is about to begin**. 会议即将开始。
be to + 动词原形	表示计划中约定的或按职责、义务和要求必须做的事或即将发生的动作	The French President **is to visit** China. 法国总统即将访华。 You **are to be** back by 9 o'clock. 你必须在九点前回来。
be + 现在分词	表示按计划即将发生的事,这种用行时表将来的结构仅限于如下几个动词:come、go、start、begin、leave、arrive、do、have、take 等	They **are coming** soon. 他们马上要来了。 We **are having** a meeting this morning. 今天早上我们要开个会。
一般现在时	一般现在时也可表将来,常用在一些条件句和时间状语从句中;一般现在时也用于动词为 arrive、begin、be、go、leave 和 stay 等简单句中,表示这些动作是事先安排好的,不会轻易改变	We will not go to the Summer Palace if it **snows** tomorrow. 如果明天下雪,我们就不去颐和园了。 There **is** a lecture on English literature this evening. 今晚有一场英国文学方面的报告。

(2) 将来完成时和将来完成进行时

时态	将来完成时	将来完成进行时
形式	shall/will have done	shall/will have been doing
定义	表示将来某时间之前或某动作发生之前将会完成的动作	表示某种情况下一直持续到说话人所提及的时间,往往与将来的时间连用
常用状语	before, by + 固定时间, in + 某段时间	
区别	将来完成时强调在另一件事前一个动作的完成。 I **shall have finished** reading the book by the end of this week. 到本周末,我将读完这本书了。	将来完成进行时强调在将来某时某个动作已经进行多久了。 By the end of the year she **will have been acting** for twenty years. 到今年年底她演戏将满二十年。

(四) 过去将来时和过去将来完成时

由于过去将来进行时和过去将来完成进行时使用较少,本章节只对过去将来时和过去将来完成时进行对比讲解。

时态	过去将来时	过去将来完成时
形式	would do	would have done
定义	表示从过去某时看来将要发生的动作或存在的状态,常用于主句谓语动词为过去时的间接引语中(即宾语从句中)	表示从过去观点看将来时某动作已完成。通常主要用于转述方面,即用于与过去情况相反的虚拟语气及间接引语中
例句	He said that he **would wait** for us at the bus stop. 他说他将在公共汽车站等我们。 He assured me that he **would support** us. 他向我保证他会支持我们。	I thought she **would have told** you the accident. 我想她会已告诉你这个事故。 By the time he arrived, his wife **would have gone** home. 他到时他的妻子会已经回家。
用于虚拟语气	涉及现在时间的虚拟条件:即条件从句所涉及的内容是现在的不真实情况,此时从句的谓语用一般过去时,而主句谓语用"would + 动词原形"(当然根据情况也可用should, might, could)。如: If I were taller, I **would become** a basketball play. 如果我个子再高一点,我就当篮球运动员。 涉及将来时间的虚拟条件:即条件从句所涉及的内容是将来的不真实情况,或很可能是将来的不真实情况。 If... + 一般过去时(be通常用were) + should + 动词原形 + were to + 动词原形 } would + 动词原形 (主句用过去将来时) (根据情况也可用should, might, could)。如: If you took a taxi, you **would get** there quicker. 如果你叫一辆出租汽车,你就会快点儿到那儿。	涉及过去事实相反的虚拟语气,此时条件从句的谓语用过去完成时(had + 过去分词),而主句谓语则通常用过去完成时(would + have + 过去分词),主句谓语也可根据情况使用"should(could, might) + have + 过去分词"。如: If he had left sooner, he **would have been** there on time. 要是他早点离开,他就准时到了。(但他离开太晚了,没有准时到达) I **would have forgotten** her birthday if you hadn't reminded me. 要不是你提醒我,我就会忘记她的生日。

注意：其他表示过去将来时的形式及用法。

表示过去将来时的句式	例句
"was/were going to + 动词原形"表示过去的打算或过去即将发生的事	I **was going to** buy a car then. 我那时正要去买辆车。 There **was going to be** a thunderstorm. 将要有一场雷暴。
"was/were about + 不定式"表示过去正要做的事或将发生的事	He **was about to say** something more, and then checked himself. 他还想说几句，却又止住了。
"was/were + 不定式"表示曾计划做某事或"后来注定,结果"	He said that he **was to go** abroad then. 他说他那时曾经打算去国外。 At that time he did not know that taking the job **was to become** a turning point in his life. 那时他不知道接受那份工作会是他生活的一个转折点。
"was/were + 现在分词"表示按过去将要发生的事,这种用进行时表将来的结构仅限于如下几个动词：come, go, start, begin, leave, arrive, do, have, take 等	They said they **were leaving** for America soon. 他说他们马上就要去美国了。

三、时态小结

英语句子用何种时态主要看谓语动词所处的时间（现在、过去、将来、过去将来）及状态（一般式、进行式、完成式、完成进行式）。在主从复合句中，从句谓语动词的时态，常常受到主句时态的影响和制约，这种现象称为"时态呼应"，其基本规则如下：

①如果主句谓语动词的时态是现在时或将来时，从句可根据具体情况选用适当的时态。

I **know** he **is**（**was**,**will be**,**has been**）in charge of the class.
我知道他(曾,将,一直)主管这个班。

He **will tell** you when they **arrived**（**will arrive**）.
他将告诉你他们是何时抵达的(将于何时抵达)。

②如果主句谓语动词的时态是过去时，从句通常用过去范畴的时态。

I **did not know** where she **was**. 我不知道她在哪。

The professor **said** that the students **were taking** an exam. 那位教授说学生们正在考试。

She **knew** that he **had forgotten** his promise. 她知道他已忘了他的诺言。

John **hoped** that the boss **would give** him a promotion. 约翰希望老板会提升他。

③如果从句表示的是客观事实或真理时，其时态通常用一般现在时，不受主句时态的影响。

Kepler proved that the sun **is** the center of the solar system.
开普勒证明了太阳是太阳系的中心。（真理）

The professor said that Persian **belongs to** the Indo-European group of languages.

教授说波斯语属于印欧语系。（事实）

Mother told me that honesty **is** the best policy. 母亲告诉我诚实是上策。（谚语）

Grammar Exercises
语法训练

Ⅰ. Fill in each blank with one word. 填空。(5%)

1. "I am having lunch," he said.
   He said that he _____ _____ lunch.
2. "I have seen the film," Tina said to me.
   Tina told me that she _____ _____ the film.
3. By the end of this month, he will have taken 2 000 pictures.
   By the end of last month, he _____ _____ _____ 2 000 pictures.
4. She says that she will buy a laptop computer (笔记本电脑) in two weeks.
   She said that she _____ _____ a laptop computer in two weeks.
5. The teacher said, "The sun is bigger than the earth."
   The teacher said that the sun _____ bigger than the earth.

Ⅱ. Fill in the blanks with the proper forms of the given verbs in the bracket. 用括号中所给动词的适当形式填空。(10%)

1. He _____ swimming in the river every day in summer. (go)
2. Look, the children _____ basketball on the playground. (play)
3. He _____ to the music when I came in? (listen)
4. — I need some paper.
   — I _____ some for you. (bring)
5. I can't find my pen. Who _____ it? (take)
6. He said that he _____ back in five minutes. (come)
7. I didn't meet him. He _____ when I got there. (leave)
8. I _____ my bike, so I have to walk to school. (lose)
9. He is not here. He _____ to the post office. (go)
10. We will not go to the cinema if it _____ tomorrow. (rain)

Ⅲ. Error identification. 错误辨识。(20%)

1. (A) Prof. Wang explained (B) to us that light (C) travelled faster (D) than sound.
2. I (A) watch the sunrise (B) on the top of (C) the Mountain Tai (D) this time tomorrow.
3. My mom (A) is always (B) say I (C) don't help (D) enough.
4. It was (A) the last time (B) that she (C) has been (D) at home.
5. (A) If you (B) heat water (C) to 100 degree, it (D) boil.
6. I (A) have started (B) to learn English (C) when I (D) was six.
7. (A) By the year of 2030, the percentage of the population (B) aged 65 (C) will rise to (D) more than 30%.

8. She (A) will be arriving (B) at the airport (C) at 6 am (D) tomorrow.
9. When (A) the patient was sent to (B) the nearest hospital, he (C) has been dead (D) for two hours.
10. I (A) shall finished (B) reading the novel he (C) gave me (D) by this weekend.

IV. Multiple choice. 单项选择。(30%)

1. John isn't here. He _____ the classroom.
   A. has been to   B. has gone to   C. went to   D. goes
2. I will tell him as soon as he _____ back.
   A. come   B. comes   C. will come   D. came
3. _____ your mother _____ some cleaning on Sundays?
   A. Does; does   B. Do; does   C. Does; do   D. Do; do
4. You can join us. We _____ a special English course now.
   A. are setting up   B. have set up   C. were setting up   D. sets up
5. Mr. Smith _____ short stories, but he _____ a TV play these days.
   A. is writing; is writing   B. is writing; writes
   C. writes; is writing   D. writes; writes
6. It _____ dark as the team made its way to the village.
   A. got   B. had got   C. was getting   D. was got
7. There _____ any lecture next week.
   A. is not going to have   B. will not be going to be
   C. is not going to be   D. won't be going to have
8. —_____ you _____ out for a walk after supper?
   —Yes, I _____.
   A. Did; went; went   B. Did; go; went   C. Did; went; did   D. Did; go; did
9. We _____ our breakfast when an old man came to the door.
   A. just have had   B. have just had   C. just had   D. had just had
10. We _____ for Tom at ten last Sunday. He often kept us _____.
    A. were waiting; waiting   B. were waiting; wait
    C. waited; waiting   D. waited; wait
11. I have been studying here for four years; by next summer I _____.
    A. shall graduate   B. shall be graduating
    C. shall have graduated   D. might be graduated
12. She _____ that she _____ her best to help them the next term.
    A. says; will do   B. said; will do
    C. said; would do   D. says; would do
13. She ought to stop working; she has a headache because she _____ too long.
    A. has been reading   B. had read   C. is reading   D. read
14. We were all surprised when he made it clear that he _____ office soon.
    A. leaves   B. would leave   C. left   D. had left

15. Tom _____ up into the tree. Look, he _____ high up there!
    A. has got; is   B. has climbed; was
    C. got; was   D. climbed; is

16. Jack _____ over five lessons by seven o'clock. Then he _____ a test.
    A. went; took   B. went; had taken
    C. had gone; took   D. had gone; had taken

17. They _____ each other since childhood.
    A. have been knowing   B. knew
    C. have known   D. had know

18. He promised his boss that he _____ the work by the end of that month.
    A. would finish   B. will finish
    C. have finished   D. had finished

19. By the time this talk is over, we _____ a lot about planes.
    A. shall be learning   B. are learning
    C. would learn   D. shall have learnt

20. He _____ tired because he _____ for a long time.
    A. had got; had walked   B. got; walked
    C. had got; walked   D. got; had walked

V. Fill in the blanks with the correct forms of the given verbs. 填写所给动词的正确形式。(20%)

Rose is one of the funniest girls in her class. She (1) _____ (look) like a boy, and she is good at performing. So she (2) _____ (choose) to play Harry Potter by her classmates last week. She said happily, "I'm sure that I (3) _____ (be) able to do the job well because I (4) _____ (see) the movie many times already."

Dick, one of Rose's best classmates, is also an actor in the play. He (5) _____ (like) to perform the play with Rose. He (6) _____ (say), "We are confident that we (7) _____ (do) well in our school art festival next week."

Mrs. Smith, their teacher, (8) _____ (pay) much attention to their play. She often (9) _____ (encourage) them. Yesterday afternoon when she (10) _____ (watch) their performance, she took photos of them.

VI. Translate the following sentences into English. 将下列句子译成英语。(15%)

1. 当我们赶到时,足球赛已经开始。
2. 现在李先生正在纽约参加一个会议。
3. 大卫说他不久就要结婚了。
4. 到这个学期末,这些学生将已学习英语六年了。
5. 这是我第二次到北京。

第十一章 被动语态

一、被动语态的构成

被动语态(Passive Voice)是以"be 动词 + 过去分词"的形式来表达的,如果要特别强调动作或行为的执行者时,句子后面需接 by...,译为"被/由……"。

被动语态的句型见下表。

肯定句	主语 + be + 过去分词 +(by...).
否定句	主语 + be not + 过去分词 +(by...).
一般疑问句	Be +主语 + 过去分词 +(by...)?
特殊疑问句	疑问词 + be + 主语 + 过去分词 + (by...)?

二、被动语态的时态

	一般	进行	完成
过去	was/were done The present **was given** by her father yesterday. 这礼物是昨天她爸爸给的。	was/were being done The roads **were being widened** at that time. 道路那时正在加宽。	had been done When I got there, all the tickets **had been sold out**. 当我到那的时候,所有的票都卖光了。
现在	am/is/are done History **is made** by the people. 历史是由人民创造的。	am/is/are being done Look! He **is being punished** by the teacher. 看!老师在惩罚他。	has/have been done She **has been sent** to work in Beijing. 她已经被派到北京工作。
将来	shall/will be done This city **will be destroyed** one day if people do not live in peace. 如果人们不和平共处,这座城市总有一天会被毁掉。		shall/will have been done The work **will have been done** by the time I come back. 到我回来时此工作将已完成。
过去将来	should/would be done Yesterday, he said that the project **would be completed** in two years. 昨天他说工程将会在两年内完成。		should/would have been done It was said that the new library **would have been built** by the end of next month. 据说新图书馆到下月末将已竣工。

注意：主动语态变被动语态的方法，如下：

My friend   invited   me   to her home.
　执行者　　谓语　　承受者

变为→　 I　was invited（by my friend）to her home.
　　承受者　　谓语　　by + 执行者

1) 把主动语态的宾语变成被动语态的主语。
2) 把主动语态的谓语变成被动语态的 be + 过去分词，时态要与原句保持一致。
3) 把主动语态的主语变为介词 by 的宾语，放在被动语态谓语动词之后，by 短语可以省略。

三、被动语态的几种类型

类型	分类	主动句	被动句
由及物动词构成的被动语态	有一个宾语（SVO）的句子	She wrote this poem days ago. 几日前她写了这首诗。	This poem **was written** by her days ago. 这首诗是她几日前写的。
	有两个宾语（SVOO）的句子	He lent me a bike. 他借给我一辆自行车。	1) I **was lent** a bike（by him）. 我被(他)借给了一辆自行车。 2) A bike **was lent to** me（by him）. 一辆自行车被(他)借给了我。
	含有宾语补足语（SVOC）的句子	We saw a thief steal something from the room. 我们看见一个小偷从屋子里偷了东西。	A thief **was seen** to steal something from the room. 一个小偷被看见从屋子里偷了东西。
祈使句	肯定祈使句	Let us do the work at once. 让我们立即完成工作。	Let the work **be done** at once. 立即完成工作。
	否定祈使句	Don't tell him the truth. 不要告诉他事情真相。	Don't let the truth **be told** to him. 别告诉他事情真相。
由"不及物动词 + 介词或副词"构成的被动语态		He looks after his grandmother. 他照顾她的奶奶。	His grandmother **is looked after** by him. 他的奶奶由他照顾。
由情态动词构成的被动语态，情态助动词要保留		You ought to clean this classroom. 你应该打扫这间教室。	This classroom **ought to be cleaned**. 这间教室应该被打扫。

注意：

1) 有些"静态"动词不能用于被动语态，如：have、cost、last、own、suit、hold、fit、belong to 和 agree with 等。如：

The trip lasts six weeks. 本次旅行持续了6个星期。

These English - Chinese dictionaries belong to the children who love study.
这些英汉字典属于爱学习的孩子们。

2) 有些不及物动词的主动形式可以用来表示被动意义，如：cut、wash、write、sell 和 wear 等。如：

This kind of clothes sells well. 这种衣服很畅销。

The pen that my mother gave me writes smoothly. 妈妈送我的那只笔书写很流畅。

3) 谓语是及物动词 leave、enter、reach、suit、have、benefit、lack 和 own 等。如：

She entered the office and answered the phone. （正确）她走进办公室接了电话。

The office was entered by her and the phone was answered. （错误）

4) 有些词组的主动形式表示被动意义，如：be worth doing 和 need doing 等。如：

The bike there **needs repairing**.　=　The bike there **needs to be repaired**.

那边那辆自行车需要修理。

The stamp **is not worth collecting**. 这张邮票不值得收藏。

5) 感官系动词一般用主动形式表示被动意义，如：feel、look、seem、taste、sound 和 remain 等。如：

It sounds a good idea. 听起来真是一个好主意。

These flowers smell very sweet. 这些花闻起来很香。

6) 在汉语中，有一类句子不出现主语，在英语中一般可用被动结构来表示。如：

汉语	英语句式
据说……	It is said that…
据报道……	It is reported that…
据推测……	It is supposed that…
希望……	It is hoped that…
普遍认为……	It is generally considered that…
有人建议……	It is suggested that…
众所周知……	It is well known that…

Grammar Exercises
语法训练

Ⅰ．Fill in the blanks with the right forms. 用正确形式填空。（5%）

1. The novel _____ (translate) into many languages since it was published.

2. His education was stopped when the money _____ (use up).

3. All his time _____ (spend) on his cell phone every day.

4. The candidates _____ (interview) in two months.

5. It _____ (report) that the temperature will decline in one or two days.

Ⅱ．Change the following sentences into passive voice. 请将下列句子变成被动语态。（10%）

1. In the old days people used teapots（茶壶）to make tea.

2. The workers are building the longest bridge now.

3. I will turn off the TV as soon as the football game ends.
   _____

4. The doctor told him to take the medicine three times a day.
   _____

5. You cannot use a calculator（计算器）in the maths test.
   _____

6. The little girl was sad because some boys laughed at her.
   _____

7. My friend has taken many pictures since he got his first camera.
   _____

8. She said that she would remember the day forever.
   _____

9. Nature made human beings have early fires on the earth.
   _____

10. My sister was washing her clothes at seven yesterday evening.
    _____

Ⅲ. Error identification. 错误辨识。(20%)

1. (A) Good dishes (B) are preparing (C) for dinner by mothers (D) at the weekend.
2. (A) 3 000 new cars (B) are going to (C) produce (D) next year.
3. (A) The great project (B) has started (C) to send water from the river (D) to the city.
4. Rainforests (A) cut and burned (B) at such a speed that they (C) will disappear (D) from the earth.
5. (A) The rooms (B) are being painting (C) by the workers (D) now.
6. The manager (A) came into the office and (B) was happy to know that (C) the five sixths of the tickets (D) had booked.
7. If one (A) is noticed (B) overcome by pride, he (C) will refuse (D) useful advice and friendly help.
8. (A) The uneducated (B) should not (C) look down upon (D) by common people.
9. (A) The plan to take a trip to Yunnan (B) have been (C) given up (D) during the vacation.
10. Some day the environment (A) will be completely damaged (B) if (C) no proper measures (D) take.

Ⅳ. Multiple choice. 单项选择。(30%)

1. My bike _____ last night.
   A. was stolen　　B. were stolen　　C. was stealing　　D. were stealing
2. The project _____ finished next month.
   A. is going to　　B. will　　C. will be　　D. is
3. The young generations _____ better opportunities to improve and develop themselves.
   A. has been given
   B. have been given
   C. have been giving
   D. has been giving

4. The Great Opera House _____ now; it _____ in three years.
   A. is being built; will be completed
   B. is built; is completed
   C. will be built; will be completed
   D. is being built; is completed

5. By the end of next year, English _____ in the college for 30 years.
   A. is taught
   B. has been taught
   C. was taught
   D. will have been taught

6. Great changes _____ in China in the last two decades.
   A. have taken place
   B. has taken place
   C. have been taken place
   D. has been taken place

7. The new computers, with artificial intelligence, _____ and perfected now.
   A. will have been developed
   B. have developed
   C. are being developed
   D. developed

8. By the time the old man retired, he _____ a teacher for 40 years.
   A. is
   B. was
   C. had been
   D. be

9. We all know that the People's Republic of China _____ on October 1st, 1949.
   A. found
   B. was founded
   C. was found
   D. founded

10. Mary _____ a job in an international company, but she didn't take it.
    A. offered
    B. was offered
    C. is offered
    D. has offered

11. She told me that she _____ to take a trip to New York on business.
    A. had been asked
    B. is asked
    C. has been asked
    D. are asked

12. By the time she comes back from her travel, we _____ writing the report required by the manager.
    A. will finish
    B. will have finished
    C. have finished
    D. will be finishing

13. He _____ to have information which will be useful to the police.
    A. said   B. says   C. is said   D. was said

14. They recommended that water-proof glass _____ in this field.
    A. is used
    B. use
    C. is using
    D. should be used

15. Do you know when the message _____ to the old lady yesterday?
    A. delivered
    B. was delivered
    C. was delivering
    D. has been delivered

16. The river smells terrible and people must _____ rubbish into it.
    A. be stopped from throwing
    B. stop from throwing
    C. be stopped to throw
    D. stop to throw

17. A movie is going to _____ tonight.
    A. see   B. saw   C. be seen   D. is seeing
18. —What _____ the take _____ from?
    —Rice.
    A. was; made   B. is; making   C. was; making   D. be; made
19. He told us that the whole article _____ by the end of next week.
    A. will have been done   B. was done
    C. is done   D. would have been done
20. The window _____ by those naught boys last month.
    A. broke   B. is broken   C. was broken   D. is breaking

Ⅴ. Fill in the blanks with the correct forms of verbs. 填写动词的正确形式。(20%)

On Sundays, hundreds of people (1) _____ (come) from the city to (2) _____ (see) our town and to walk through the woods. Visitors (3) _____ (ask) to keep the woods clean and tidy. Litter baskets (4) _____ (place) under the trees, but people still (5) _____ (throw) their rubbish everywhere. Last Wednesday, I (6) _____ (go) for a walk in the woods. What I saw made me very sad. I counted seven old cars and three old refrigerators. The litter baskets (7) _____ (be) empty and the ground (8) _____ (cover) with pieces of paper, cigarette ends, old tyres, empty bottles and rusty tins. Among the rubbish, I (9) _____ (find) a sign which said, "Anyone who litters in these woods will (10) _____ (punish)."

Ⅵ. Translate the following sentences into English. 将下列句子译成英语。(15%)
1. 这座图书馆到去年年底前已经建成了。
2. 不要担心,你的汽车正在修理。
3. 据报道,今年的价格已经增长了10%。
4. 你和他之间的问题应该被及时解决。
5. 下周这个重要的会议将在北京召开。

第十二章 非谓语动词

一、非谓语动词

非谓语动词(Non-finite Verbs)是动词的特殊形式,在句中可以作除谓语外的所有成分,非谓语动词没有人称和数的变化。非谓语动词包括三种形式:

a. 动词不定式 Her job is **to clean** the hall. 她的工作是打扫大厅。

b. 动名词 **Climbing mountains** is interesting. 爬山很有趣。

c. 分词(现在分词和过去分词)

The room **facing south** is our classroom. 朝南的房间是我们的教室。

二、非谓语动词的分类

(一)动词不定式

(1)动词不定式的形式

动词不定式(Infinitive)是非谓语动词的一种格式,由不定式符号(to)加动词原形构成。

形式	主动	被动
一般式	to do She likes **to read books**. 她喜欢读书。	to be done The books are not allowed **to be taken** out of the reading room. 这些书不许带出阅览室。
完成式	to have done The students seem **to have cleaned** the classroom. 好像学生们已经打扫过教室了。	to have been done The man is said **to have been sent** to hospital yesterday. 据说这个男人昨天已经被送到医院了。
进行式	to be doing She seemed **to be reading something** at that time. 她那时候似乎在读什么东西。	

（2）动词不定式的用法

序号	句法成分	例句
1	主语	**To watch too much TV** is bad for your eyes. 看太多电视对你的眼睛不好。
2	宾语	The boy promised **to study hard** from then on. 男孩答应从此努力学习。
3	宾语补足语	The police man told us **not to play football** on the street again. 警察告诉我们不要再在街上踢足球。
4	定语	I have something **to tell you**. 我有事情要告诉你。
5	主语补足语	She is known **to have been studying** on the problem for many years. 据说她研究这个问题很多年了。
6	状语	We were very excited **to hear the news**. 听到这个消息我们很高兴。

注意：only to 作为固定结构，一般位于后半句，表示一系列中"较晚"发生的事情。这种不定式经常用来描写出乎意料的或者是不受欢迎的事件。如：

He returned after the war, **only to** find that his wife had been dead.
他战后归来，却发现妻子已经去世。

（3）it 代替 to do 作形式主语和形式宾语

"it"用作形式主语当不定式（短语）、动名词（短语）或从句在某个句子中作主语时，为保持句子结构前后平衡，避免头重脚轻而常用 it 作形式主语置于句首，将真正的主语放在句尾。此时 it 只起先行引导作用。当不定式（短语）、动名词（短语）或从句在某个句子中作宾语时，为保持句子结构平衡，避免句式结构的混乱，常用 it 作形式宾语，而将真正的宾语放在句尾。此时 it 仍只起先行引导作用，本身无词义。

成分	句型	例句
形式主语	It + v. + to do	**It** often takes me about two hours to do my homework every day. 我每天大概花两小时做作业。
	It's + n. + to do	**It** is my duty to teach you English. 教你们英语是我的职责。
	It's + adj. + for sb. to do sth.	**It** is easy for him to finish this work before ten. 对于他来说十点前完成这项工作不难。
	It's + adj. + of sb. to do sth.	**It** is impolite of you to speak to your mother like that. 你那样对你妈妈说话不礼貌。
	注意：It's + adj. + (of/for) sb to do sth. 意思为"（某人）做某事是……的"，It 是形式主语而不定式是真正主语。如果形容词表示人的品质，即 sb. 和 adj. 有主系表关系时使用 of，如：It was stupid **of** him to refuse the invitation. (= He is stupid.) 拒绝这个邀请，他太傻了。如果当形容词仅是描述事物，即 sb. 和 adj. 没有主系表关系时用 for，如：It is dangerous **for** children to cross the busy street. (= To cross the busy street is dangerous.) 对于孩子们来说，横穿这条繁忙的街道很危险。	
形式宾语	主语 + find/think/feel/consider… it + adj./n + to do sth.	We think **it** important to obey the law. 我们认为遵守法律是很重要的。 I know **it** impossible to finish so much work in a day. 我知道一天之内完成这么多工作是不可能的。

(4) 不定式 to 的省略

序号	分类	例句
1	不定式在表示知觉的感官动词 feel、hear、listen to、see、look at、watch、observe、notice 和 find 后作宾补，to 要省略	I **heard** her **cry** in the room last night. 昨晚我听见她在房间里哭。 Her neighbors **saw** her **grow up** from childhood. 邻居们看着她长大。
2	使役动词 let、make 和 have 后，不定式作宾补，to 要省略	Don't **make** your little sister **cry**. 不要把你妹妹惹哭。 The teacher **let** me **tell** the truth. 老师让我说出真相。
3	谓语动词是 help，后面作宾语补足语的不定式可以带 to，也可以不带 to	I often **help** him **(to) clean** the room. 经常帮他打扫房间。

注意：这类句子变为被动结构时，不定式前加 to。如：
{ We often hear her **sing this song**. 我们经常听到她唱这首歌。
{ She is often heard **to sing this song**. 她经常被听到唱这首歌。

(二) 动名词

动名词(Gerund)是由动词原形加词尾 ing 构成的，它与动词的现在分词形式相同，它具有动词和名词的特征。

(1) 动名词的形式

形式	主动语态	被动语态
一般式	doing **Travelling** is interesting but tiring. 旅行是有趣的，但是使人疲劳。	being done He doesn't like **being laughed at**. 他不喜欢被嘲笑。
完成式	having done She denied **having stolen** anything. 她否认偷过任何东西。	having been done I don't remember **having ever been given** a chance to do it. 我不记得曾经有人给过我机会去做这件事情。

(2) 动名词的用法

序号	句法成分	例句
1	主语	**Reading** aloud is good in learning English. 大声朗读对学英语有好处。
2	宾语	Do you mind **opening** the windows? 你介意打开窗户吗？
3	表语	What I should do today is **looking after** my sister. 今天我该做的是照顾我妹妹。
4	定语	Do you have a **swimming** pool in your school? 你们学校有游泳池吗？

(3)必须使用动名词的结构
①介词后的宾语
能接动名词的短语有：

think of/about 考虑	dream about 梦到	prevent/keep/stop…from 阻止
hear of 听说	set about 开始	succeed（in）成功做……
worry about 担忧	burst out 迸发	depend on 依赖
be/get used to 习惯……	devote…to… 致力于……	look forward to 期望
insist on 坚持	pay attention to 注意	get down to 处理
be good at 擅长	be fond of 喜爱	do well in ……做得好
be interested in 对……感兴趣	be tired of 厌烦	be afraid of 害怕
spend…(in) 花费……做	prefer…to…喜欢……而不是	feel like 想要

We are thinking of **making** a new plan for the next term.
我们正考虑为下学期制定新的计划。
Ann has been looking forward to **coming** to China for a long time.
安好久以来就盼望着来中国。

②特殊动词后的宾语
只能接动名词的动词有：finish、enjoy、mind、suggest、practise、admit、advise、allow、appreciate、avoid、consider、delay、deny、discuss、dislike、escape、excuse、fancy、forbid、forgive、give up、imagine、keep、mention、miss、pardon、permit、prevent、put off、report、risk 和 understand 等。如：

I advise **waiting** a few more days. 我建议再等几天。

I admit **breaking** the window. 我承认窗子是我打破的。

Try to imagine **being** on the moon. 设法想象你是在月球上。

He tried to escape **being** punished. 他设法逃避惩罚。

③动名词结构
动名词作主语放后，it 是形式主语的特殊句型，如：

句型	例句
It is no use doing sth. 做某事没用/只是白费力气	It is no use **crying** over spilt milk. 覆水难收。（谚语）
It is no good doing sth. 做某事没用	It is no good **telling** him the truth. 告诉他真相是无济于事的。
It is a waste of time/money doing sth. 做某事是白费 时间/金钱	It is a waste of time **persuading** him to have a rest. 劝他休息是浪费时间。
It is fun doing sth. 做某事很有趣	It is fun **playing** golf. 打高尔夫球很有趣。

(4)动名词与动词不定式的区别
①作主语或表语时
动词不定式和动名词都可以用作主语，在意义上相近，但动名词多用来表示泛指的抽象的动作或经常性的动作；不定式多用来表示特指或具体的动作，特别是将来的动作。比较：
Smoking is not good for health. 抽烟对身体不好。

It is not good for you **to smoke** so much. 抽这么多烟对你身体不好。

{ My job is **teaching** English. 我的工作是教英语。
{ Our task now is **to increase** food production. 我们现在的任务是增加粮食产量。

②在 like,hate 和 prefer 等动词后:如果表示一般倾向,多用动名词作宾语;如指特定的或具体的某次行为,用不定式更多一些。

{ I like **reading** books in my spare time. 我喜欢在我的空闲时间阅读。
{ I like **to read** that book. 我想去读那本书。

{ They prefer **walking** to cycling. 比起骑自行车,他们更喜欢走路。
{ He prefers **to stay** at home today. 今天他偏向于待在家里。

③有些动词后即可用动名词也可用不定式作宾语,如 like、love、hate、dislike、begin、start、continue、want、need、stop、remember、forget、try 和 attempt 等。

  a. 作宾语的动名词或动词不定式,在意义上相似,无太大区别。如:
   Let's continue **working/to work**. 让我们继续工作。
   When did you begin **learning/to learn** English? 你什么时候开始学英语的?

  b. 但有时两种结构之间含义不同,如 remember、forget、regret、try、stop、mean 和 go on 等。

{ He tried **speaking** English to us. 他试着用英语和我们讲话。
{ Please **try to do** it better next time. 下次请设法做得更好些。

{ This means **setting** out at once. 这意味着立即出发。
{ He really meant **to come**. 他确实打算来的。

④在表示"需要"意思的 want、need、require 和 deserve 等动词后,当主语表事物时,其后既可用动名词的主动式也可用不定式的被动式表被动含义。

My watch needs **repairing/to be repaired**. 我的手表需要修理。
The house wants **cleaning/to be cleaned**. 房子需要打扫。

⑤在 allow、permit、advise、recommend、consider 和 forbid 等词后,常用动名词作宾语,用不定式作宾语补足语。

We don't allow **smoking** here. 我们这不允许抽烟。(宾语)
Her mother doesn't allow her **to stay up** late. 她妈妈不允许她熬夜。(宾语补足语)

(三)分词

(1)分词的形式

①现在分词

形式	主动语态	被动语态
一般式	doing This is a **pressing** problem. 这是一个紧迫的问题。	being done The problem **being discussed** is very important. 正在被讨论的问题很重要。
完成式	having done **Having finished** his homework, he went out. 做完作业后,他出去了。	having been done **Having been written** in haste, the book is full of mistakes. 这书因写得仓促,所以错误不少。

②过去分词

过去分词只有一般式,没有完成式。过去分词在意义上主要表示被动,在时间上可以表示多种关系,如表示已经发生的,表示经常性动作或泛指概念;表示与谓语动词同时发生的动作,表示现在或过去的状态。

I saw him **taken** away in an ambulance. 我看见他被救护车送走。
Moved by their speech, I was at a loss what to say. 被他们的发言感动,我不知道说什么。
They came in, **followed** by their children. 他们走了进来,后面跟着他们的孩子。

(2)分词的用法

序号	句法成分	例句
1	定语	Do you know the boy **standing** at the gate? 你认识站在门口的那个男孩?
2	表语	We were **excited** at the news. 听到这个消息我们很兴奋。
3	宾语补足语	We found the ground **covered** with snow. 我们发现大地覆盖着白雪。
4	状语	**Seen** from the hill, the village looks more beautiful. 从山上看,村庄看起来更漂亮。

(3)现在分词和过去分词的区别

现在分词和过去分词主要的区别表现在语态和时间关系上。如:

语态上不同	现在分词表示主动的意思,而过去分词多由及物动词变来,表示被动的意思。	surprising 使人感到惊讶的(主动) surprised 自己感到惊讶的(被动,即被惊讶的) an exciting story 一个令人兴奋的故事(主动) excited audience 激动的观众(被动,即被引起激动的)
时间关系上不同	一般说来,现在分词所表示的动作往往正在进行,而过去分词所表示的动作往往已经完成。	the changing world 正在变化着的世界 the changed world 已经起了变化的世界/被改变的世界 boiling water 正在沸腾的水 boiled water 已经煮开过的水(可能是凉开水)

注意:在以 when、while、if、once、though 和 unless 六个连词引导的状语从句中,若从句主语与主句的主语相同时,可省略从句的主语,并将之后的动词变成现在分词或过去分词。如:

When writing my paper, I found my mother come in.
= When I wrote my paper, I found my mother come in.
当我写论文的时候,我发现妈妈走了进来。
The flowers will die **unless watered** every day.
= The flowers will die unless they are watered every day.
如果不给这些花每天浇水,它们会死掉的。

(4)分词在独立主格结构中的应用

当分词的逻辑主语与句子的主语不同时,带逻辑主语的分词短语成为独立主格结构,在句法功能上起状语作用。

The weather **permitting**, they will go and visit the science museum.
= If the weather permits, they will go and visit the science museum.
天气允许的话,他们会去参观科学博物馆。

The meeting **being over**, they all left the room.

= After the meeting was over, they all left the room.

会议结束,他们都离开了那个房间。

The moon **appearing**, they decided to go on with their journey.

= When the moon appeared, they decided to go on with their journey.

月亮出来了,他们决定继续他们的旅行。

注意:由 There being + 主语这种结构多表示原因。

There being a lot of books to read, he used to study till midnight.

= Because there were a lot of books to read, he used to study till midnight.

因为有许多书要读,他经常学习到深夜。

Grammar Exercises
自测训练

Ⅰ. Fill in the blanks with what you have learnt. 用所学知识填空。(5%)

非谓语动词有三种形式:动词不定式,1._____和分词。非谓语动词没有2._____和数的变化。动词不定式一般由 to 加动词原形构成。动名词是由动词原形加3._____构成的,它具有4._____和名词的特征。分词则分为现在分词和5._____两种形式。

Ⅱ. Fill in the blanks with the Non-Finite Verbs' syntactic function. 填写非谓语动词的句法功能。(10%)

1. Would you mind *waiting* for me in this room? ( )
2. It is no use *spending too much money on such useless products*. ( )
3. The suggestion *made* by the foreign expert was adopted by the manager. ( )
4. *Mary's being chosen* as the most excellent student in her university made her parents very happy. ( )
5. Because of my *broken* English, I can't make myself understood. ( )
6. She didn't wish the subject *to be mentioned* in the letter. ( )
7. The policeman put down the phone, *satisfied* with a smile on his face. ( )
8. Prices of daily goods *bought* through a computer can be lower than store prices. ( )
9. The purpose of the organization is *to greet* all new comers to the city and to provide them with any necessary information. ( )
10. The girl *sitting* beside me is my cousin. ( )

Ⅲ. Error identification. 错误辨识。(20%)

1. (A) Having been warned (B) of danger in the street at night, she (C) had to go home with a friend (D) followed her.
2. (A) To accept at a college or university in the USA, Chinese and other international students (B) must have a strong ability (C) in spoken and (D) written English.
3. (A) At the shopping centre, he (B) didn't know (C) what to buy and (D) leaving with an empty bag.

4. You (A) can't imagine (B) what great trouble they have (C) solved the problem (D) being discussed.
5. (A) All the staff in our company (B) are considering (C) to go to the city centre (D) for the fashion show.
6. It is no good (A) to try to remember grammatical rules. You (B) need to (C) practise what you (D) have learned.
7. I (A) don't know the girl (B) catching in the (C) destroyed building (D) because of the earthquake.
8. John (A) did not have time (B) to visit his uncle last night (C) because he was busy (D) being prepared for his examination.
9. I am (A) examining (B) the composition he has just finished (C) correcting (D) his possible mistakes in it.
10. (A) Seeing from the top, the 2008 Olympic Stadium (B) looks (C) as if it (D) is covered by a gray net of steal.

IV. Multiple choice. 单项选择。(30%)

1. Tony lent me the money, _____ that I'd do as much for him.
   A. hoping   B. to hope   C. hoped   D. having hoped
2. The old man sat in front of the television every evening, happy _____ anything that happened to be on.
   A. to watch   B. watching   C. watched   D. to have watched
3. The policeman came up to the house with the door _____, _____ there for a while and entered it.
   A. open; stood
   B. opened; stood
   C. opening; standing
   D. opened; standing
4. When _____ for his views about his teaching job, Philip said he found it very interesting and rewarding.
   A. asking   B. asked   C. having asked   D. to be asked
5. _____ to work overtime that evening, I missed a wonderful film.
   A. Having been asked
   B. To ask
   C. Having asked
   D. To be asked
6. The decision _____ at the tomorrow's meeting will influence the future of our company.
   A. to be made
   B. being made
   C. made
   D. having been made
7. Film has a much shorter history, especially when _____ such art forms as music and painting.
   A. having compared to
   B. comparing to
   C. compare to
   D. compared to
8. One learns a language by making mistakes and _____ them.
   A. corrects   B. correct   C. to correct   D. correcting
9. _____ with care, one plastic bag will last for six weeks.

A. Use   B. Using   C. Used   D. To use

10. He spent as much time as he could _____ his son.

    A. teaching   B. teach   C. to teach   D. for teaching

11. China recently tightened its waters controls near the Huangyan Island to prevent Chinese fishing boats from _____ in the South China Sea.

    A. attacking   B. having attacking

    C. being attacked   D. having been attacked

12. Pressed from his parents, and _____ that he has wasted too much time, the boy is determined to stop playing video games.

    A. realizing   B. realized   C. to realize   D. being realized

13. Having finished her project, she was invited by the school _____ to the freshmen.

    A. speaking   B. having spoken   C. to speak   D. to have spoken

14. Everything _____ into consideration, they may have another chance.

    A. taking   B. taken   C. to take   D. to be taken

15. —What do you suppose made her worried?

    —_____ a gold ring.

    A. Lose   B. Lost   C. Losing   D. Because of losing

16. She was very glad to see her child well _____.

    A. take care of   B. taken care of   C. to take care of   D. taking care of

17. He kept _____ to his parents.

    A. putting off to write   B. to put off to write

    C. putting off writing   D. to put off writing

18. The man _____ in the chair asked me to _____.

    A. seated; seated   B. sitting; sitting

    C. seating; seat   D. seated; be seated

19. How pleased the Emperor was _____ what the cheats said!

    A. heard   B. hearing   C. hear   D. to hear

20. Whom would you rather have _____ with you, him or me?

    A. to be gone   B. gone   C. going   D. go

21. I won't go to the party even if _____.

    A. inviting   B. to be invited   C. invited   D. having invited

22. After _____ for the job, everyone will be asked to take a language test.

    A. having interviewed   B. interviewed

    C. interviewing   D. being interviewed

23. "It's such a nice place," Mother said as she sat at the table _____ for the family.

    A. to be reserved   B. having reserved   C. reserving   D. reserved

24. The old couple often take a walk after super in the park with their pet dog _____.

    A. to follow   B. following   C. followed   D. follows

25. This machine is very easy _____. Anybody can learn to use it in a few minutes.

    A. operating   B. to be operating   C. operated   D. to be operated

26. Tom took a taxi to the airport, only _____ his plane high up in the sky.
    A. finding   B. to find   C. being found   D. to have found

27. _____ an important decision more on emotion than on reason, you will regret sooner or later.
    A. Based   B. Base   C. Basing   D. To base

28. Before driving into the city, you are required to get your car _____.
    A. washed   B. wash   C. washing   D. to wash

29. No matter how bright a talker you are, there are times when it's better _____ silent.
    A. remain   B. be remaining
    C. having remained   D. to remain

30. —Where is my bag? I remember _____ it here.
    —You shouldn't have left it here. Remember _____ it with you all the time.
    A. to put; taking   B. putting; taking
    C. to put; to take   D. putting; to take

V. Fill in the blanks with the right forms of the verbs given in brackets. 用括号里动词的正确形式填空。(20%)

    Trees can be found all over the world. One tree can be the home to thousands of living things. It keeps them away from other animals and bad weather. It gives them food (1)_____ (eat) and a place to make "houses", too. All of us know that birds like living in the forests. Some birds have long and (2)_____ (point) mouths. This kind of mouth can help them to find insects in the tree. They are sure that forests are the best place for them to live in.

    Over half of the world's plants and animals live in the rainforests. But more and more trees in rainforests are (3)_____ (cut) down for wood and the rainforests have been turned into fields for (4)_____ (grow) rice and vegetables. The rainforests in some parts of the world are gone. Today, too many trees are still being cut down. The rainforests are also (5)_____ (kill) by acid rain. This is because of the smoke and dirty water from cars and some factories. The acid rain falls on the trees (6)_____ (make) the leaves dry and it stops the trees from (7)_____ (grow) well. In a few years, there (8)_____ (be) no forests at all.

    Some scientists say that one kind of animal is lost from the earth every half an hour as these rainforests (9)_____ (go). Many animals need the rainforests to live in. When the trees are cut down, they have no place to live in or to get food from. Then many animals are made (10)_____ (live) near towns and cities to get food. As a result, a lot of animals are killed by people and cars each year.

VI. Translate the following sentences into English. 将下列句子译成英语。(15%)

1. 购买我们不需要的东西是浪费金钱。
2. 非常感谢你帮助我找到丢失的钱包。
3. 看来他们家可能发生了一些出人意料的事情。
4. 他们送给我一张请帖,邀请我去参加一个生日聚会。
5. 很久没有收到父母的来信了,爱丽丝期待着收到他们的信。

第十三章 构词法

一、构词法的概述

英语中的词汇数以万计,但英语词汇并不是杂乱无章、互不相关的群体,而是一个严密的体系,在这个结构体系中,词与词之间有着各种各样的联系。英语中的许多单词往往会与其他词在结构上有联系,把这些联系的规律总结出来就是构词法(Word Formation)。

二、构词法的种类

构词法主要有以下六种。

	分类	定义
构词法	转化法 Conversion	转化法是指由一个词类转化为另一词类
	派生法 Affixation	派生法是在词根前面加前缀或在词根后面加后缀,从而构成一个与原单词意义相近或截然相反的新词
	合成法 Compounding	合成法是把两个或多个单词连在一起合成一个新词
	混合法 Blending	混合法是将两个词混合或各取一部分紧缩而形成一个新词
	缩略法 Clipping	将单词缩写,词义和词性保持不变的英语构词法称为截短法,主要有截头、去尾、截头去尾等形式
	首尾字母缩略法 Acronymy	用单词首尾字母组成一个新词的英语构词法叫作首尾字母缩略法这种形式的英语构词生成的新词,读音主要有两种形式,即各字母分别读音和作为一个单词读音

(一)转化法

序号	转化法	例句
1	名词转化为动词	**Hand** in your exercise books, please. 请交作业本。 We **breakfasted** yesterday morning. 我们昨天早晨一起吃了早点。

续表

序号	转化法	例句
2	动词转化为名词	He is a man of strong **build**. 他体格健壮。 No zuo no **die**. 不作死就不会死。
3	形容词转化为名词	The girl in **white** is my younger sister. 穿白衣服的女孩子是我的妹妹。 When will the **final** start? 决赛何时开始?
4	形容词转化为动词	We will try our best to **better** our working conditions. 我们会尽力改善工作条件。 **Dry** your hands with the towel. 用毛巾擦干你的手。

(二)派生法

(1)前缀

除少数英语前缀外,前缀一般改变单词的意义,不改变词性。

①表示否定的前缀

序号	否定前缀	例词
1	dis-	dislike 不喜欢,disappear 消失,discover 发现
2	in-	invisible 看不见的,incorrect 不正确的,incomplete 不完全的
3	im-	impolite 不礼貌的,impossible 不可能的,immoral 不道德的
4	il-	illegal 不合法的,illogical 不合逻辑的,illiterate 文盲的
5	ir-	irregular 不规则的,irresponsible 不负责任的
6	non-	nonsense 废话,nonstop 不停地,nonsmoker 不抽烟的人
7	neg-	negative 消极的,neglect 忽略
8	un-	unhappy 不快乐的,unimportant 不重要的,unable 不能的
9	mis-	misunderstand 误解,mislead 把……带错路,misrepresent 歪曲

②表示空间位置、方向关系的前缀

序号	空间和方向前缀	意义	例词
1	a-	表示"在……之上""向……"	ahead 向前,abroad 在海外
2	fore-	表示"在前面"	forehead 额头,forearm 前臂
3	in-	表示"在……里面""向内"	include 包括,indoors 在室内
4	out-	表示"在……外面""向外"	outside 在外面,output 输出
5	over-	表示"在上面""在……之外"	overhead 头顶上的,overcoat 大衣
6	under-	表示"在下面"	underground 地下的,underline 下划线
7	up-	表示"在上面""向上"	upwards 在上面,upstairs 在楼上
8	tele-	表示"远"	telephone 电话,telescope 望远镜

③表示时间、序列关系的前缀

序号	时间和序列前缀	意义	例词
1	ex-	表示"先,前,故"	ex-president 前任总统,ex-husband 前夫
2	fore-	表示"在前""预先"	foreword 前言,foresight 预见
3	mid-	表示"在……中间"	midnight 午夜,midsummer 盛夏
4	post-	表示"在……后面"	postwar 战后的,postliberation 新中国成立后的
5	pre-	表示"在……前面""提前"	preview 预示,prehistoric 史前的

④表示数量、程度的前缀

序号	数量和程度前缀	意义	例词
1	mono-	表示"一""单一"	monologue(戏剧)独白,monotone 单调的语调
2	di-, bi-	表示"二""双"	dialogue 对话,bicycle 自行车
3	deca-	表示"十"	decade 十年,decimal 十进位的
4	cent-/centi-	表示"百""百分之一"	century 世纪,centimeter 厘米
5	kilo-	表示"千"	kilometer 公里,kilogram 公斤
6	multi-	表示"许多""多数"	multimedia 多媒体,multiple 多个的
7	semi-/hemi-	表示"半""一半"	semiconductor 半导体,hemisphere 半球
8	mini-	表示"微小的"	minibus 小巴,miniskirt 超短裙
9	micro-	表示"微观上的"	microscope 显微镜,microwave 微波
10	macro-	表示"宏观上的"	macroeconomics 宏观经济学 macroevolution 大进化
11	extra-	表示"超越""额外"	extraordinary 巨大的
12	over-	表示"超过"	overcome 克服,overweight 超重的
13	super-	表示"超"	supermarket 超市,superstar 超级明星
14	re-	表示"重复"	review 回顾,recover 恢复

⑤表示其他意义的前缀

序号	其他意义的前缀	意义	例词
1	auto-	表示"自动"	automobile 汽车,autoalarm 自动报警器
2	en-	表示"使……"	enlarge 扩大,enrich 使富裕
3	trans-	表示"横过""贯通"	transport 运输,translate 翻译
4	de-	表示"除去""离去"	destroy 摧毁,depart 离开
5	bio-	表示"生命""生物"	biology 生物学,biography 传记

(2)后缀

英语后缀一般改变词类,而不引起词义的变化。

构 词 法

① 名词后缀
a. 表示人或物的后缀

序号	人或物的后缀	意义	例词
1	-er/-or	表示人或物	hunter 猎人, actor 男演员, cooker 炊具
2	-ess	表示女性或雌性	actress 女演员, waitress 女侍者, lioness 母狮
3	-ese	表示某一国家或地区的人	Japanese 日本人, Cantonese 广东人
4	-an	表示某一国家的人	American 美国人, Austrian 奥地利人, Indian 印度人
5	-ist	表示有某种专业特长的人（"……家"）	artist 艺术家, novelist 小说家, typist 打字员

b. 构成抽象名词或集合名词的后缀

序号	抽象或集合名词后缀	例词
1	-ment	movement 运动, government 政府, announcement 宣告
2	-ion/-sion/-ation/-ition	invention 发明, invitation 邀请, decision 决定
3	-ship	friendship 友谊, relationship 关系
4	-hood	childhood 童年, neighborhood 地区
5	-dom	wisdom 智慧, freedom 自由
6	-th	truth 真理, length 长度
7	-ness	illness 疾病, happiness 幸福

② 形容词后缀

序号	形容词后缀	例词
1	-able/-ible	comfortable 舒适的, enjoyable 愉快的, terrible 可怕的
2	-al	natural 自然地, national 国家的, musical 音乐的
3	-ic/-ical	electric 电的, medical 医学的
4	-ish	selfish 自私的, childish 幼稚的
5	-ful	careful 认真的, beautiful 美丽的
6	-less	careless 粗心的, useless 无用的
7	-ly	friendly 有好的, monthly 每月的, lovely 可爱的
8	-en	wooden 木制的, woolen 羊毛的, golden 金质的
9	-ern	eastern 东方的, northern 北方的
10	-y	lucky 幸运的, funny 有趣的, shiny 闪耀的, dirty 脏脏的
11	-ous	dangerous 危险的, famous 著名的, serious 严重的
12	-ant/-ent	pleasant 令人愉快的, excellent 优秀的
13	-ed	excited 兴奋的, tired 疲倦的, interested 感兴趣的
14	-ing	exciting 使人兴奋的, tiring 令人疲倦的, interesting 有趣的

③动词后缀

序号	动词后缀	例词
1	-en	quicken 增速, weaken 衰减
2	-fy	beautify 美化, purify 使纯净
3	-ish	finish 完成, establish 建立
4	-ize	modernize 使现代化, organize 组织
5	-ate	separate 分开, operate 操作

④副词后缀

序号	副词后缀	例词
1	-ly	possibly 可能地, swiftly 迅速地, slowly 缓慢地
2	-ward/-wards	downward 向下地, inwards 向内地
3	-ways	always 常常, sideways 斜着
4	-wise	otherwise 否则, clockwise 顺时针方向的

(三)合成法

(1)合成名词

序号	合成名词	例词
1	名词 + 名词	teahouse 茶室, chairman 主席, postman 邮递员
2	代词 + 名词	she-wolf 母狼, he-sparrow 雄麻雀
3	形容词 + 名词	blackboard 黑板, greenhouse 温室
4	副词 + 名词	outhouse 外屋, uptown 住宅区
5	动词 + 名词	pickpocket 扒手, runtime 运行时间
6	V-ing + 名词	reading-room 阅览室, swimming-pool 游泳池
7	V-ed + 名词	spoken-English 英语口语, written-English 书面英语
8	名词 + V-ing	handwriting 书法, sun-bathing 日光浴
9	名词 + 介词 + 名词	daughter-in-law 儿媳, father-in-law 岳父

(2)合成形容词

序号	合成形容词	例词
1	名词 + 形容词	duty-free 免税的, ice-cold 冰冷的
2	名词 + V-ing	peace-loving 爱好和平的, English-speaking 说英语的
3	名词 + V-ed	snow-covered 被雪覆盖的, man-made 人造的
4	名词 + 名词 + ed	iron-hearted 铁石心肠的, iron-willed 意志坚强的
5	形容词 + 名词 + ed	warm-hearted 热心肠的, middle-aged 中年的
6	形容词 + 名词	long-distance 长途的, color-blind 色盲的

(3) 合成动词

序号	合成动词	例词
1	副词 + 动词	overcome 克服,ill-treat 虐待
2	名词/代词 + 动词	self-pollinate 自授花粉,mass-produce 大规模生产
3	形容词 + 动词	safe-guard 保卫,whitewash 粉刷

(4) 合成副词

序号	合成副词	例词
1	形容词 + 名词	hotfoot 匆忙地,downstairs 在楼下,downtown 在商业区
2	代词 + 副词	everywhere 到处,anywhere 任何地方
3	副词 + 副词	however 尽管如此,furthermore 此外
4	介词 + 名词	beforehand 事先,alongside 在……旁边
5	介词 + 副词	forever 永远,nearby 附近地

(5) 合成代词

everybody 每人　　　　everything 每件事物　　　　everyone 每个人
nobody 没有人　　　　nothing 没有事情　　　　　　no one 没有人
somebody 某人　　　　something 某些事物　　　　　someone 某人
anybody 任何人　　　　anything 任何事物　　　　　anyone 任何人

(四) 混合法

在混合法中,将两个词混合、剪切拼接而形成一个新词,新词形式上保留了原来两个词的一部分。这种构词法就是把一个词与另一个词"混合一体"来构成合成词的方法。从形态结构看,大致可分成以下四类。

序号	混合方式	例词
1	取第一个词的首部接第二个词的尾部	motor + hotel→motel 汽车旅馆 breakfast + lunch→brunch 早午餐
2	保持第一个词的原形,删去第二个词的首部	news + broadcast→newscast 新闻报道 cheese + hamburger→cheeseburger 芝士汉堡包
3	保持第二个词的原形,删去第一个词的尾部	medical + care→medicare 医疗照顾方案 parachute + troops→paratroops 空降部队
4	取第一个词的首部接第二个词的首部	international police→interpol 国际警察 communications + satellite→comsat 通信卫星

(五)缩略法

序号	缩略方式	例词
1	剪切原词的开头部分	telephone→phone 电话 airplane/aeroplane→plane 飞机
2	剪切原词的末尾部分	examination→exam 考试,taxicab→taxi 出租车 laboratory→lab 实验室,advertisement→ad 广告
3	剪切原词的中间部分	foot/feet→ft 英尺,year→yr 年
4	剪切原词的两端,保留中间部分	refrigerator→fridge 冰箱

(六)首尾字母缩略法

首字母缩略法是指一种取词组中每个词的第一个字母代表这个词组构成新词的方法。首字母缩略构词法具有以下特点:

①单个单词截取其首字母;
②多个单词构成的词组截取其各个单词的首字母;
③不含虚词的词组,截取各个单词首字母;
④含虚词的词组,一般截取实词首字母,虚词省略。

	按首字母拼读的缩略语	像单词一样拼读的缩略语
首尾字母缩略法	British Broadcast Corporation→BBC 英国广播公司 United States of America→USA 美国 Unidentified Flying Object→UFO 不明飞行物 very important person→VIP 贵宾 Information Technology→IT 信息技术 Computer Assisted Design→CAD 计算机辅助设计 World Trade Organization→WTO 世界贸易组织	North Atlantic Treaty Organization→NATO 北大西洋公约组织 the United Nations Educational, Scientific and Cultural Organization→UNESCO 联合国教科文组织 lightwave amplification by stimulated emission of radiation→laser 激光 acquired immunity deficiency syndrome→AIDS 艾滋病 Asian Pacific Economic Cooperation→APEC 亚太经贸合作组织 International English Language Testing System→IELTS 雅思考试

Grammar Exercises
语法训练

Ⅰ. **Change the word form according to the requirement.** 按照要求变词形。(5%)

1. happy (形容词) _____ (名词)
2. honest (形容词) _____ (反义词)
3. Europe(名词) _____ (形容词)

4. pure（形容词）＿＿＿＿＿＿＿＿＿＿＿＿＿＿＿＿（动词）
5. move（动词）＿＿＿＿＿＿＿＿＿＿＿＿＿＿＿＿（名词）

Ⅱ. **Fill in the blanks with right forms.** 用正确形式填空。（10%）
1. The hero died for his country, so his ＿＿＿＿＿＿＿ (die) is heavier than Mount Tai.
2. The little boy looked ＿＿＿＿＿＿＿ (sad) at his father who was badly wounded.
3. To everyone's ＿＿＿＿＿＿＿ (satisfy), the manager finished her job well.
4. My radio is out of order. Can you tell me the ＿＿＿＿＿＿＿ (late) news about Tiangong 2?
5. No one should enter without the ＿＿＿＿＿＿＿ (permit) of the police.
6. The letter "b" in the word "climb" is ＿＿＿＿＿＿＿ (silence).
7. The black people were against slavery and fought for their ＿＿＿＿＿＿＿ (free) bravely.
8. ＿＿＿＿＿＿＿ (honest) speaking, I didn't want to hurt you on purpose.
9. You'd better give up smoking if you want to be ＿＿＿＿＿＿＿ (health).
10. I believe travelling can broaden our mind, and that music can ＿＿＿＿＿＿＿ (rich) our life.

Ⅲ. **Error identification.** 错误辨识。（20%）
1. The mobile phone (A) that (B) my younger sister lost is (C) very expensive and it is (D) of great valuable.
2. (A) How foolish my nephew is! He (B) is always acting (C) fool. He is really (D) a fool.
3. We (A) are exciting (B) that our team has won (C) the championship (D) in the final.
4. The boss (A) listened to (B) the complain from (C) the angry customer (D) patiently.
5. (A) Seeing that he was reading (B) attentively, his mother (C) opened and closed the door (D) quiet.
6. We all (A) know that he is (B) an expert (C) at chemistry and he is called (D) a chemical.
7. (A) It takes (B) the man-make satellite (C) 48 hours (D) to orbit the planet around.
8. She explains (A) why Easter（复活节）, (B) a region and social festival, (C) is popular (D) in those countries.
9. I'd just like to (A) emphasis (B) how important (C) it is for people to learn (D) a foreign language.
10. My grandmother is (A) as energy as a young woman and (B) dislikes (C) sitting around (D) doing nothing at all.

Ⅳ. **Multiple choice.** 单项选择。（30%）
1. We have measured the wall and the wall is more than 5 meters in ＿＿＿＿＿＿＿.
   A. long　　　　B. longer　　　　C. length　　　　D. longing
2. She got the job finally because she had the right ＿＿＿＿＿＿＿ for the job.
   A. qualify　　　B. qualification　　C. qualified　　　D. quantity
3. The worker was so ＿＿＿＿＿＿＿ that he was fired by his factory.
   A. careless　　　B. careful　　　　C. care　　　　D. carefulness
4. The song sounds ＿＿＿＿＿＿＿ and we are all listening ＿＿＿＿＿＿＿.
   A. moving; careful　　　　　　B. beautifully; carefully
   C. happily; careful　　　　　　D. beautiful; carefully

5. I can't go _____ because I have to pick up my sister at the airport after work.
   A. anywhere else　　　　　　　　　　B. somewhere else
   C. to else anywhere　　　　　　　　　D. to somewhere else
6. The little boy did not want to _____ his parents, so he told them a lie.
   A. disappointing　　　　　　　　　　B. disappointed
   C. disappoint　　　　　　　　　　　　D. disappointment
7. We are still in _____ and we must leave here as soon as possible.
   A. dangerous　　B. danger　　　　C. endanger　　　　D. dangerless
8. The price of the furniture is _____, so I cannot afford it.
   A. reason　　　　B. reasonable　　C. unreasonable　　D. reasonably
9. My uncle is a _____ person. He does not think that anyone can be successful without _____.
   A. working-hard; work hard　　　　B. working-hard; hard work
   C. hard-working; work hard　　　　D. hard-working; hard work
10. During the _____ experiment, the teacher told her students what was happening.
    A. science　　　B. scientific　　　C. scientist　　　　D. scientificly
11. Although they are twins, there is no _____ between them except for their appearance.
    A. silimar　　　B. similarly　　　C. same　　　　　　D. similarity
12. Jane decided to lose _____ by eating less and doing more exercise.
    A. weight　　　B. weigh　　　　　C. height　　　　　　D. heavy
13. My old grandmother lives _____ in her eighties, but she doesn't feel _____.
    A. lonely; lonely　　　　　　　　　B. alone; alone
    C. alone; lonely　　　　　　　　　　D. lonely; alone
14. Scientists around the world are working to _____ the treatment of AIDS.
    A. discovery　　　　　　　　　　　　B. discover
    C. invent　　　　　　　　　　　　　　D. invention
15. It was the government that helped the _____ people build their own houses.
    A. homeless　　B. homely　　　　C. home　　　　　　D. homed
16. —What does your father do?
    —He is a skillful _____ in a local restaurant.
    A. cook　　　　B. cooker　　　　C. cooking　　　　　D. cooked
17. For our homework today, we have to write a _____ of the school where we study.
    A. describe　　B. descriptive　　C. description　　　D. descriptor
18. The second lesson is the most _____ part in the book.
    A. enjoy　　　　B. enjoyable　　　C. enjoyment　　　　D. enjoying
19. Difficulties _____ the mind, as labor does the body.
    A. strong　　　B. strength　　　　C. strongly　　　　　D. strengthen
20. The gold medal winner said that he owes much of his _____ to his coach.
    A. succeed　　B. successful　　　C. successfully　　　D. success

第十三章 构词法

V. Fill in the blanks with the correct forms of words in the following passage. 填写正确形式。(20%)

Elizabeth Blackwell was born in England in 1821, and moved to New York City when she was ten years old. One day, she (1) _____ (decision) that she wanted to become a doctor. That was nearly (2) _____ (possible) for a woman in the middle of the nineteenth century. After writing many letters asking for (3) _____ (admit) to medical schools, she was (4) _____ (final) accepted by a doctor in Philadelphia. She was so (5) _____ (determine) that she taught in school and gave music lessons to get money for the cost of schooling.

In 1849, after she (6) _____ (graduation) from medical school, she made up her mind to further her (7) _____ (educate) in Paris. She wanted to be a surgeon (外科医生), but a (8) _____ (seriously) eye problem forced her to give up the idea.

Upon returning to (9) _____ (American), she found it (10) _____ (difficulty) to start her own practice because she was a woman. By 1857 Elizabeth and her sister, also a doctor, along with another woman doctor, managed to open a new hospital, the first for women and children. Besides being the first woman physician and founding her own hospital, she also set up the first medical school for women.

VI. Translate the following sentences into English. 将下列句子译成英语。(15%)

1. 尽管她出生在美国, 但是她还是一个中国人。
2. 这些研究表明0.2%的女人是色盲。
3. 大多数人都对这个有趣的故事感兴趣。
4. 前几天雾霾(haze)如此严重导致许多孩子生病。
5. ——那位歌手看上去非常紧张。
   ——我们也紧张地看着他呀。

词　　法

第十四章　陈述句和感叹句

一、陈述句

(一)陈述句概述

句子按照功能分为陈述句、感叹句、祈使句和疑问句。而陈述句主要说明一个事实或陈述说话人的看法。如：

The sun rises in the east. 太阳在东方升起。（说明事实）

I like watching movies. 我喜欢看电影。（陈述看法）

(二)陈述句的否定形式

	时态	肯定句	否定句
主谓陈述句	一般现在时	A smart phone **plays** an important role in people's lives. 智能手机在人们生活中发挥重要作用。 We **cycle** to work every day. 我们每天骑车去上班。	A smart phone **doesn't play** an important role in people's lives. 智能手机在人们生活中没有发挥重要作用。 We **don't cycle** to work every day. 我们每天不骑车上班。
	现在进行时	The population of the world **is increasing** very fast. 世界人口正增长的非常快。	The population of the world **is not increasing** very fast. 世界人口增长得不快。
	一般过去时	The audience **threw** flowers onto the stage. 观众把花扔上了舞台。	The audience **didn't throw** flowers onto the stage. 观众没把花扔上了舞台。
	一般将来时	My elder brother **will** go abroad for further study next month. 我哥哥下个月要出国进修。	My elder brother **will not** go abroad for further study next month. 我哥哥下个月不出国进修。
主系表陈述句	一般现在时	My nephew **is** a 6th grader. 我侄子是六年级学生。 These birds **are** from the south. 这些鸟儿来自南方。	My nephew **is** not a 6th grader. 我侄子不是六年级学生。 These birds **are** not from the south. 这些鸟儿不是来自南方。

第十四章 陈述句和感叹句

续表

	时态	肯定句	否定句
主系表陈述句	一般过去时	She **was** a movie fan three years ago. 她三年前是电影迷。 His parents **were** teachers. 他的父母是老师。	She **was not** a movie fan three years ago. 我三年前不是电影迷。 His parents **were not** teachers. 他的父母不是老师。
含有情态动词的陈述句	在情态动词后加 not	You **must** hand in your homework tomorrow. 你一定要明天交作业。 David **can** play the guitar. 戴维会弹吉他。	You **needn't** hand in your homework tomorrow. 你明天不必交作业。（must作"必须"讲时，否定形式是 needn't。） David **cannot** play the guitar. 戴维不会弹吉他。

注意：陈述句中的否定形式是在 be 动词、助动词 do、does、did、have/has、will、shall 等或情态动词 can、may、must 等后面加 not。如果陈述句中的谓语动词只有行为动词而没有助动词或情态动词时，要根据时态找出其相应的助动词。

二、感叹句

(一)感叹句概述

感叹句是用来表达人的喜、怒、哀、乐等强烈感情的句子。句尾用感叹号"！"，读时用降调。在口语中常省略句，后面的主语与谓语也往往省略。

①感叹句可以是一个单词，如：
  Ouch! 哎哟！
  Wonderful! 妙极了！
②感叹句可以是一个短语构成的独立句。如：
  My God! 我的天呀！
  Well done! 干得不错啊！
③感叹句也可以是一个分句。如：
  If only I were a millionaire! 我要是个百万富翁多好啊！
  As if I had owed you! 好像我欠了你钱似的！
④感叹句也可以是一句话。如：
  How time flies! 时间过得多快！
  What good news it is! 多好的消息啊！

(二)感叹句的形式

英语中最常见的感叹句是由 what 和 how 引导的，what 主要用来感叹名词，how 主要用来感叹形容词和副词。

（1）what 引导的感叹句

用法	例句
What + a(an) + 形容词 + 单数名词 + 主语 + 谓语！	What a new book it is! 好新的一本书啊！ What a terrible day it is! 多么糟糕的一天！
What + 形容词 + 复数名词或不可数名词 + 主语 + 谓语！	What silly questions you asked! 你问的问题真傻！ What bad weather it is! 多么糟糕的天气啊！
What + 名词短语！ （在口语中常常省略主语和谓语。）	What an interesting movie! 多么有趣的电影啊！ What educational lectures! 多么有教育意义的讲座啊！

（2）how 引导的感叹句

用法	例句
How + 形容词（副词） + 主语 + 谓语！	How hard they are working! 他们工作多么努力啊！ How soft Mary's voice is! 玛丽的嗓音是多么轻柔啊！
How + 形容词 + a(an)/the + 单数名词 + 主语 + 谓语！	How amazing the movie is! 这电影多么棒啊！ How cool a car it is! 一辆好酷的车！

（3）其他形式的感叹句

what 和 how 引导的感叹句本质上是通过倒装的形式，以强化语气，表达强烈感情的句型。如：

"It is a cute girl."是一句陈述句，通过把名词短语 a cute girl 前置，倒装为：What a cute girl she is!

把形容词 cute 前置，倒装为：How cute the girl is! 或 How cute a girl she is!

对于一个短小的句子也可以通过倒装的形式表达强烈的感情，这样的句子也可以算是感叹句的一种类型。如：

Aren't they awesome!（= They are really awesome.）他们太棒了！

Here comes my turn!（= My turn finally comes here.）终于轮到我了！

Grammar Exercises
语法训练

I. Turn the following sentences into negative sentences. 将下列句子变成否定句。（5%）

1. They must go to work every day.

2. Mrs. Black usually takes an umbrella with her when she goes out.

3. These students can speak Japanese very well.

4. The guide will take you to the Summer Palace.
   _____

5. Jessica wrote an email to her professor last Sunday.
   _____

Ⅱ. **Turn the following sentences into exclamatory sentences.** 将下列各句变成感叹句。（10%）

1. This is a very inspiring story. _____
2. She is a very hospitable housewife. _____
3. The news is exciting. _____
4. His grandpa gets up early every day. _____
5. These cars are very expensive. _____
6. They did very excellently in the examination. _____
7. She drives her car very carelessly. _____
8. They are watching an exciting football game now. _____
9. The weather in Kunming is comfortable. _____
10. We had a good time in summer vacation. _____

Ⅲ. **Error identification.** 错误辨识。（20%）

1. （A）What （B）hard （C）it is （D）raining!
2. （A）What fast （B）time （C）flies! （D）We have not seen each other for five years.
3. Tom together （A）with his coach （B）don't （C）tell me （D）the message last night.
4. （A）How （B）a beautiful （C）flower （D）it is!
5. （A）Anyway, （B）I can't cheat him. （C）It's not against （D）all my principles.
6. （A）We didn't know （B）when would these volcanoes （C）erupt （D）in the following years.
7. I （A）hasn't given my son （B）any money （C）since we quarreled with （D）each other last time.
8. Nothing （A）cannot be （B）more important （C）than staying with family （D）during the holidays.
9. （A）You'd better （B）don't （C）drive to work （D）during the rush time.
10. （A）Alice doesn't （B）go shopping （C）with Mrs. Baker （D）in the downtown tomorrow.

Ⅳ. **Multiple choice.** 单项选择。（30%）

1. _____ noises they are making!
   A. What   B. How   C. What a   D. How a

2. _____ heavy snow!
   A. How   B. What   C. What a   D. How a

3. _____ old coat Li Lei is wearing!
   A. How   B. What an   C. What a   D. How a

4. _____ exciting moment it is!
   A. How a   B. How an
   C. What an   D. What a

5. _____ the water in the river is!

   A. What a clean   B. How clean

   C. What   D. How a clean

6. _____ fine weather it is today!

   A. How a   B. What a   C. What   D. How much

7. _____ fast the boys are running!

   A. What   B. What a   C. How   D. How a

8. _____ the moon is!

   A. How round   B. What round

   C. What a round   D. How a round

9. _____ surprising news it is!

   A. How   B. What   C. What a   D. How a

10. _____ they love their country!

    A. What   B. How   C. What a   D. How very

11. —Please bring your homework to school tomorrow, John.

    —OK, I _____.

    A. don't   B. won't   C. do   D. will

12. This peach _____, and you _____ like it.

    A. taste good; will   B. tastes well; won't

    C. tastes good; will   D. taste well; won't

13. What he has told us about the situation in the South Korea _____.

    A. don't make any value   B. don't make any sense

    C. doesn't make any value   D. doesn't make any sense

14. —_____ I take a message?

    —Yes, can you ask Davis _____ me back this evening.

    A. Can; to call   B. Cannot; to call

    C. Can; call   D. Cannot; call

15. The TV is too loud. You _____.

    A. have to turn it up   B. needn't turn it down

    C. must turn it down   D. can turn it up

16. The children _____ cross the road until the traffic lights turned green.

    A. shall not   B. wouldn't   C. doesn't   D. don't

17. My leg is aching. Jack always _____ me _____ my schoolbag.

    A. helps; not to carry   B. help; not to carry

    C. helps; carry   D. help; carry

18. To protect the environment, the local government _____ a lot of signs to warn the citizens _____ litter (乱扔垃圾).

    A. put up; of   B. put up; against

    C. has put up; to   D. has put up; not to

19. You had better _____ here _____ the heavy storm.
   A. not leave; because of
   B. not leave; because
   C. not to leave; because
   D. not to leave; because of

20. English _____ a large vocabulary. When knowing more words and expressions, you _____ it easier to read and communicate.
   A. has; find
   B. have; will find
   C. has; will find
   D. have; find

V. Cloze. 完形填空。(20%)

　　Marx had a remarkable talent for languages. He could __1__ all European languages and write in three, German, French and English, in a __2__ that won the praise of all who knew these languages well. Having __3__ "Capital" in German, he translated it into French himself. He was fond of saying, "A foreign language is a weapon in the __4__ of life." When he was already fifty, he began to learn Russian. He made __5__ progress that in six months he was able to __6__ reading Russian poets and writers.

　　__7__ reading foreign poems and novels, Marx had __8__ remarkable way of rest in—mathematics. In the most unhappy moments of his life, when he was unable to go on __9__ his usual scientific work, he turned to mathematics. Mathematicians have a very high opinion of the work he has done. __10__ talent Marx is!

1. A. listen   B. read   C. hear   D. tell
2. A. way   B. road   C. book   D. story
3. A. seen   B. read   C. written   D. found
4. A. struggle   B. period   C. time   D. way
5. A. many   B. much   C. so   D. such
6. A. like   B. enjoy   C. go   D. watch
7. A. Except   B. But   C. Beside   D. Besides
8. A. another   B. other   C. else   D. rest
9. A. to   B. for   C. with   D. at
10. A. How a   B. How   C. What a   D. What

VI. Translate the following sentences into English. 将下列句子译成英语。(15%)

1. ——我这个月必须要完成这项计划吗?
   ——不,你不必。
2. 老妇人走得多慢啊!
3. 她既说汉语又说英语。是一个多么聪明的姑娘啊!
4. 老年人不用贵的手机。
5. 新疆到北京路程好长啊!

第十五章 祈使句和疑问句

一、祈使句

表示请求、命令、叮嘱、邀请或劝告的句子叫祈使句。祈使句常以动词原形开头,主语(you)一般省略。根据说话者的语气不同,句末用感叹号或句号,且用降调朗读。

用法	例句
"V 原形"结构(动态句): 行为动词原形 V + 宾语 + 其他成分	**Open** the window, please. 请开窗。 Please **fasten** your seat belt. 请系好安全带。 **Look out**! **Mind** your steps! 小心!当心脚下!
"Be"结构(静态句): Be + 表语(名词、形容词) + 其他成分	**Be quiet**! 请安静! **Be a good student**. 要做一个好学生。
"Let"结构(使役句): Let + 人称代词宾格 + 动词原形 + 其他成分	**Let him cry**. 让他哭吧。 **Let me help** you. 我来帮你吧。 **Let's go skating** together. 咱们一起去滑冰吧。(包括对方) **Let us go** home. 让我们回家吧。(不包括对方)
祈使句的否定形式:Don't + 无人称祈使句 　　　　　　　Let's + not + 动词原形 　　　　　　　No + doing(动名词)	**Don't follow** me! 别跟着我! **Don't be** late next time! 下次别迟到了! **Let's** not play the computer games. 咱们别玩电脑游戏了。 **No smoking**. 禁止吸烟。

二、疑问句

用来提出问题的句子叫疑问句。英语中的疑问句有四种形式:一般疑问句、特殊疑问句、选择疑问句和反义疑问句。

(一)一般疑问句

一般疑问句用来询问一件事或一种情况是否属实,其结构是将助动词、情态动词或 be

动词置于主语之前,句末用问号,通常以 yes 或 no 来回答(有时也用 certainly,perhaps,not at all 等来回答),读升调。

用法	例句
以系动词(be)开头的疑问句	— **Are** you a student? 你是学生吗? — No, I am not. I am a teacher. 不,我是老师。
以助动词开头的疑问句	**Do** you **learn** from your mistakes? 你从错误中学习吗? **Does** he **go to the gym** every day? 他每天去健身房吗? **Did** you **have** trouble in finding the exit yesterday? 昨天你找出口有困难吗? — **Have** you ever **told** the children your story? 你给孩子们讲过你的故事吗? — No, never. 不,从未讲过。
以情态动词开头的疑问句	— **Can** you drive a car? 你会开车吗? — Yes, I can. 是的,我会。 — **Must** we finish our homework tomorrow? 我们明天必须完成作业吗? — No, you needn't. 不,不必。 — **Would** you mind if I turn off the air conditioner? 我关空调你介意吗? — Not at all. 不。

(二)特殊疑问句

特殊疑问句是以疑问词 who、whom、whose、which、what、when、where、why 和 how 等开头,对句子中某一部分提问。基本结构是:特殊疑问词 + 一般疑问句。特殊疑问句不能用 yes 或 no 来回答,要根据所提问的内容回答,句末读降调。例如:

Which do you like? — I like the blue one. ——你喜欢哪个? ——我喜欢蓝色的那个。
What is your name? — My name is Jack. ——你叫什么名字? ——我叫杰克。
Where do you come from? — I come from Germany. ——你来自哪儿? ——我来自德国。

注意:特殊疑问句用陈述语序有两种情况。

①疑问词作主语时

What made you cry? 什么事让你哭了?
Who is the most charming lady in the world? 谁是世界上最迷人的女士?

②whose/what/which/how many 等和所修饰的成分一起作主语时

Whose book was left in the meeting room? 谁的书落在会议室了?
Which plane leaves for Urumqi? 哪一架飞机开往乌鲁木齐?

(三)选择疑问句

提出两种或两种以上的情况,要求对方选择一种情况给予回答,不能用 yes 或 no 来回答。选择疑问句可分为两种:一般选择疑问句和特殊选择疑问句。

用法	例句
一般选择疑问句的构成： 一般疑问句 + or + 被选择的内容	— Are you a ↗teacher or a bank ↘clerk？你是老师还是银行职员？ — I'm a bank clerk. 我是银行职员。 — Shall we go there, by ↗bus or by ↘subway？ 我们怎么去那里，乘公共汽车还是地铁？ — We shall go there by subway. 我们将乘地铁去那里。
特殊选择疑问句的构成： 特殊疑问句 + A or B？	Which do you like better, ↗the rock music or ↘the country music？ 摇滚和乡村音乐，你更喜欢哪个？ What's your hobby, ↗reading or ↘listening to music？ 你的爱好是什么，读书还是听音乐？

(四)反义疑问句

反义疑问句是附在陈述句之后，对陈述句所叙述的事实提出相反的疑问。

(1)反义疑问句的用法

反义疑问句提出情况和看法，问对方同不同意。前一部分用陈述句形式，后一部分附着一个简短的问句。如果前一部分为肯定形式，后一部分通常为否定形式；前一部分是否定形式，后一部分就用肯定形式，两部分的人称、数和时态要保持一致。当陈述部分的主语是名词或代词时，疑问部分要用相应的人称代词。如：

Miss Li teaches you English, **doesn't she**？李老师教你们英语，不是吗？
They often go to the cinema, **don't they**？他们经常去电影院，不是吗？
She speaks English very fluently, **doesn't she**？她说英语非常流利，不是吗？
Mr. Brown has been to China, **hasn't he**？布朗先生去过中国，不是吗？

(2)反义疑问句的回答

用法	例句
如果答语是肯定的，就用"Yes + 肯定结构" 如果答语是否定的，就用"No + 否定结构"	— She **is** a nurse, **isn't she**？ 她是一名护士，对吗？ — **Yes, she is**. 是的，她是护士。 — **No, she isn't**. 不，她不是护士。
陈述部分为否定句，后面反义疑问句为肯定的，回答时，yes译为"不"；no译为"是"	—Kate **didn't go** to the hospital yesterday, **did she**？凯特昨天没去医院，是吗？ —**No, she didn't**. Because she took medicine and felt better. 是的，她没去。因为她服药了，感觉好些了。

(3)反义疑问句的特殊形式
①陈述句反义疑问句的特殊形式

用法	例句
陈述句是"I am..."，反义疑问句用 aren't	**I am** your best friend, **aren't I**？我是你最好的朋友，对吗？
当陈述句中含有 never、seldom、hardly、few、little、nothing、nobody、none、neither 等否定或部分否定词时，反义疑问句用肯定形式	The dream will never die, **will it**？梦想永不止息，是吧？ Jim is a stranger here. He **has no** friends here, **does he**？ 吉姆是新来的，他在这没有朋友，对吗？

续表

用法	例句
如果陈述部分有否定前缀(im-, ir-, in-, un-, dis-等),该陈述部分作肯定处理,反意问句仍用否定形式	Grandpa **is unhappy** today, **isn't** he? 爷爷今天不高兴,是吗? Tom **dislikes** the blues, **doesn't** he? 汤姆不喜欢蓝调音乐,对不对?

②祈使句反义疑问句的特殊形式

祈使句后面的附加疑问句不表示反问,而是表示一种语气,其形式有:

用法	例句
否定祈使句 + will you	**Don't** yell out, **will you**? 别喊出来,好不好?
肯定祈使句 + will you/won't you?	**Switch off** the lights, **will you/won't you**? 把灯关了,好吗?
Let's +其他,shall we?	**Let's** recite the text together, **shall we**? 咱们一块背诵课文吧,好吗?
Let us +其他,will you?	**Let us** close the door, **will you**? 我们关门吧,好吗?

注意:

1)若陈述部分为肯定祈使句,反义疑问句通常 will you 和 won't you 两者都可以用。如:
Open the window, **will you**? 把窗打开,好吗?
Follow the tour guide, **won't you**? 跟着导游走,好吗?

2)若陈述部分为否定式,则反义疑问句部分只能用 will you。如:
Don't forget to turn off the light, **will you**? 请别忘关灯。
Don't make this kind of mistake again, **will you**? 请别再犯这样的错误了。

③含有情态动词 must 的反义疑问句

用法	例句
当 must 表推测时,反意问句的动词形式要根据 must 后面的动词形式和时态来确定	The girl **must be** very hungry, **isn't she**? 女孩一定很饿了,是吗? English **must have** the largest number of speakers, **doesn't it**? 说英语的人一定最多,对不对? He **must have finished the work** yesterday, **didn't he**? 他一定是昨天完成的工作,是吗?(强调动作发生在过去) You **must have been** to London, **haven't you**? 你一定去过伦敦,不是吗?(强调动作已完成)
当 must 表示"必须""必要"时,反意问句用 mustn't 或 needn't	You **must** hand in your homework at once, **mustn't you**? 你必须马上交作业,对不对? I **must** call you this evening, **needn't I**? 我必须今晚给你打电话,是吗?
当 mustn't 表示"禁止"时,反意问句用 must	You **must not** speak ill of others, **must you**? 你不能说别人坏话,不是吗? You **mustn't** smoke in public places, **must you**? 你不能在公众场所抽烟,不是吗?

④其他特殊形式的反义疑问句

用法	例句
当陈述部分含有情态动词 had better 时,反意问句用 had	You **had better** go to bed early, **hadn't you**? 你最好早点上床,行吗?
当陈述部分是 there be 结构时,反义疑问句的主语用 there	**There is** little water in the cup, **is there**? 杯子里几乎没有水了,是吗? **There are** many new inventions in modern life, **aren't there**? 现代生活中有许多新发明,不是吗?
当陈述部分含有 used to 时,反义疑问句用一般使用 didn't,也可以用 usedn't	Your parents **used to** go to work by bike, **didn't/usedn't they**? 你父母过去常常骑自行车去上班,是吗? **There used to** be a post office in this street, **didn't/usedn't there**? 这条街上过去有个邮局,不是吗?
当陈述部分的主语是指示代词 this 或 that 时,反义疑问句部分的主语用 it;陈述部分的主语是指示代词 these 或 those 时,反义疑问句的主语用 they	**This is** a newly-built block, **isn't it**? 这是一个新建街区,是吗? **These** are Chinese high-speed trains, **aren't they**? 这些是中国制造的高铁,对吗?
当陈述部分的主语是 someone、somebody、anyone、everyone、nobody、no one 等复合不定代词时,反义疑问句的主语用 they	**Everyone has** a dream, **don't they**? 人人都有梦想,不是吗? **Nobody** will succeed without confidence or perseverance, **will they**? 没有信心和坚持没人会成功,不是吗?
当陈述部分的主语是 something、anyone、everything、nothing 等复合不定代词时,反义疑问句的主语通常用 it	**Everything** is OK, **isn't it**? 一切进展顺利,是吧?
当陈述部分带有宾语从句时,反问部分的主语要随主句的主语而变化;但是当主句的谓语动词是"imagine、believe、suppose、think、expect 等",且主语为第一人称时,反意问句要与宾语从句的主语、谓语及其时态保持对应关系	**Mary** said I could borrow money from her, **didn't she**? 玛丽说她会借给我一些钱,是吧? **I suppose** he is honest, **isn't he**? 我认为他是诚实的,不是吗? **I don't think** he is right, **is he**? 我认为他不对,是吧?

Grammar Exercises
语法训练

I. **Complete the following imperative sentences. 完成下列祈使句。**(5%)
1. _____ a rest. (我们休息一下吧[包括我]。)
2. _____ leave. (让他走吧。)
3. _____ day. (记住这个有意义的日子。)
4. Please _____. (请带上这把伞。)
5. _____ the lawn. (不要践踏草坪。)

第十五章 祈使句和疑问句

II. Add tag questions to the following sentences. 完成下列反义疑问句。（10%）
1. This computer doesn't work well, _____?
2. Nothing can stop us from pursuing our dreams, _____?
3. She used to live in her hometown, _____?
4. Rose would like to go shopping with us, _____?
5. Professor Smith seldom has lunch at school, _____?
6. Your answer is incorrect, _____?
7. Such things ought not to be allowed, _____?
8. Robert has picked up a lot of English when he worked in London, _____?
9. I think that those are your daughter's colour pens, _____?
10. Everyone knows the answer, _____?

III. Error identification. 错误辨识。（20%）
1. (A) What age (B) you would like to (C) live to (D) if you could choose?
2. (A) How does (B) all work and no play (C) makes (D) Jack a dull boy?
3. (A) Where did (B) Jody got the money (C) to buy (D) the box of chocolate?
4. (A) Where (B) will you (C) explain your mistake today, (D) at 8:00 or 9:00 o'clock?
5. (A) Please help me (B) with the homework. (C) Let us (D) do it together.
6. (A) Not (B) play football (C) in the street. It is (D) very dangerous.
7. Don't (A) silent, (B) please. We (C) are waiting for (D) your answer.
8. (A) Let Xiao Wang (B) teaches (C) her (D) English.
9. Let's (A) read (B) English (C) aloud, (D) will you?
10. (A) What (B) he said (C) is true, (D) aren't they?

IV. Multiple choice. 单项选择。（30%）
1. The houses where they lived are being rebuilt, _____?
   A. wasn't they   B. didn't they   C. weren't they   D. aren't they
2. She likes chatting on Wechat, _____?
   A. is she   B. isn't she   C. does she   D. doesn't she
3. He wishes everything would be all right, _____?
   A. doesn't he   B. wouldn't it   C. wouldn't they   D. aren't they
4. I believe he knows the answer to the question, _____?
   A. does he   B. doesn't he   C. don't I   D. do I
5. They had a wonderful train trip that day, _____?
   A. don't they   B. had they   C. didn't they   D. did they
6. Mary must be in the dining-room, _____?
   A. isn't Mary   B. isn't she
   C. mustn't Mary   D. mustn't she
7. Nothing will make him give in, _____?
   A. will there   B. won't there   C. will it   D. won't it
8. I think you know the secret of this thing, _____?
   A. don't I   B. do I   C. don't you   D. do you

9. We knew little about the accident, _____?
   A. didn't we   B. hadn't we   C. did we   D. had we
10. Don't speak so much nonsense, _____?
    A. do you   B. will you   C. won't you   D. is it
11. Let us go to the museum, _____?
    A. will you   B. shall we   C. won't you   D. shan't we
12. —_____ did you choose to work in a kindergarten?
    —Well, you know, dancing is my _____. So it is my best choice.
    A. How often; talent   B. Why; strength
    C. What reason; ability   D. How soon; skill
13. There are lots of books in our university library, _____?
    A. aren't they   B. are they   C. are there   D. aren't there
14. Those are some fruits from Hainan, _____?
    A. aren't they   B. aren't those   C. are they   D. aren't those
15. —_____ do you learn Spanish?
    —I learn it by myself.
    A. With which   B. For which   C. How   D. What
16. _____ do you have for lunch, noodles or rice?
    A. How   B. When   C. Whose   D. What
17. _____ do you prefer, the blue one or the yellow one?
    A. What   B. Which   C. How   D. What color
18. —_____ will Prime Minister come back?
    —In three days.
    A. How soon   B. How long
    C. How often   D. How much time
19. —_____ is the weather like today?
    —It's cloudy.
    A. How   B. What   C. When   D. What time
20. —_____ do you call your parents?
    —Once two days.
    A. What time   B. How often   C. How long   D. How soon

Ⅴ. Cloze. 完形填空。(20%)

A few weeks after arriving in China I received an e-mail informing us foreigners how to look after ourselves in summer, including a warning not to eat cold food.

Why are cold foods __1__? According to traditional Chinese medical beliefs, cold food should be avoided in summer in case one __2__ a "summer disease", which sounds to me a bit __3__ a cocktail you might drink at a pool party.

The idea of food being linked to well-being is hardly __4__ to China. But in the West we think __5__ of the rules of what is and isn't good for you. It seems each week there is new studying praising the __6__ of tomatoes or claiming animal fats are bad for you. The next week another expert will swear you should __7__ away from tomatoes and eat more beef. The __8__ things to do is to pay attention to the ones you agree with and __9__ the ones you don't, eventually __10__ a strict diet of dark chocolate and red wine.

In China, however, there is a range of __11__ beliefs about food and how __12__ you eat impacts your health. There is __13__ a saying — a good __14__ should first be a good cook.

To an outsider, these rules can seem a little strange, and __15__ most of the reasons for eating certain foods are fairly __16__, others can seem puzzled if they are not the simple philosophies you are __17__ to. So I ignored the __18__ mail, continuing to eat cold food at __19__ throughout the summer. So far, so good. Anyway, a cold food is just the medicine to __20__ the summer heat.

1. A. warned   B. forbidden   C. bad   D. improper
2. A. catches   B. prevents   C. keeps   D. grasps
3. A. by   B. with   C. like   D. as
4. A. common   B. unusual   C. unique   D. unnecessary
5. A. few   B. high   C. much   D. little
6. A. virtues   B. qualities   C. taste   D. size
7. A. throw   B. send   C. give   D. stay
8. A. last   B. best   C. perfect   D. superior
9. A. neglect   B. consider   C. treasure   D. scan
10. A. going   B. finding   C. developing   D. solving
11. A. old   B. good   C. wrong   D. set
12. A. which   B. that   C. what   D. when
13. A. even   B. so   C. once   D. therefore
14. A. leader   B. doctor   C. teacher   D. worker
15. A. since   B. because   C. while   D. after
16. A. sound   B. possible   C. imaginative   D. unreasonable
17. A. used   B. told   C. taught   D. persuaded
18. A. absurd   B. well-meaning   C. time-wasting   D. troublesome
19. A. range   B. random   C. ease   D. will
20. A. refuse   B. beat   C. avoid   D. hide

VI. Translate the following sentences into English. 将下列句子译成英语。（15%）
1. 我们怎么去办公室？乘公交车还是步行？
2. 永远不要停止对阅读的热爱。因为书在我们的生活中不仅是好朋友还是明智的老师。
3. ——今天几号？
   ——今天6月2号。
4. ——今天星期几？
   ——今天星期三。
5. 健康太重要了！让我们动起来吧！

第十六章　主谓一致

一、主谓一致的概述

主谓一致(Agreement)是指在英语句子里,谓语受主语支配,其动词或系动词必须和主语在人称和数上保持一致的语法现象。如:

Reading aloud **helps** you a lot in your study. 大声朗读可以让你在学习中受益匪浅。

Although she **was** very tired, she still finished her task.
尽管她疲惫不堪,仍然完成了任务。

It **is** really a piece of good news that my friend survived the earthquake.
真是好消息,我的朋友在地震中幸免于难。

There **are** only several pieces of bread in the refrigerator. 冰箱里只有几片面包。

注意:一定要在句子中确定主语,动词或系动词在人称和单、复数形式上必须和主语保持一致。

二、主谓一致的种类

主谓一致指"人称"和"数"方面的一致关系。一般情况下,主语和谓语之间的一致关系应遵循以下三个原则:

	分类	定义	例句
主谓一致	语法一致 Grammatical Concord	谓语与主语要一致	He **goes** to school on foot every day. 他每天走路上学。
	意义一致 Notional Concord	谓语的单复数形式与主语意义上的单复数形式一致	Ten years **is** a long period of time in one's life. 十年是人的一生中很长一段时间。 (十年表示一个整体的概念)
	就近一致 Principle of Proximity	谓语动词的单复形式取决于最靠近它的主语	Not only the students but also their teacher **is** confident of success. 不但学生们而且他们的老师都有信心成功。

注意:"主谓一致"考查内容涉及名词单数或复数作主语、不可数名词作主语、不定代词作主语、并列结构作主语、特殊名词作主语时,考点在谓语动词或系动词的单复数上。

主谓一致

（一）语法一致

主语和谓语从语法形式上取得一致：主语是单数形式，谓语也采取单数形式；主语是复数形式，谓语也采取复数形式。在语法一致中需要注意以下分类。

序号	分类	例句
1	以单数名词或第三人称单数主格代词、主语从句、动词不定式短语或动名词短语作主语时，谓语动词一般用单数形式	Our homework **is** to write a composition. 我们的家庭作业是要写一篇作文。 When we have many choices, it **is** hard for us to make a decision. 当我们有许多选择的时候，就很难做决定。 To see **is** to believe. 眼见为实。 Reading books **is** a good hobby. 读书是一个好的爱好。
2	主语为单数名词或代词，尽管后面跟有介词 with、except、but、as well as 和 including 等短语，谓语动词仍用单数形式；若主语为复数，谓语用复数形式	The father with his children **likes** watching TV at home. 这位父亲和孩子们喜欢在家看电视。 His colleagues but the journalist **have** a New Year's plan. 除了这位记者，他的同事们也有新年计划。
3	由 "a lot of、lots of、plenty of、the rest of + 名词"构成的短语，以及由"分数或百分数 + 名词"构成的短语作主语，短语中的名词是不可数名词时，谓语动词为单数；短语中的名词为可数名词复数时，则谓语动词为复数	Five sixths of tourists **are** from China. 六分之五的游客来自中国。 A lot of cheese **is** imported from France. 大量的奶酪是从法国进口的。
4	either、neither、each、every 或 no + 单数名词，以及由 some、any、no、every 构成的复合不定代词，都作单数看待	Neither of us **agrees** with what you said. 我们俩都不同意你所说的。 Each teacher **has** his own teaching methods. 每位教师都有自己的教学方法。 Everything **is** ready. 一切就绪。
5	在定语从句中，关系代词 that、who、which 等在从句中作主语时，其谓语动词的数应与先行词的数一致	She is one of my roommates who **study** English. 她是我学习英语的室友之一。 She is the only one of my roommates who **studies** English. 她是我唯一一个学习英语的室友。
6	由连接词 and 或 both ... and 连接起来的合成主语后面，要用复数形式的谓语动词	Both the man and his wife **are** basketball players. 这位男士和他的妻子都是篮球运动员。
7	在倒装句中，谓语动词的数应与其后的主语一致	On the table **are** several baskets. 桌子上有几个篮子。 There **comes** my classmate. 我的同学走了过来。

注意：

①由 what 引导的主语从句，后面的谓语动词多数情况用单数形式，但若表语是复数或 what 从句是一个带有复数意义的并列结构时，主句的谓语动词用复数形式。比较：

What he gave me **was** one battery. 他给我的是一个电池。

What I borrowed from him **are** three dictionaries. 我从他那里借的是三本字典。

What he says and what he does **do** not agree. 他所说和他所做的不一致。

②如果 and 所连接的两个词是指同一个人或事物时,后面的谓语动词就应用单数形式。如果由 and 连接的并列单数主语前如果分别有 no、each 或 every 修饰时,其谓语动词要用单数形式。如:

The famous singer and dancer **is** going to visit our school next month.（同一个人）

这位著名的歌手兼舞者将于下月来我校。

比较:

The famous singer and the dancer **are** going to visit our school next month.（两个人）

那位著名的歌手和那位舞者将于下月来我校。

Every man and every woman in the room **was** shocked when hearing the news.

听到这个消息,房间中的每一位男士女士都惊愕不已。

③使用 none of 修饰主语的时候,主语是不可数名词,它的谓语动词就要用单数;若后面的主语是可数名词的复数,它的谓语动词用单数或复数都可以。如:

None of them **is/are** tired of listening to music. 他们中没有人厌倦听音乐。

④a number of 表示"一些",作定语修饰复数名词,谓语用复数;the number of 用于表示"……的数量",主语是一个整体"number",谓语用单数。

A number of policemen **work** over time on weekends. 许多警察周末加班。

The number of policemen **is** 12 in the local police station.

这个派出所的警察人数为 12 人。

⑤如果主语有 more than one 或 many a 修饰的时候,尽管从意义上看是复数内容,但它的谓语动词仍用单数形式。

More than one boy **likes** playing badminton. 不止一个男孩子喜欢打羽毛球。

Many a man **works** hard to meet life's challenges. 许多人努力工作以迎接生活的挑战。

(二)意义一致

有时主语形式上为单数,但意义上却是复数,那么谓语也用复数形式;而有时主语形式上为复数,但意义上却是单数,那么谓语也用单数形式。意义一致的情况如下表:

序号	分类	例句
1	"定冠词 + 形容词"即"the + 形容词"作主语时,指一类人则应该看作是复数,那么谓语动词也应该用复数	The old **are** always respected by the young. 年轻人总是尊敬老人。
2	集体名词若指的是整个集体,它的谓语动词用单数;集体名词若用于强调集体的成员,其谓语动词就用复数形式。如:family, class, committee, population, audience, cattle, people 和 police	Our class **is** made up of 65 students. 我们班由 65 个学生组成。（强调集体） Our class **are** from 32 minorities. 我们班学生来自于 32 个少数民族。（强调成员）

续表

序号	分类	例句
3	表示时间、金钱、距离、体积、重量、面积、数字等词语作主语时,其意义若是指总量应看作单数,谓语动词用单数	Twenty days **is** not enough for us to finish the work. 我们不能二十天完成这项工作。 Five dollars **is** too expensive for the snack. 这个小吃要五美元,太贵了。
4	主语是书名、片名、格言、剧名、报名、国名等的复数形式,其谓语动词通常用单数形式	The United States of America **consists of** 50 states. 美国由五十个州组成。
5	一些以-s 结尾的名词或以-ics 结尾的学科和疾病名词,都属于形式上是复数的名词,实际意义为单数名词,它们作主语时,其谓语动词要用单数形式。如:news、works、mathematics、politics 和 physics 等	No news **is** good news. 没有消息就是好消息。 Mathematics **is** only taught in the first term of the school year. 数学只在本学年第一学期上课。
6	trousers、glasses、clothes、shoes 等词作主语时,谓语用复数,但如果这些词前有 a/the pair of 等量词修饰时,谓语动词用单数	Your shoes **are** under the bed. 你的鞋在床下。 How much **does** the pair of trousers cost? 这条裤子多少钱?
6	what,who,which,any,more,all 等代词可以是单数,也可以是复数,主要靠意思来决定	Which **is** your notebook? 哪本是你的笔记本? Which **are** your notebooks? 哪些是你的笔记本?
7	当 and 连接两个并列主语在意义上指同一人、同一物、同一事或者同一概念时,应看作单数,谓语动词用单数	Bread and butter **is** what Americans have for breakfast. 黄油面包是美国人早餐的食物。

(三)就近一致

虽然有两个主语,但是谓语动词的形式与它紧邻的名词或代词保持一致,即谓语遵循就近原则,与最靠近它的主语保持一致。

序号	分类	例句
1	either…or…	Either her husband or her children **support** her. 不是丈夫就是孩子们支持她。 Either her children or her husband **supports** her. 不是孩子们就是丈夫支持她。
2	neither…or…	Neither they nor she **is** wrong. 他们和她都没有错。 Neither she nor they **are** wrong. 她和他们都没有错。
3	…or…	One or two friends **were** invited to his birthday party. 有一、两个朋友被邀请参加了他的生日宴会。
4	not only…but also…	Not only Jane but also her parents **are** going to move. 不但简而且她的父母都打算搬家。 Not only her parents but also Jane **is** going to move. 不但父母而且简都打算搬家。

续表

序号	分类	例句
5	there be 或 here be 句型	There **is** one computer and several keyboards on the desk. 桌子上有一台电脑和几个键盘。 There **are** several keyboards and one computer on the desk. 桌子上有几个键盘和一台电脑。 Here **is** a letter and some presents for you. 这里有你一封信和几份礼物。 Here **are** some presents and a letter for you. 这里有你几份礼物和一封信。

Grammar Exercises
语法训练

Ⅰ. Fill in the blanks with what you have learnt. 用所学知识填空。(5%)

主谓一致强调的是主语为单数形式,谓语动词用1._____;主语为复数形式,谓语动词也用2._____,即谓语动词或系动词必须和主语在人称和数上保持3._____的语法现象。一般情况下,主语和谓语之间的一致关系由以下三种原则的组成:语法一致,4._____和5._____。

Ⅱ. Fill in the blanks with the correct forms. 填写正确形式。(10%)

1. Three days _____ (be) not enough for her to finish the work and she needs five days.
2. Now either Tom or his brothers _____ (be) watching TV at home.
3. It is reported that cell phones of this kind _____ (be) sold well.
4. Many a student _____ (have) realized the importance of learning a foreign language.
5. Last night nothing but one desk and six chairs _____ (be) left in the room.
6. Neither Li Ping nor I _____ (be) a baseball player.
7. About 75 percent of the students _____ (be) from the south, while the rest of them are from the north.
8. The secretary and engineer _____ (be) making a speech at the meeting now.
9. Between the two roads _____ (stand) a TV tower called "Oriental Pearl Tower"(东方明珠塔).
10. Either of the twins _____ (be) going to the party tonight.

Ⅲ. Error identification. 错误辨识。(20%)

1. (A) Two thirds of the area (B) are covered with green trees and about (C) 60 percent of the trees (D) have been watered.
2. The number of (A) the students in school (B) have greatly increased since (C) last term and a number of the students (D) were from the countryside.
3. (A) What he wants to buy (B) is a digital camera, (C) while what his wife wants to buy

（D） is several pictures.
4. （A） Each time he comes here, he is always the only （B） one of the editors who （C） have come here （D） on time.
5. We each（A） has weak points, and （B） what's more （C） each of us also （D） has strong points.
6. Jogging （A） are （B） of great help （C） to health although you run （D） at a slow speed.
7. —（A） Is there anybody in the reading room?
   —No, the librarian （B） together with some students （C） have gone to （D） the playground.
8. （A） Either the leader or his assistant （B） have to （C） be responsible for （D） the incident.
9. We were （A） so tired that we could not （B） go any farther and ten miles （C） were a long way （D） to cover.
10. Sometimes （A） there is （B） only one answer, but here more than one answer （C） have been given （D） to the question.

IV. Multiple choice. 单项选择。（30%）

1. Besides the machines, the factory _____ destroyed in the flood and all the workers including my father _____ willing to rebuild it.
   A. was; was   B. were; were   C. was; were   D. were; was
2. It is during the holiday that half of the visitors _____ from Europe.
   A. is   B. are   C. was   D. were
3. In any country, every man and every woman _____ to have free medical care.
   A. intends   B. intend   C. enjoys   D. enjoy
4. What our parents have done _____ of great importance to us.
   A. are   B. is   C. will   D. maybe
5. At that time nobody but my younger sister and me _____ at home when my mother and father worked outside.
   A. is   B. are   C. were   D. was
6. The accountant and the engineer _____ to England several times since the company was founded.
   A. are   B. is   C. have been   D. has been
7. Not only I but also my brothers _____ tired of listening to the same story again and again.
   A. is   B. be   C. am   D. are
8. A garden with six hundred trees _____ by the local government now.
   A. is being built   B. have built   C. are built   D. has built
9. He is the only one of the workers who _____ a winner in the match for 5 years.
   A. have been   B. has been   C. is   D. are
10. The number of the guests invited to the party _____ twenty, but a number of them _____ absent for different reasons.
    A. was; were
    C. was; was
    B. were; was
    D. were; were

11. On top of the mountain _____ the stone you're looking for.
    A. are   B. is   C. has   D. have

12. This is one of the most interesting movies that _____ watched.
    A. have   B. has   C. have been   D. has been

13. After the air crash occurred, the wounded _____ sent to the nearest hospital.
    A. is   B. are   C. was   D. were

14. We each _____ advantages, but each of us on the other hand _____ disadvantages.
    A. has; has   B. have; have
    C. have; has   D. has; have

15. Physics _____ my favorite subject.
    A. is   B. am   C. are   D. be

16. Her family _____ all very nice and friendly and above all, her family _____ a happy one.
    A. is; are   B. is; is   C. are; are   D. are; is

17. In fact, he as well as his parents, _____ hurt in the car accident.
    A. were   B. are   C. was   D. had

18. Neither my friend nor I _____ able to sing this English song.
    A. has been   B. am   C. is   D. are

19. We all know that about 20 percent of the work _____ done last night.
    A. was   B. were   C. has   D. have

20. This pair of shoes _____ sold only in the store near my company.
    A. is   B. are   C. were   D. will

V. Fill in the blanks with the correct forms in the following passage. 在短文中填写正确形式。(20%)

Coffee and tea (1) _____ (be) the most popular drinks in the world. Coffee (2) _____ (be) a favorite drink of Canadians. Many Canadians like to start their day with a cup of coffee. At work, they may take a coffee break. Coffee break (3) _____ (be) a time to stop and relax for a few minutes over a cup of coffee or a snack.

Why is coffee so popular? For one thing, it (4) _____ (have) a rich, strong taste that many people like. It is served hot, with milk, cream or sugar. Many people (5) _____ (like) coffee in the morning because it (6) _____ (help) them wake up. Coffee has caffeine (咖啡因) in it and caffeine (7) _____ (give) people more energy.

Every day, millions of people all over the world drink tea. Tea is the national drink of China, Japan, England and Russia. In England, it is a custom to drink tea in the afternoon. In Japan, drinking tea (8) _____ (be) also a social custom and there (9) _____ (be) special rules for tea drinking. Tea (10) _____ (come) from tea leaves. We make tea by pouring boiled water on dried tea leaves. People usually drink hot tea, but it can be served cold. Some people like to drink tea with milk or cream. Other people hate milk or cream in tea, but they put in honey, sugar or lemon. Tea also has some caffeine in it.

Ⅵ. Translate the following sentences into English. 将下列句子译成英语。(15%)

1. 无论何时,阅读是一项必要的技能。
2. 英雄们所做的一切被历史和他们的国家铭记。
3. 当人们身处困境,除了他们自己没有人能真正帮助他们走出困境。
4. 不是他就是他的邻居们已经被数次邀请参加圣诞节的晚会了。
5. ——这个盒子里有什么?
　　——这个盒子里只有一些大米。

第十七章 名词性从句

一、名词性从句的概述

名词性从句(Nominal Clause)是指在复合句中起名词性作用的从句。在名词性从句中，句子要用陈述句的语序，即"引导词 + 主语 + 谓语动词 + 其他成分"。如果引导词作主语，则语序应为"引导词(主语) + 谓语动词 + 其他成分"。名词或名词词组在句子中主要充当主语、宾语、表语和同位语，所以名词性从句又可以分为主语从句、宾语从句、表语从句和同位语从句。

	分类	例句
名词性从句	主语从句	**That they would have ten days off** made them happy. 他们要休假十天，这让他们很高兴。
	宾语从句	We don't know **whether it is going to snow**. 我们不知道是否会下雪。
	表语从句	What we want to know is **what made him angry**. 我们想知道什么事让他生气。
	同位语从句	The news **that he won the game** is exciting. 他赢得比赛的消息令人激动。

注意：关于名词性从句，最常见的考点是名词性从句的语序和名词性从句的引导词。

二、主语从句

在复合句中充当主语的句子叫作主语从句。

(一)主语从句的引导词

主语从句的引导词可以分成四类：第一类是 that，that 在从句中只起连接作用，不充当成分，没有意义，不能省略；第二类是 whether，whether 在从句中只起连接作用，不充当成分，表示是否的含义；第三类是连接代词 what、whatever、who、whoever、whom、whomever、which、whichever 和 whose 等，连接代词在从句中可以充当主语、宾语或者定语；第四类是连接副词 when、where、why 和 how 等，连接副词在从句中充当状语。主语从句的引导词通常都不能省略。如：

名词性从句

引导词	用法	例句
that	只起连接作用,不充当成分没有意义,不能省略	<u>That they passed the exam</u> excited them all. 他们通过了考试,这让他们很激动。 <u>That we work hard every day</u> is very important. 我们每天努力工作很重要。
whether	只起连接作用,不充当成分,表示是否的含义	<u>Whether it is going to rain</u> is not clear. 是否会下雨,还不清楚。 <u>Whether the meeting should be put off</u> is not noticed. 会议是否应该被推迟,还没有通知。
what	在从句中作宾语或主语	<u>What he will do</u> is not the key. 他会做什么不是关键。 <u>What made him angry</u> was her lie. 让他生气的是她的谎言。
who	在从句中作主语	<u>Who will come to help us</u> is a mystery. 谁会来帮我们是一个秘密。
which	在从句中作主语、宾语或者定语	<u>Which is his favourite film</u> is an open secret. 哪部电影是他的最爱是个公开的秘密
how	在从句中作状语	<u>How they will carry out the plan</u> is being discussed now. 他们将怎么执行这个计划,现在正在被讨论。
why	在从句中作状语	<u>Why she laughed at the end of the movie</u> was not explained. 她为什么在电影结束时笑了,没有被解释。
when	在从句中作状语	<u>When we will have sports meeting</u> will be decided tomorrow. 我们什么时候开运动会将会在明天决定。
where	在从句中作状语	<u>Where they will meet this Saturday</u> is not known. 他们这个周六在哪碰面,并不清楚。

(二) it 作形式主语的主语从句

在包含有主语从句的复合句中,由于主语是一个句子,一般都比较长,所以常用 it 作形式主语,放在句首,而把主语从句后置。如:

<u>That they passed the exam</u> excited them all. = **It** excited them all <u>that they passed the exam.</u>

<u>Why she laughed at the end of the movie</u> was not explained.

= **It** was not explained <u>why she laughed at the end of the movie.</u>

(1) It is + 名词 + 从句

It is a fact that... "……是事实"

It is good news that ... "……是好消息"

It is a pity that ... "……是个遗憾"

It is common knowledge that ... "……是常识"

类似的名词还有:a wonder、a good thing 和 a surprise 等。如:

It is a question **how we can find him**. 我们怎么能找到他是个问题。

It is common knowledge **that the moon travels around the earth**.

月亮绕着地球转，这是常识。

It was a surprise **that they came to my birthday party**.

他们来参加我的生日聚会，是个惊喜。

(2) It is + 形容词 + 从句

It is strange that… "奇怪的是……"

It is interesting that… "有趣的是……"

It is certain that… "肯定的是……"

类似的形容词还有：likely、natural、necessary、essential、true、good、wonderful、possible、unlikely、unusual、clear 和 surprising 等。如：

It is strange **that she didn't ask us for help**. 奇怪的是她没有向我们求助。

It is unlikely **that she is reluctant to come**. 她不太可能不愿意来。

It was really surprising **that your team won the championship**.

你们队获得了冠军真是令人惊讶。

(3) It is + 过去分词 + 从句

It is said that … "据说……"

It is reported that … "据报道……"

It must be pointed out that… "必须指出……"

类似的过去分词还有：advised、known、expected、believed、thought、hoped、noted、discussed、required、decided 和 suggested 等。如：

It is suggested **that we should leave for Shanghai at once**.

大家建议我们立刻前往上海。

It is reported **that leaders from over two hundred countries attended the summit**.

据报道，超过两百个国家的领导人出席了这次峰会。

It is said **that he has written over twenty books**. 据说他写了二十多本书。

(三) 主语从句的数

在包含有主语从句的复合句中，谓语动词或系动词通常用单数形式。如：

Whether we will be late **is** not clear. 我们是否会迟到，还不清楚。

但是，what 引导主语从句时，系动词的单复数取决于其后面的表语。如：

What they want **is** a book. 他们要的是一本书。

What they want **are** some books. 他们要的是一些书。

两个或者两个以上的主语从句并列作主语时，如果表达的是同一个意思，谓语动词或系动词用单数；如果表达的是不同的意思，谓语动词或系动词用复数。如：

What they said and what they did **was** none of your business.

他们所说所做和你无关。

What they said and what they did **were** not the same. 他们说的和做的并不一样。

三、宾语从句

在复合句中充当宾语的句子叫作宾语从句。宾语从句既可以作动词的宾语,也可以作介词的宾语。

(一)宾语从句的引导词

常用的宾语从句的引导词有 that, whether, if, what, who, whom, which, whose, when, where, why 和 how 等。如:

引导词	用法	例句
that	只起连接作用,不充当成分没有意义,不能省略	They know **that they passed the exam**. 他们知道他们通过了考试。 We understand **that it is necessary for us to work hard every day**. 我们明白每天努力工作很重要。
whether/if	只起连接作用,不充当成分,表示是否的含义	Can you tell me **whether/if you like the film**? 你能告诉我你是否喜欢那部电影吗? We are not sure about **whether the meeting will be put off**. 我们不确定会议是否会被推迟。(介词后只能用 whether)
what	在从句中作主语或者宾语	They are curious about **what he has found in the bag**. 他们对他在那个包里找到了什么很好奇。 No one can tell **what the secret of his success is**. 没有人能说出他成功的秘诀。
who	在从句中作主语	Can you guess **who will come to help us**? 你能猜猜谁会来帮我们吗?
how	在从句中作状语	They are discussing **how they will carry out the plan** now. 他们现在正在讨论将怎么执行这个计划。
why	在从句中作状语	She didn't tell us **why she laughed at the end of the movie**. 她没有告诉我们她为什么在电影结束时笑了。
when	在从句中作状语	We will discuss **when we will have sports meeting tomorrow**. 我们将会在明天讨论什么时候开运动会。
where	在从句中作状语	She doesn't know **where they will meet this Saturday**. 她不知道他们这个周六在哪碰面。

(二)宾语从句引导词的特殊用法

①宾语从句可以作动词的宾语,也可以作介词的宾语,但是 that 引导的宾语从句不能作

介词的宾语。如：

Everyone paid attention to that the speaker did.（错误）

Everyone paid attention to **what the speaker did.**（正确）

大家都注意到了那个演讲者做了什么。

②if 在引导宾语从句时，不能放在介词后面，也不能和 or not 连用，而 whether 都可以。如：

I am worried about if they can come on time.（错误）

I am worried about **whether they can come on time.**（正确）

我担心他们是否能准时来。

Tell us if you like to swim or not.（错误）

Tell us **whether you like to swim or not.**（正确）告诉我们你是否喜欢游泳。

(三) 宾语从句时态呼应

在包含有宾语从句的复合句中，如果主句用了现在的时态，从句不受限制，可以用任何时态；如果主句用了过去的时态，那么宾语从句一定要用相应的过去的时态。如：

We hope that we will meet again soon. 我们希望能很快再见面。

They said that they would go abroad this year. 他们说他们今年会出国。

注意：如果从句表述的是客观事实、真理、公式等，则还用一般现在时。如：

The teacher taught us that light **travels** faster than sound. 老师教了我们，光比声音传播得快。

(四) it 作形式宾语的宾语从句

it 不仅可以作为形式主语，还可以作形式宾语，而真正的 that 宾语从句则放在句尾。如：

We all take **it** for granted that every child should go to school.

我们认为每个孩子都要上学是理所当然的。

The teacher made **it** clear that we would have a test next month.

老师说得很清楚，我们下个月将会有一场考试。

They think **it** necessary that children get enough sleep.

他们认为孩子们获得充足的睡眠是有必要的。

四、表语从句

在复合句中充当系动词后面的表语的句子叫作表语从句。所以，判断表语从句的关键在于系动词，英语中常用的系动词有 be、look、appear 和 seem 等。

引导表语从句的引导词有：that，whether，who，whom，what，which，when，where，how，why，because，as if/as though 等。如：

引导词	用法	例句
that	只起连接作用,不充当成分没有意义,不能省略	The good news is **that they passed the exam**. 好消息是他们通过了考试。 It seems **that we will work ten hours tomorrow**. 似乎我们明天要工作十个小时。
whether	只起连接作用,不充当成分,表示是否的含义	The question is **whether you want to see the film**? 问题是你是否想看那部电影。 What we don't know is **whether the meeting will be put off**. 我们不知道的是会议是否会被推迟。
what	在从句中作主语或者宾语	This is **what he has found in the bag**. 这就是他在包里找到的东西。 Her success is **what has made her father happy**. 她的成功是让她父亲高兴的事。
who	在从句中作主语	The key to the problem is **who will come to help us**. 这个问题的关键是谁会来帮我们。
how	在从句中作状语	What we want to know is **how they will carry out the plan**. 我们想知道的是他们将怎么执行这个计划。
why	在从句中作状语	This is exactly **why she laughed at the end of the movie**. 这就是她为什么在电影结束时笑了的原因。
when	在从句中作状语	The focus is **when we will have the sports meet**. 焦点是我们什么时候开运动会。
where	在从句中作状语	The Summer Palace is **where they will meet this Saturday**. 颐和园是他们这个周六碰面的地方。
as if/ as though	在从句中作状语	It seems **as though it is going to rain**. 看上去似乎要下雨了。 He looks **as if he is the boss of the company**. 他看上去似乎是公司老板。

注意:当主语是 reason 时,表语从句的引导词不能用 because。如:
The reason for his lateness was because he missed the first bus. (错误)
The reason for his lateness was **that he missed the first bus**. (正确)
他迟到的原因是他错过了第一趟公共汽车。

五、同位语从句

(一)同位语概述

在英语当中,当一个句子成分对另外一个句子成分(通常是名词或者代词)进行解释或者补充说明时,这个句子成分就是**同位语**。如果去掉句子中的同位语成分,基本不影响该句的整体意思。同位语通常由名词、代词或者从句来充当,并且常常和它所修饰的成分紧紧挨在一起使用。如:

Mr. Smith, **our English teacher**, often runs in the park.

史密斯先生——我们的英语老师——常常在公园跑步。
(our English teacher 是主语 Mr. Smith 的同位语,指同一人。)
Do you know the man, **the most famous singer** in China?
你认识那个男子——中国最有名的歌手吗?
(the most famous singer in China 是宾语 the man 的同位语,指同一人。)

(二)同位语从句概述

在复合句中充当同位语的句子叫作同位语从句。同位语从句的引导词主要是 that,但是 whether、who、whom、what、which、when、where 和 how 等引导词也可以引导同位语从句。如果去掉同位语从句,主句仍然是正确的句子,具有完整的句子成分。同位语从句所修饰的名词通常被称为先行词,先行词通常是抽象名词。常见的先行词有 fact、news、idea、plan、hope、report、opinion、truth、question、decision、command、order、promise、suggestion 和 advice 等。如:

The idea **that money means everything** is popular but wrong.
钱是万能的想法很流行,但是是错的。
He told everyone the news **that our team won the first prize**.
他告诉了所有人我们队获得第一名的消息。
The advice **that she should stay in bed** is right. 她应该卧床休息的建议是正确的。
The question **who will come to help** is not answered. 谁会来帮忙的问题并没有回答。
The question **whether this plan will work** remains to be answered.
这个计划是否有用的问题还有待解答。

(三)同位语从句和定语从句的区别

同位语从句和定语从句有着相同的结构,都是"先行词+引导词+从句",其中的引导词都可以是 that,这是它们之间的相同之处。它们之间的主要区别如下:

	同位语从句	定语从句
从句和先行词之间的关系	同位语从句对先行词进行解释或补充说明,和先行词是同位关系	定语从句对先行词进行修饰或限定,和先行词是修饰和被修饰的关系
that 的用法	that 只是引导词,在从中不充当成分,不能省略	that 是关系代词,在从句中必须充当成分,只有作宾语时可以省略

如:
The news **that we will have a meeting on Thursday** is true.
我们周四要开会这一消息是真的。
(同位语从句,用来说明先行词的内容,that 不能省略。)
The news **that he told me just now** is true. 他刚才告诉我的消息是真的。
(定语从句,对先行词起修饰限制作用,that 可以省略。)
You have to accept the order **that you should go to Shanghai at once**.
你必须接受你要立刻去上海的命令。(同位语从句,that 在从句中不充当任何成分。)

You have to accept the order **that your mother gave you**.

你必须接受你妈妈给你的命令。(定语从句,that 在从句中作 gave 的宾语,可以省略。)

(四)同位语从句的特殊句型

英语中,有一些特殊的句型也包含有同位语从句。如:

1)sb + have/has/had + no idea (that,when,where,how 等) + 从句

They had no idea **that they would miss the train**. 他们不知道他们会错过火车。

2)There is/was + little/no + doubt/possibility + that + 从句

There is little doubt **that he will get the first place in the competition**.

毫无疑问,他将会在比赛中获得第一名。

Grammar Exercises
语法训练

I. Fill in the blanks by choosing proper words from the brackets. 选词填空。(5%)

1. The reason for her success is _____ (why/that) she studied extremely hard.
2. I wonder _____ (that/how) Tom is getting along with his work.
3. I'm thinking _____ (that/what) I should say to him next.
4. There's no doubt _____ (that/whether) your baby will be taken good care of here.
5. His grandparents were among the first to settle in _____ (where/what) is now a famous place.

II. Decide what clause the underlined part is. 判断画线部分是哪种从句。(10%)

1. He asked how much I paid for the car. (   )
2. They want to know what they can do to help solve the problem. (   )
3. What you have done might harm others. (   )
4. I have no idea what our classroom will look like. (   )
5. Whoever leaves the house last should close the windows. (   )
6. That Jean failed the last English exam was quite unexpected. (   )
7. It is not likely that they will come back this year. (   )
8. What computers can give out is just what has been stored in them by man. (   )
9. We all heard the news that the Chinese women volleyball team had won the Olympic Gold Medal. (   )
10. What he has said is what made her so angry. (   )

III. Error identification. 错误辨识。(20%)

1. (A) It was (B) where he was born (C) and grew up (D) what surprised all of us.
2. (A) Because she (B) was not invited to the party (C) made her (D) very angry.
3. (A) That they (B) are planning to do (C) has never been done (D) before.
4. (A) I'm not sure (B) whether he (C) could have done (D) to my car.
5. The doctor (A) couldn't answer (B) the question (C) if the patient (D) could survive the

disease.

6. I firmly believe (A) that (B) what he (C) did in class (D) were not proper.
7. (A) What he was trying to (B) prove to the police (C) was (D) when he did last night.
8. My mother (A) left word (B) with my roommate (C) she would call again (D) in the afternoon.
9. At the meeting, we (A) talked about (B) if or not we (C) should employ (D) more workers.
10. (A) It seems (B) that (C) no one knows (D) how has happened in the park.

IV. Multiple choice. 单项选择。(30%)

1. The other day, my brother drove his car down the street at _____ I thought was a dangerous speed.
   A. as   B. which   C. what   D. that

2. It is pretty well understood _____ controls the flow of carbon dioxide in and out the atmosphere today.
   A. that   B. when   C. what   D. how

3. _____ made this school proud was _____ more than 80% of the students had been admitted to key universities.
   A. What; because   B. What; that   C. That; what   D. That; because

4. Perseverance is a kind of quality — and that's _____ it takes to do anything well.
   A. what   B. that   C. which   D. why

5. _____ more and more students showed interest in her lectures was _____ made her happy.
   A. What; why B. That; what   C. What; because   D. Why; that

6. A man's worth lies not so much in _____ he has as in _____ he is.
   A. that; what B. what; what   C. that; that   D. what; that

7. Our hometown is no longer _____ it used to be.
   A. which   B. that   C. as   D. what

8. _____ we can't get always seems to be better than the things _____ we have.
   A. What; what B. What; that   C. That; that   D. That; what

9. I will do _____ you want me _____.
   A. whether; to do
   B. what; doing
   C. that; done
   D. whatever; to do

10. — _____ you must do?
    — No, as a matter of fact, I don't need to.
    A. Is that what   B. Is what that   C. What is that   D. Is that which

11. We took it for granted _____.
    A. that they were not coming
    B. that were they not coming
    C. they were coming not
    D. were they not coming

12. They want us to know _____ to help us.
    A. what can they
    B. what they can

C. how they can   D. how can they

13. We must put _____ into practice.
    A. what we have learned   B. that we have learned
    C. that have we learned   D. what have we learned

14. _____ they will come here hasn't been decided yet.
    A. What   B. That   C. When   D. Where

15. It is not common _____ she has left without saying a word.
    A. that   B. what   C. why   D. how

16. It is very clear _____ our policy is a correct one.
    A. what   B. that   C. why   D. where

17. _____ is troubling me is _____ I don't understand _____ he said
    A. What; that; what   B. What; what; what
    C. That; that; what   D. Why; that; which

18. Energy is _____ makes things work.
    A. what   B. something   C. anything   D. that

19. Information has been provided _____ more high school graduates are short-sighted (近视的).
    A. while   B. that   C. when   D. as

20. This is _____ the Shenzhou Ⅷ Spaceship landed.
    A. there   B. in which   C. where   D. when

V. Fill in the blanks with proper conjunctions. 用适当的引导词填空。(20%)

I read a newspaper last night. In the newspaper there was a piece of news (1)_____ aroused my attention. It said (2)_____ ten cars crashed at a busy cross and (3)_____ seven people died and dozens of people were seriously injured in the accident. But I forget (4)_____ or not the accident happened at 7 p.m. (5)_____ astonished me most is (6)_____ two babies lost their lives. It is still now clear (7)_____ caused the accident. However, I don't know (8)_____ or not the government has taken some measures to deal with it. In my opinion, (9)_____ the accident has taught us is the lesson (10)_____ we should obey the traffic rules.

Ⅵ. Translate the following sentences into English. 将下列句子译成英语。(15%)

1. 我们都同意我们一起去旅游的计划。
2. 他们认为无论在哪儿开晚会都可以。
3. 汤姆说的和他做的不同。
4. 据说我们公司将会举办一次大聚会。
5. 她一直在担心她是否会失业。

第十八章　定语从句

一、定语从句概述

在句中修饰名词或代词的成分叫作定语。定语可以是单个词、短语,也可以是句子。用作定语的句子,叫作定语从句(Attributive Clause)。如:

定语	例句
单词作定语	He is a **young** man. 他是个青年人。
短语作定语	That is a paper **on translation**. 那是一篇翻译方面的论文。
从句作定语	This computer is the one **which my mother gave to me last year**. 这台电脑是我妈妈去年给我的。
注意:从以上例句中可以看出,单个词作定语时,常放在被修饰词的前面;短语或从句作定语时,则一定放在被修饰词的后面,但是译成汉语时通常还是放在被修饰词的前面。	

二、定语从句结构

定语从句所修饰的词叫**先行词**;引导定语从句的词叫**关系词**(也叫**引导词**)。关系词一般紧跟在先行词之后,引导定语从句。定语从句的结构通常为:

定语从句结构	例句
先行词 +(关系词 + 定语从句主体部分)	Thanks for your **cooperation**(**that you gave me**). 谢谢你配合我。 **The man**(**who lives upstairs**)is a taxi driver. 住在楼上的那位先生是一位出租车司机。

注意:关系词分为两种,关系代词和关系副词。常用的关系代词有 that、which、who、whom 和 whose;常用的关系副词有 where、when 和 why。

三、定语从句常见关系词

	关系词	用法	作用	例句
关系代词	who	先行词是人	作主语	The student **who got the first price at the sports meeting** was Tom. 在运动会上拿第一的学生是汤姆。
	whom	先行词是人	作宾语	The professor **with whom you talk** is his sister. 和你说话的那个教授是他的姐姐。
	which	先行词是物	作主语或宾语	Please give me the bag **which you found yesterday**. 请给我你昨天找到的那个包。 The necklace **which is gold** is a present. 这条金项链是一个礼物。
	that	先行词是人或物	作主语或宾语	That is the most exciting news **that I have ever heard**. 这是我听过的最振奋人心的新闻。 This is the best car **that he has ever seen**. 这是他见过最好的车。
	whose	先行词是人或物,但后边要接名词,表示所有关系	作定语	Lisa **whose eyes are blue** is from Europe. 丽萨是蓝眼睛的欧洲人。 There is a girl **whose hair you like**. 这有个梳着你喜欢的发型的女孩儿。
关系副词	when	先行词表示时间	作状语	I began to learn English in the year **when I was 6 years old**. 我从六岁开始学习英语。
	where	先行词表示地点	作状语	I often come to my hometown **where my aunt lives**. 我经常去姑妈居住的故乡。
	why	先行词表示原因	作状语	Do you know the reason **why she looks so young**? 你知道她看起来年轻的原因吗?

从上表可以看出,关系词在句中不仅起到连接作用,而且还必须在从句中充当一个成分。如:

例句	释义
This is the book **which I borrowed yesterday**. 这是昨天我借的书。	引导定语从句的关系代词 which,除连接主句和从句外,它还(替代先行词 the book)作从句中谓语动词 borrowed 的宾语
This is the reason **why I didn't come here**. 这就是我为什么没来这里的原因。	引导定语从句的关系副词 why,除连接主句和从句外,还作从句的原因状语

(一)关系代词 who

关系代词 who	例句
一般说来,如果先行词所指的人不那么具体,不那么确定,关系代词用 who 或 that 都可以	People usually don't like women **who/that gossip a lot**. 人们通常不喜欢爱讲闲话的女人。
如果所指的人较为具体或确定,关系代词用 who 的时候较多	This is the athlete **who won the gold medal**. 这就是赢得金牌的运动员。
指人的不定代词 all、anybody、many、most、somebody、some 和 those 之后,关系代词多用 who	Anybody **who wants to participate in my party** is welcome. 谁想来参加我的派对都欢迎。

(二)关系代词 which

如果先行词所指的是物,关系代词用 that 或 which 都可以。如:
Tom was not on the train **that/which arrived just now**.
汤姆不在刚到达的那列火车上。

(三)关系代词 that

关系代词 that	例句
先行词是不定代词 all、anything、everything、nothing 和 something 等,或受限定词 all、any、every、no、only 和 some 等修饰的时候	Is there anything **that I can help you**? 有什么我可以帮你吗?
先行词受最高级形容词修饰的时候	The museum is the most famous building **that has ever been established**. 这个博物馆是最著名的建筑物。
先行词受序数词修饰的时候	The first thing **that I should know** is your name. 我首先应该了解的是你的名字。
关系从句为"系动词 be + 补语"结构的时候	It is a song **that will be very popular**. 这是一首将广受欢迎的歌曲。
当先行词既有人又有物的时候	They talked of persons and things **that they had met in the journey to Britain**. 他们谈论着去英国的旅行中遇到的那些人和事。

(四)关系副词 when

在表示时间的一些特定名词如 time、day、morning、month 和 year 等之后,可接一个由

when 引导的限制性定语从句。when 的意思相当于 at which、in which 和 on which 等,可以互相替代。如：

Monday is the day **when (= on which) students usually go to school**.
星期一是学生通常上学的日子。

(五) 关系副词 where

关系副词 where	例句
在表示地点的一些特定名词如 place、room 和 street 等之后,可接一个由 where 引导的限制性定语从句。它的意思相当于 at which、on which 和 to which 等,可以相互替代	I know a park **where (= to which) few people ever go**. 我知道一个公园,那里很少有人去。
where 还可用在有地点含义的抽象名词如 situation、state、point 和 stage 等词之后,表达 in which 和 at which 等意思	I've reached the point **where (= at which) I'm about ready to retire**. 我已到了即将退休的时候。

(六) 关系副词 why

在名词 reason 后,可用 why 来表达 for which 的意思。如：

Is there any particular reason **why you are late**? 你迟到有什么特殊原因吗？

四、定语从句的种类

定语从句分为限制性定语从句(Restrictive Attributive Clause)和非限制性定语从句(Non-restrictive Attributive Clause)。以下为限制性定语从句和非限制性定语从句的区别。

(一) 限制性定语从句

这种从句用于修饰和限定先行词,它与先行词关系密切,不能去掉。如果去掉,意思就不清楚。书写时,主句和从句不用逗号分开。译成汉语时,通常从句的末尾有"的"字,并把从句放在所修饰的名词前面。如：

This is the picture **that I took yesterday**. 这是我昨天拍的照片。
I always remember the day **when I met my teacher**.
我永远都记得和老师见面的那一天。
I like the girl **who works hard**. 我喜欢努力工作的女孩。
That is the reason **why he wants to go home**. 那就是他想回家的原因。

(二) 非限制性定语从句

非限制性定语从句与所修饰的先行词关系松弛,只提供有关该先行词的补充情况或附加说明。非限制性定语从句不能省略关系代词,也不能由 that 引导。即使去掉从句,主句的意思仍然清楚。非限制性定语从句主要用于书面语,书写时往往用逗号与主句分开。译成汉语时是否移到它修饰的名词前面,要看具体情况。如:

The mobile phone, **which he bought yesterday**, is very popular.

这款手机很流行,是他昨天买的。

The young man, **who is in the office**, wants to have a job.

那个青年想有一份工作,他在办公室里。

Tom is the manager of that company, **which is a famous foreign company**.

汤姆是那家公司的经理,那家公司是有名的外企。

(1)非限制性定语从中的 which

非限制性定语从中的 which	例句
指物时,关系代词一概用 which	He gave me a piece of cake, **which was made by himself**. 他给了我一块蛋糕,那是他亲自做的。
非限制性定语从句还能以整个主句作为先行词,用关系代词 which 引导。这时候的 which 并不是修饰某一个确定的名词,而是概括整个主句的意思	There are twelve months in a year, **which is very important**. 一年有十二个月,这很重要。 (which 指的是"一年有十二个月"这件事,这时从句中的谓语动词要用第三人称单数。)
在与介词连用时,介词总是位于关系代词之前。如果介词为短语动词不可分割的一部分,则不能提前	The President visited the new university, **in which he delivered a speech**. 总统参观了那所新大学,在那里他发表了演讲。

(2)非限制性定语从中的 who 和 whom

指人时,先行词若在非限制性定语从句中作主语,用 who;先行词若在从句中作宾语,用 whom。如:

Your brother, **who is busy now**, will pick you up as soon as possible.

你哥哥现在在忙,他会尽快来接你。

Sarah, **whom you met this morning**, is an outstanding entrepreneur.

莎拉博士你早上见过,她是个杰出的企业家。

(3)非限制性定语从中的 whose、when 和 where

whose 以及 when、where 也可用于非限制性定语从句。如:

Wilson is playing basketball with a boy, **whose hair is red**.

威尔逊正在和一个男孩打篮球,那个男孩的头发是红色的。

China held the Olympic Games in 2008, **when I was in Africa**.

中国在2008年举办了奥运会,那年我在非洲。

One of my friends came from Shanghai, **where I had worked for three years**.

我有个朋友来自上海,我曾在那里工作过三年。

(三)限制性定语从句与非限制性定语从句的区别

限制性定语从句	非限制性定语从句
和先行词的关系密切(去掉后影响整个意义的表达)	和先行词的关系不密切(去掉后不影响整个意义的表达)
不用逗号分开	一般使用逗号分开
可以用关系代词 that	不可以用关系代词 that
关系代词有时候可省略(that, who, which 在从句中担任宾语时可以省略)	关系代词不可省略
关系代词可以替代(whom 作宾语时,可用 who 或 that 替代)	关系代词不可以替代
读时不停顿	读时要停顿
不可以修饰整个主句	可以修饰整个主句

限制性定语从句和非限制性定语从句从结构上有以下对比:

There are many people **who come from foreign countries**.
这里有很多来自国外的人。(限制性定语从句)
There are many people, **who come from foreign countries**.
这里有很多人,这些人都来自国外。(非限制性定语从句)

This is our new house **which we moved in last month**.
这是我们上个月新搬入的房子。(限制性定语从句)
The new house, **which we moved in last month**, is very nice.
这幢房子很漂亮,我们上个月刚搬进去的。(非限制性定语从句)

五、"介词 + 关系代词"引导的定语从句

That is the house **where my classmates live**. 那是我同学们住的房子。
在这个例句中可以用 in which 来替代关系副词 where,也可以将这个句子改写成:
That is the house **in which my classmates live**.
改写后的句子中关系代词"which"代表"house",和介词 in 构成短语,像 where 一样,作状语,说明 live 的地点。这种由 in which 一类介词短语引导的从句就是"介词 + 关系代词"引导的定语从句。

在限制性定语从句中,"介词 + 关系代词"的结构中的介词可以放在从句之尾,关系代词有时可以省略,但介词一定不能省略。请看下列表格中的例句:

介词 + 关系代词	关系代词可省略,介词后置
The city **in which he lives** is Tokyo. 他所居住的城市是东京。	The city (**which**) he lives in is Tokyo.

续表

介词+关系代词	关系代词可省略,介词后置
The professor **about whom we often talk** will come to our school this afternoon. 我们常谈论的那位教授今天下午要来我们学校。	The professor (**whom**) **we often talk about** will come to our school this afternoon.
The young man **with whom you just shook hands** is Jay Chou. 你刚才握手的那位年轻人是周杰伦。	The young man (**whom**) **you just shook hands with** is Jay Chou.
There wasn't a single person **with whom she could communicate**. 连一个能和她交谈的人都没有。	There wasn't a single person (**whom**) **she could communicate with**.

注意:定语从句中的关系副词 when、where 和 why 可用"介词+which"代替,如:

when = in (on, at) + which

where = in (at, to) + which

why = for + which

此外,在非限制性的定语从句中,关系代词前的介词不能后置,介词和关系代词都不能省略。如:

October 1st is the National Day of China, **on which** we have a day off.

十月一日是中国的国庆节,在那天我们放假。(on 不可后置,on which 不可以省)

Grammar Exercises
语法训练

Ⅰ. Use attributive clauses to connect the following sentences. 用定语从句连接句子。(5%)

1. I'm writing a letter to Mike. Mike's mother is ill.

_____

2. This happened in 1947. I was a baby in 1947.

_____

3. This is the reason. I didn't come here for that reason.

_____

4. The city is Chengdu. He lives in Chengdu.

_____

5. The house is very nice. We bought the house last month.

_____

Ⅱ. Replace the words in italics by when, where or why. 用 when, where 或 why 代替句中斜体部分单词。(10%)

1. The days *in which* _____ you could travel without a passport are a thing of the past.

2. In time we reached a stage *at which* _____ we had more black readers than white ones.

3. I want to know the reason *for which* _____ you were late this morning and the time *at which* you came.
4. This was the sort of morning *on which* _____ everything goes wrong.
5. The place *at which* _____ they dump（倾倒）the rubbish has become very dirty and smelly.
6. He remembered several occasions *on which* _____ he had experienced a similar feeling.
7. I've always longed for the time *in which* _____ I should be able to be independent.
8. You cannot go to the house *in which* _____ no one lived.
9. This is the hour *at which* _____ the place is always full of women and children.
10. I can't think of any reason *for which* _____ you should take all the blame for what happened.

Ⅲ. **Error identification.** 错误辨识。（20%）
1. Mr. Brown (A) is talking (B) to the students (C) who (D) comes from Canada.
2. The factory (A) which we (B) are going to work (C) is (D) far from here.
3. This (A) is the room (B) in that we (C) lived (D) last year.
4. They (A) talked of things and people (B) who they (C) remembered (D) in the hospital.
5. All (A) which (B) Iraqi people (C) want (D) is peace.
6. Anyone (A) that (B) breaks the rule (C) will (D) be punished.
7. This (A) is (B) the child (C) who father (D) died of SARS.
8. I (A) have lost my (B) pen, (C) that I like (D) very much.
9. I (A) went to the library (B) but I didn't find the book (C) that I (D) needed it.
10. (A) This is the (B) person (C) who you are (D) looking for.

Ⅳ. **Multiple choice.** 单项选择。（30%）
1. The silk _____ is made in Hangzhou sells well.
   A. that   B. who   C. what   D. /
2. The man _____ today left this message for you.
   A. called   B. has called   C. whom called   D. who called
3. Do you live near the building _____ colour is yellow?
   A. that   B. which   C. whose   D. its
4. He helped his father on the farm _____ they lived.
   A. which   B. that   C. when   D. where
5. I'm one of the boys _____ never late for school.
   A. that is   B. who is   C. who are   D. who am
6. All _____ should be done has been done.
   A. what   B. which   C. that   D. whatever
7. Jack told me everything _____ he knew about it.
   A. what   B. that   C. which   D. who
8. My father works in the factory _____ this type of truck is made.
   A. in where   B. in which   C. from which   D. of which

9. The school _____ we visited last week was built in 1956.
    A. /   B. where   C. that   D. both A and C
10. This is one of the best films _____ I have ever seen.
    A. which   B. that   C. of which   D. of that
11. In fact the Swede did not understand the three questions _____ were asked in French.
    A. where   B. who   C. in which   D. which
12. He paid the boy $10 for cleaning ten windows, most of _____ hadn't been cleaned for at least a year.
    A. these   B. those   C. that   D. which
13. His parents wouldn't let him marry anyone _____ family was poor.
    A. of whom   B. whom   C. of whose   D. whose
14. God helps those _____ help themselves.
    A. whom   B. whose   C. who   D. which
15. My parents talked of persons and things _____ they had met in the US.
    A. that   B. who   C. which   D. whom
16. She heard a terrible noise, _____ brought her heart into her mouth.
    A. it   B. which   C. this   D. that
17. Nearly all the streets are in straight lines, _____ from east to west. Those _____ run from north to south are called avenues.
    A. running; that B. run; who   C. running; who   D. run; that
18. This is the city _____ he's had all his money stolen.
    A. when   B. where   C. that   D. on which
19. Mr. Smith paid a visit to Beijing in 2008, _____ we enjoyed the 2008 Olympic Games.
    A. where   B. why   C. which   D. that
20. October 15th is my birthday, _____ I will never forget.
    A. when   B. that   C. what   D. which

V. Fill in the blanks with the correct relatives. 填写正确的关系词。(20%)

1. I'm retiring at the end of the year, and the dentist _____ will be taking my place is Mr. Steven Brown.
2. The three men _____ the police wish to interview are all aged 22~25.
3. Yet colleges and graduate schools continue every year to turn out highly trained people to compete for jobs _____ aren't there.
4. At the end of the month the Post Office will send him an enormous bill _____ he won't be able to pay.
5. According to the article _____ I read, the police have arrested the man _____ robbed the First National Bank.
6. The only thing _____ I can suggest is that you consult your lawyer about it.
7. I let him have it without asking for a receipt, _____ is a big mistake.
8. Many of the labor saving devices _____ we all take for granted today did not exist before

· 144 ·

the war.

9. The relief agencies have promised to do all _____ lies in their power to bring food to the starving（饥饿的）population.
10. Those _____ would like to go on the trip should put their names on the list.

VI. Translate the following sentences into English. 将下列句子译成英语。（15%）
1. Here is the knife _____（你昨天丢失的）。
2. This is the best novel _____（我曾读过的）。
3. I have lost the dictionary _____（我姐姐给我买的）。
4. Rice is a plant _____（中国南方种植的）。
5. The woman _____（上周六给他们做报告的）is Tom's mother.

第十九章 状语从句

一、状语从句的概述

在主从复合句中起副词状语作用的从句叫作副词性从句,又叫作状语从句(Adverbial Clause)。状语从句一般分为如下几类。

序号	状语从句类别	例句
1	让步状语从句	**Although she got up late**, she was never late for school. 虽然她起床晚,但是她上学从不迟到。
2	原因状语从句	I don't trust him, **because he has cheated me**. 我不相信他,因为他曾经骗过我。
3	方式状语从句	I take life **as it comes**. 我随遇而安。
4	目的状语从句	**In order that the company gets over the trouble**, we need to be united. 为了公司度过困难,我们需要团结。
5	结果状语从句	John changed his job **so that he could get more free time**. 约翰换了份工作,这样他能够有多一点的空闲时间。
6	地点状语从句	**Where there is life**, there is hope. 只要活着,就有希望。
7	时间状语从句	**When you need help**, just call me. 你需要帮助的时候,就给我打电话。
8	条件状语从句	Shall we fly a kite **if it is windy tomorrow**? 如果明天有风的话,我们可以去放风筝吗?

二、状语从句的种类

(一)让步状语从句

序号	引导词	例句
1	although/though	**Although /Though he is poor**, he is happy. 虽然他很穷,但是他很快乐。
2	as	**Young as he is**, he has won several prizes. 尽管还年轻,他已经获奖多次。
3	while	**While we don't agree with each other**, we respect each other. 虽然我们不同意对方,但我们都尊敬对方。

续表

序号	引导词	例句
4	even if/ even though	**Even if /Even though Tom can't speak English**, I think he will still visit London. 尽管汤姆不会说英语,我认为他仍然会去伦敦的。
5	whatever	**Whatever you do**, I won't forgive you. = **No matter what you do**, I won't forgive you. 无论你做什么,我都不会原谅你。
6	however	**However hard the question is**, he can answer it. = **No matter how hard the question is**, he can answer it. 无论这道题有多难,他都能回答上来。
7	wherever	**Wherever you go**, I will be right here waiting for you. = **No matter where you go**, I will be right here waiting for you. 无论你去哪里,我都会一直在这里等你。
8	whoever	**Whoever you are**, you should obey the rules. = **No matter who you are**, you should obey the rules. 无论你是谁,你都应该遵守规则。

注意:

1) despite 和 in spite of 是介词(短语),后接名词或者动名词,引导让步状语。从语法上来说,它们引导的成分并不是状语从句,但表达的意思和 although 等连词引导的状语从句类似,故在此一并列出,如:

<u>Despite /In spite of</u> the bad weather, we enjoyed our holiday.
= <u>Although</u> it was bad weather, we enjoyed our holiday.
尽管天气恶劣,我们度假仍然很愉快。

2) as 和 though 引导的让步状语从句,有相似的句型结构,如:

as/though 引导让步状语句型	例句
名词 + as/though + 主语 + 动词 (位于句首的名词前不用冠词)	**Girl as/though she is**, she likes to play with boys. 她虽是女孩,却喜欢与男孩玩。
形容词 + as/though + 主语 + 动词	**Old as/though he was**, he still worked six hours a day. 尽管年事已高,他仍一天工作六个小时。
副词 + as/though + 主语 + 动词	**Hard as/though he studied**, he did not pass the test. 尽管他努力学习,但是还是没有通过考试。
动词原形 + as/though + 主语 + 动词	**Try as/though he might**, he couldn't solve the problem. 尽管他想方设法,却未解决这个问题。

(二)原因状语从句

引导词	例句
because	**Because he got up late**, he didn't catch the bus. 因为他起晚了,他没有赶上公共汽车。
for	We don't talk regularly **for we don't like each other**. 我们平常不怎么说话,因为我们不喜欢对方。
since	**Since you are interested**, I'll tell you the story. 既然你感兴趣,我就把故事讲给你听听。
as	**As she's been ill**, perhaps she'll need some help. 她生病了,可能需要些帮助。
now that	**Now that you have finished the homework**, you can watch TV for a while. 既然你已经完成作业了,你可以看会儿电视。
in that	Human beings are superior to animals **in that they can make and use tools**. 人类比动物高级,因为他们可以制造和使用工具。(in that 不能放句首,只能放句尾。)

注意:

1)引导原因状语从句的 because,since,as 和 for 在用法和语气上有所不同,解释如下:

引导词	释义	例句
because	表示直接原因,其语气最强,常用来回答 why 的提问,一般放于主句之后	We can trust those products **because the quality never changes**. 我们可以信赖那些产品,因为其质量从来不变。
since	侧重主句,从句表示显然的或已为人所知的理由,常译为"因为"或"既然",语气比 because 稍弱,通常置于句首,表示一种含有勉强语气的原因	**Since everyone is here**, let's start. 既然大家都到了,我们出发吧!
as	表示的"原因"是双方已知的事实或显而易见的原因,或者理由不是很重要,常译为"由于,鉴于"	**As she had a cold**, she was absent from work. 由于她感冒了,所以没去上班。
for	表现的因果关系不像 because 那样强烈,它引导的原因状语从句并不说明主句行为发生的直接原因,只提供一些辅助性的补充说明	He could not have seen me at home, **for I was out**. 他不可能在家看到我,因为我不在家。

2)引导原因状语的还有 because of、thanks to、due to 和 owing to 等,它们都是介词短语,后接名词或者动名词。从语法上来说,它们引导的成分并不是状语从句,但表达的意思和 because 等连词引导的状语从句类似,故在此一并列出。

because of	**Because of his laziness**, he failed in the exam. = Because he was lazy, he failed in the exam. 因为懒惰,他考试没及格。
thanks to	**Thanks to getting his support**, we finished the task successfully. = As he gave us support, we finished the task successfully. 由于他的支持,我们成功完成了任务。
due to/ owing to	The restaurant made great success **due to /owing to its new manager**. 这家饭店大获成功是因为它的新经理。

(三)方式状语从句

引导词	例句
as	They did it **as they had promised**. 他们兑现了承诺。(他们按照承诺那样去做了。) You should have done it **as I showed you**. 你应该按我教你那样去做
as if/ as though	The house looks **as if/as though it is going to fall down**. 这个房子看起来好像即将要倒塌。 I remember the whole thing **as if /as though it had happened yesterday**. 我记得整件事情,就好像它发生在昨天一样。

注意:在比较正式的语体中,like 作"好像"意思讲的时候,一般用作介词,后接名词或者动名词。但在比较随意的语体中,like 也可以用作连词,像 as 一样,后接从句,如:
They did it **like/as they had promised**. 他们兑现了承诺。(他们按照承诺那样去做了。)
She is a teacher **like me**. 像我一样,她也是老师。
Walking on the floor is just **like walking on the ice**.
在这地板上走就好像在冰上走一样。

(四)目的状语从句

引导词	例句
in order that	I am saving **in order that I can buy a car**. 为了买辆汽车,我正在攒钱。
so that	They used a microphone **so that everyone could hear**. 为了使人人都听到,他们使用了扩音器。

注意:可以连接目的状语的还有 for、in order to 和 so as to,它们所引导的成分并不是状语从句,后面不能接句子。但是 for 是介词,后接名词、动名词。in order to 和 so as to 可以简写为 to,即动词不定式,后接动词原形,如:

目的状语	例句
for	I am saving **for a car**. 为了(买辆)汽车,我正在攒钱。
(in order) to	I am saving **(in order) to buy a car**. 为了买辆汽车,我正在攒钱。
(so as) to	We picked apples **(so as) to make a pie**. 我们摘苹果,以便做苹果馅饼。

(五)结果状语从句

引导词	例句
so that	He studies medicine **so that he may become a doctor**. 他学习医药,以便成为医生。
so… that…	The stone is **so heavy that I can't move it**. 这块石头太沉了,我搬不动。
such… that…	It is **such a heavy stone that I can't move it**. 这真是一块沉重的石头,我搬不动。

注意:

1) so that、so… that… 和 such… that… 意思是"如此……以至于……",都是连词短语,后接结果状语从句。so… that… 句型中 so 后面接形容词或者副词,而 such… that… 句型中,such 后面接名词或者名词短语,如:

He runs **so fast that others can't catch up with him**. 他跑得如此之快,没人追得上他。

He is **such a fast runner that others can't catch up with him**.
他是一个跑得飞快的运动员,没人追得上他。

2) 引导结果状语的 too…to… 表示"太……而不能……",本质上也是动词不定式的句型,如:

The stone is **too** heavy for me **to** move. 对我来说,这块石头太沉,我搬不动。

(六)地点状语从句

引导词	例句
where	**Where there is a will**, there is a way. = In the place **where** there is a will, there is a way. 有志者,事竟成。(有决心的地方就有方法。) You'd better make a mark **where you have any question**. = You'd better make a mark at the place **where** you have any question. 在有问题的地方,你最好做个标记。
wherever	Sit **wherever** you like. = Sit at any place that you like. 请随便坐。(请坐在任何你喜欢的地方。) Garlic is a plant that grows **wherever** there is warm climate. = Garlic is a plant that grows in any place where there is warm climate. 大蒜是一种植物,可以生长在任何气候温暖的地方。

（七）时间状语从句

序号	引导词	例句
1	every time	**Every time** our school holds sports meet, it will rain. 每次我们学校举行运动会，就会下雨。
2	next time	**Next time** you visit me, phone first, please. 下次你来看我，先打个电话。
3	the last time	**The last time** I saw him, he looked old. 上一次我见到他，他看起来很老。
4	just as/ as soon as / immediately/ the moment	It started to snow **just as** we were about to leave for school. = It started to snow **as soon as** we were about to leave for school. = It started to snow **immediately** we were about to leave for school. = It started to snow **the moment** we were about to leave for school. 我们刚要出去上学，天就下雪了。

注意：just as 和 as soon as 是连词短语，后面引导状语从句。immediately 本是副词，the moment 本是名词短语，在这里均转化为连词，后面引导状语从句。

| 5 | no sooner... than...
hardly... when... | He had **no sooner** arrived at Tibet **than** he fell sick.
= He had **hardly** arrived at Tibet **when** he fell sick.
他刚刚到达西藏就病倒了。 |

注意：no sooner... than...和 hardly... when...这两个句型只能用于过去的情况，而且时态是固定的：主句用过去完成时（had done），从句用一般过去时（did）。此外，两个句型还可使用部分倒装：
No sooner had he arrived at Tibet **than** he fell sick. = **Hardly** had he arrived at Tibet **when** he fell sick.

6	until/not until	Keep working here **until/till** I come back. 在这工作，直到我回来。 You shall **not** leave **until/till** I come back. 直到我回来，你才可以走。
7	by the time	Jerry will have finished the housework **by the time** his parents reach home. 到爸爸妈妈到家的时候，杰瑞会把家务都做完。
8	before	The American Civil War lasted four years **before** the North won. 美国内战持续了四年，北方才取得胜利。 It was only ten minutes **before** she knew she was cheated. 才十分钟，她就知道到她被欺骗了。 （before 是"在……之前"的意思，有时中文翻译为"才"或者"就"更通顺。）

注意：

1）till 和 until 既可用作介词也可用作连词引导时间状语从句，until 是 till 的强调形式，但是它们表达的意义基本是相同的。till 是指直到某一特定事件发生的时候，而在那个时刻之后，该事情或状况仍将持续。until 是指直到某一特定事件发生的时候，而讲话的人在自己心里认为，在那个时刻之后，该事情或该状况将中止（不怎么可能持续），如：

分类	till/until
用于肯定句作"直到……为止",主句的动词一般是延续到 till/until 所表示的时间为止	He waits **till/until** his children are asleep. 他等着直到孩子们睡熟。
用于否定句作"在……以前""直到才",主句的动词一般是非延续性的,它所表示的动作直到 till/until 所表示的时间才发生	He didn't arrive **till/until** the game had begun. 直到比赛开始他才到。
用于延续性动词的肯定或否定句中,till/until 和 not…till/until…其含义不同	The meeting continued **till/until** 9 a.m. 会议一直开到九点。 We didn't have the meeting **till/until** 9 a.m. 直到九点我们才开始会议。
not until 放在句首时,句子要倒装,其中的 until 不能改为 till	**Not until** the last moment did he tell me the truth. 直到最后一刻他才告诉我真相。
句首通常只用 until,不用 till	**Until** you told me I had no idea of it. 在你告诉我之前,我对此一无所知。

2) by 和 by the time 都是"到……为止"的意思,主句通常用完成时。by 是介词,后接名词或者动名词;by the time 是连词短语,后接状语从句。

I will have arrived **by** 11 o'clock. 到11点,我将到达。

All the books had been sold out **by** yesterday afternoon.
截至昨天下午,所有的书都卖光了。

(八)条件状语从句

序号	引导词	例句
1	if	**If** he studies hard next term, he will pass the exam. 如果他下学期努力学习,他会通过考试的。
2	unless	He won't be late **unless** there is a traffic jam. 除非堵车,否则他不会迟到。
3	as long as/ so long as	**As long as/So long as** you are happy, it doesn't matter what you do. 只要你高兴,你做什么都无所谓。
4	lest	He spoke in whispers **lest** the servants should hear him. 他小声说话,以免服务员听到他。 (引导的状语从句中,用"should + 动词原形",should 可以省略。)
5	for fear (that)	I daren't tell you what he did **for fear (that)** he should be angry with me. 我不敢告诉你他所做的事,以免他对我发脾气。 (引导的状语从句中,用"should + 动词原形",should 可以省略。)
6	in case	The football referee wears two watches **in case** one of them stops. 这个足球裁判戴两块手表,防止其中一块不走。

注意：lest、in case 和 for fear (that) 都是连词，后接条件状语从句；in case of 和 for fear of 是介词短语，后面接名词或者动名词，如：

In case of fire, ring the bell. 如遇火灾，请按警铃。

He is studying hard **for fear of** failure. 他学习努力，以免不及格。

Grammar Exercises
语法训练

I. Choose the right word. 选择正确的词。(5%)

1. They would like to meet the challenge _____ (though; despite) all the troubles.
2. _____ (Thanks to; Since) she is keen on her job, she doesn't care too much about the money.
3. The government is trying everything _____ (in order to; in order that) the air pollution can be greatly reduced.
4. _____ (By the time; By) he got his Ph. D., many of his classmates had been married.
5. She hurried back to school _____ (for fear of; for fear that) missing too many classes.

II. Fill in the blanks with the words in the box. 选词填空。(10%)

| due to | so long as | in spite of | before | now that |
| by the time | in case | even if | as though | however |

1. _____ the hardness of his bed, he fell asleep fast.
2. Take care of yourself. It may be many years _____ we meet again.
3. If Emma likes something, she'll buy it _____ much it costs.
4. _____ the ambulance arrived, a crowd of onlookers had gathered.
5. He looked at me angrily _____ it was I who had stolen his dictionary.
6. He still lagged behind other runners _____ he tried his best.
7. The company's financial losses (财务损失) were made _____ poor management.
8. I do believe in people being able to do what they want to do, _____ they're not hurting someone else.
9. Hide the Coca Cola _____ the children see it.
10. _____ we've got a few minutes to wait for the train, let's have a cup of coffee.

III. Error identification. 错误辨识。(20%)

1. (A) Despite of the (B) heavy traffic, I (C) still arrived (D) on time.
2. (A) However (B) careful she does the homework, she (C) will still make (D) some mistakes.
3. (A) A lot of people get their (B) success just (C) due to they are (D) lucky dogs.
4. (A) Although I (B) enjoyed the holiday but I was (C) quite glad (D) to be home.
5. I (A) don't like Norma (B) since she talks (C) as for she (D) knew everything.
6. The homework (A) is (B) too much for us (C) to finish (D) it tonight.
7. There is (A) an old saying that (B) goes "Where (C) there is smoke, (D) it has fire".

8. Hardly (A) had she locked the door (B) than she (C) realized she had left the key (D) inside.

9. I (A) have posted the letter (B) today and they (C) will receive it by (D) Monday.

10. Please (A) tell us what (B) to do (C) in case an (D) emergency.

IV. Multiple choice. 单项选择。(30%)

1. _____ I understand what you say, I don't agree with you.
   A. While   B. Despite   C. Whatever   D. As

2. _____ great achievement, Einstein kept modest (谦虚的) all through his life.
   A. Although   B. However   C. Thanks to   D. In spite of

3. _____ your argument is, I shall stick to my decision.
   A. Whatever   B. However   C. Wherever   D. Whoever

4. The family are so hospitable (热情好客的) that they welcome _____ comes to their home.
   A. who   B. whoever   C. whom   D. whose

5. _____ he admired her looks and manners, he had no wish to marry her.
   A. Although   B. Since   C. As long as   D. As

6. Many accidents happen nowadays _____ fast-speed driving.
   A. since   B. now that   C. owing to   D. therefore

7. You may keep the book a further week _____ no one else requires it.
   A. unless   B. if   C. lest   D. for

8. Peter, I think we'd better go now _____ rain.
   A. lest   B. in case of   C. due to   D. as though

9. My uncle was _____ busy in working _____ he often forgot meals or rest.
   A. very; that   B. enough; as   C. such; that   D. so; that

10. It looks _____ her effort to lose weight makes a difference.
    A. before   B. until   C. as though   D. even though

11. Don't touch the vase (花瓶). Leave it _____ it stands.
    A. before   B. as   C. since   D. like

12. As a good student, he is good at making a mark _____.
    A. where he has questions   B. where he has questions in
    C. the place which he has questions D. in the place which he has questions

13. He came to school _____ he heard the news.
    A. every time   B. hardly when   C. immediately   D. until

14. She _____ into the bath than the telephone started ringing.
    A. no sooner got B. had no sooner got C. hardly got   D. had hardly got

15. The shop doesn't close _____ 2 o'clock in the morning.
    A. until   B. not until   C. by   D. by the time

16. I haven't finished even a quarter of the homework _____ the summer vacation is coming to an end.

A. before   B. after   C. than   D. unless

17. All the roses _____ out by the noon of the Valentine's Day last year.
    A. sold   B. were sold   C. have been sold   D. had been sold

18. I'll discuss the question with you _____ you like.
    A. whichever   B. whenever
    C. no matter how   D. no matter who

19. He injured his foot _____ he was unable to play in the match.
    A. in order to   B. for   C. such that   D. so that

20. _____ you begin to speak, he gives you his full attention.
    A. By the time   B. Thanks to   C. The moment   D. In spite of

Ⅴ. Choose the proper conjunction. 选择正确的连词。（20%）

Mr. Boxell was just shutting his shoe shop at the end of the day (1) _____ (when; where) a man in a well-cut suit walked in and asked for an expensive pair of shoes. There was something about the man (2) _____ (because; that) made Mr. Boxell suspicious (怀疑). He felt (3) _____ (if; as if) he had seen him before somewhere, and then remembered —he had been on TV! The man was a wanted criminal (通缉犯)! The man tried on a few pairs of shoes (4) _____ (before; by the time) he bought a pair that Mr. Boxell strongly recommended (推荐).

"They are a bit tight," the man complained.

"They'll stretch (撑大), sir," Mr. Boxell said.

(5) _____ (Even though; As though) the man was a little dissatisfied, he bought the shoes.

The man came into the shop next day to complain about the shoes (6) _____ (as; because) Mr. Boxell had expected. (7) _____ (In order that; As soon as) he entered the shop, he was surrounded by police and Mr. Boxell closed up the door immediately (8) _____ (lest; in case of) the man should escape.

(9) _____ (In order to; As to) catch the criminal, Mr. Boxell had deliberately (故意地) sold the man a pair of shoes (10) _____ (which; whose) were a size too small, knowing he would return them the next day.

Ⅵ. Translate the following sentences into English. 将下列句子译成英语。（15%）

1. 无论发生什么，就待在这别出声。
2. 那个小孩跟我们讲话，就好像个大人一样。
3. 一些学生在手机上花的时间太多了，以至于他们都没时间学习了。
4. 他直到五十岁才开始学习俄语。
5. 只要我们还活着，我们就绝不放弃。

第二十章 强 调

一、强调的定义

在英语的句子中,强调(Emphasis)就是使句子的某一部分显得更加重要。而在语言表达中,强调的部分就会用特殊的句式或者形式突出表现出来。如:

We **do believe** you. 我们确实相信你。

It was in the area that scientists found a new insect.
就是在这个地区,科学家们发现了一种新昆虫。

Only in this way can you get along well with your colleagues.
只有用这种方式,你才能和你的同事相处融洽。

二、强调的种类

根据使用的强调方式,可以有以下分类。

	分类	定义	例句
强调	it 强调句	It is (was) + 被强调的部分 + that (who) + 句子的其他成分	**It is the news that** he wants to share with us. 就是这条新闻,他想与我们一起分享。
	词汇手段强调	利用助动词 do (does,did) 强调谓语动词的语气,或者添加其他词汇进行强调,并在句中要重读	He **did** come to the party yesterday. 昨天他确实来参加了舞会。 We **do** trust you. 我们确实相信你。
	倒装强调	为了强调句子中的某一成分,或者用来描绘动作和抒发情感,为保持句子的平稳而使用倒装句	**There** comes our boss. 我们老板来了。

注意:

①there/here 放句首时,当主语是指物的名词时,采用全部倒装。如:

The bus comes here. = **Here comes** the bus. 汽车来了。

②there/here 放句首时,主语是人称代词时,其基本语序是"There/Here 主语 + 谓语",如:

Here you are. 给你。

There they go. 他们走了。

三、it 强调句

it 强调句的基本结构为:It is(was) + 被强调的部分 + that(who) + 句子的其他成分;如果把这种强调句型结构去掉后,应该是一个完整的句子,这也是区别强调句型与其他从句的方法。强调句只有两种时态的形式表示:

强调句型	形式	时态
	It is + 被强调的部分 + that(who)	表示现在时或将来时的形式时使用
	It was + 被强调的部分 + that(who)	表达过去时的各种形式时态时使用

而这种强调句不能强调谓语动词,它只能强调主语、宾语、状语等句法成分。如果被强调的主语或宾语是人时,可用 that 也可用 who。

例句	强调的句法成分	强调句
The boy started to collect stamps when he was six years old. 这个男孩在六岁的时候开始集邮。	主语	**It was** the boy **that/who** started to collect stamps when he was six years old. 就是这个男孩在六岁的时候开始集邮。
	宾语	**It was** stamps **that** the boy started to collect when he was six years old. 当这个男孩六岁的时候,他开始收集的是邮票。
	状语	**It was** when he was six years old **that** the boy started to collect stamps. 就是在他六岁的时候,这个男孩开始集邮。

在使用强调句型的时候,需要注意以下几点:

① 如果被强调的是人或人称代词,that 和 who 可以互换使用,但是 who 只能用于强调人或人称代词;该人称代词如果是句子中的主语则用主格形式,强调的人称代词是宾语则一定用宾格形式。如:

He directed the film. → **It was he who/that** directed the film.
就是他导演了这部电影。(强调主语)

They are helping **me** at present. → **It is me who/that** they are helping at present.
他们目前在帮的人是我。(强调动词的宾语)

② 如果原句中含有 not...until 的状语从句的时候,转变成强调状语从句的句型结构为 It is(was) not until...that + 主句(肯定句)。如:

You cannot leave until the test is over. → **It is not until the test is over that** you can leave.
直到考试结束,你才可以离开。

He did not fall asleep until his mother left for work.
→ **It was not until his mother left for work that** he fell asleep.
直到他母亲出门上班,他才睡着。

③ 如果强调句变为一般疑问句,其强调结构为:Is(was) it + 被强调的部分 + that...?

肯定句：It is three times a day that the patient takes the medicine.

这位病人要一天三次服用这种药物。

一般疑问句：**Is it three times a day that** the patient takes the medicine?

这位病人要一天三次服用这种药物吗？

如果强调句变为特殊疑问句,其强调结构为:特殊疑问词 + is（was）it that…? 如：

肯定句：It is **at nine o'clock** that we begin to work at office.

我们在九点开始在办公室工作。

特殊疑问句：**When is it** that you begin to work at office? 你们何时在办公室开始工作？

肯定句：It was **because of his illness** that he became blind. 正是由于疾病,他才失明了。

特殊疑问句：**Why was it** that he became blind? 是因为什么原因他失明了？

四、词汇手段强调

(一)助动词强调

强调谓语动词的时候,需要借助英语中的助动词 do、does 和 did 来完成,并要在句中重读,被强调的动词使用原形。使用助动词强调谓语动词必须符合以下两个条件：

①句子是肯定句；

②句子是一般现在时或一般过去时,此时用助动词 do 和 does 强调现在时的动词,而 did 用来强调过去时的动词,这些强调动词的助动词则可以理解为"的确""确实""真的"或"一定"等。

助动词	例句
do	You **do** look happy today. 你今天看起来真的很高兴。
does	Everybody **does** have his secrets. 每个人确实都有自己的秘密。
did	We **did** feel that the film was boring. 我们的确觉得这部电影好无趣。

在祈使句中,有时使用助动词 do 来表示请求并非命令,这样的强调结构可以使邀请或请求的态度更加恳切、热情、友好和亲切,此时的 do 可译为"一定""务必"等。

Do come to our New Year's Party. 请一定要来参加我们的新年晚会。

Do be careful about your diet. 务必小心你的饮食。

(二)"very"表强调

使用 very 进行强调的时候,very 只能用在名词前,加强名词的语意,意为"正是""就是""仅仅""甚至"等。

At this **very** moment, he rushed in the burning building.

就在这个时候,他冲进了着火的楼房里。

He came up with the **very** idea we wanted. 他想出了我们想要的主意。

She is the **very** person who can solve the difficult problem.

她正是那个可以解决难题的人。

（三）"only"表强调

使用 only 进行强调的时候，only 常放置于被强调部分的前面，加强语气，意为"唯一的""仅有的""只有的""最合适的"等。

①only 置于单数名词之前，以加强名词的意思表达，如：

This was the **only** gift he wanted to buy his daughter. 这是他正想给女儿买的礼物。

Mr. Smith is the **only** person for that position. 史密斯先生是那个职位的最佳人选。

②only 可以置于状语前进行强调，但是如果 only 引导的状语放在句首时，则后面的主句要倒装。如：

倒装强调	例句
Only ＋ 状语/状语从句 ＋ 主句倒装	His parents work **only** on the nearest farm. **Only** on the nearest farm do his parents work. 他的父母只在最近的农场工作。 He visited his uncle **only** yesterday. **Only** yesterday did he visit his uncle. 他只在昨天看望了他的叔叔。

五、倒装强调

改变正常语序，将所强调的部分置于句首。

序号	倒装强调	例句
1	这一类倒装句通常以状语开始，谓语动词是 come, sit, lie, stand, walk 等不及物动词。其语序通常是动词在前，主语在后，不借用助动词 do	**In a corner of the room sat** a little girl. 房间的角落里坐着一个小女孩。 **On the top of the mountain stands** a TV tower. 电视塔屹立在这座山顶上。
2	这一类倒装句以否定副词开句，never, not only, hardly, no sooner, at no time, in no way, seldom 等。句子的倒装要借用助动词 do/does/did 或 have/has/had 来构成	**Hardly** had she left her office when it rained. 她还没离开办公室就下起了雨。 **Not only** do we know this song, but we can also sing it. 我们不仅知道这首歌，还会唱。 **Seldom** do the graduates watch TV at home. 这些毕业生很少在家看电视。

对于 not only ... but also... 的使用，需要注意以下规则：

①为了强调，可将 not only 置于句首，此时其后的句子通常要用部分倒装的形式。如：

Not only has she been late five times, but also she has done no work.

她不仅仅迟到了五次，她还不干活。

Not only do they need clothing, but also they lack food.

他们不但需要衣服，而且还缺少食物。

②如果 not only... but also...连接两个主语放句首,后面的句子不倒装,而且谓语动词要和与其最近的主语保持人称和数的一致。

Not only the students but also the teacher **was for the plan.**
不仅学生们而且这位老师也支持这个计划。

Not only the teacher but also the students **were** for the plan.
不仅这位老师而且学生们都支持这个计划。

Grammar Exercises
语法训练

Ⅰ. **Fill in the blanks with what you have learnt.** 用所学知识填空。(5%)

在英语中,强调就是使句子的某一部分比一般情况下显得更加重要。其中 it 强调句的基本结构为:It is (was) + 1.＿＿＿＿＿＿ + that (who) + 句子的其他成分,而这种强调句是不能强调 2.＿＿＿＿＿＿,它只能强调 3.＿＿＿＿＿＿、宾语、状语等句法成分。强调谓语动词的时候,则需要借助英语中的助动词 do、4.＿＿＿＿＿＿和 did 来完成,并要在句中重读,被强调的动词使用 5.＿＿＿＿＿＿。

Ⅱ. **Choose the correct forms to fill in the blanks.** 选择正确形式填空。(10%)

1. Was it during the First World War ＿＿＿＿＿ (that/when) his uncle was wounded?
2. She said that she would send him her new CD and she ＿＿＿＿＿ (does/did) send it.
3. It was in school ＿＿＿＿＿ (where/that) she learned biology.
4. At present, we ＿＿＿＿＿ (did/do) accept English as an international language.
5. It ＿＿＿＿＿ (is/was) not until 1920 that regular radio broadcasts began.
6. Only in this way ＿＿＿＿＿ (we can/can we) book train tickets online.
7. ＿＿＿＿＿ (That/It) was his mother who helped him review what he had learned.
8. As a result, it was what you did ＿＿＿＿＿ (that/which) impressed me most.
9. When doing researches, the scientists ＿＿＿＿＿ (does/do) need to be serious.
10. What was it ＿＿＿＿＿ (that/why) led her to be late again?

Ⅲ. **Error identification.** 错误辨识。(20%)

1. (A) This was Tom and Jack (B) who helped (C) the old woman (D) a few days ago.
2. (A) It was (B) not until he was eighteen years old (C) when he got (D) his first mobile phone.
3. (A) My younger sister said (B) she would (C) have a holiday and she (D) does have it.
4. Only (A) with the help of the local guide (B) those mountain climbers were saved (C) finally when they were (D) in danger.
5. (A) Was this in 1969 (B) that the American astronaut (C) succeeded in (D) landing on the moon?
6. (A) It was (B) because of bad weather (C) so that the flight (D) had to be postponed.
7. No sooner (A) the little boy had (B) gone to school (C) than he wanted to (D) quit school.
8. (A) It is I that (B) is taking care of (C) my younger brother when (D) he stays at home.

9. —What (A) happened to you in that accident?
   —Not only (B) we lost our money, but (C) our lives were also (D) in danger.
10. (A) It was from him, (B) her physics teacher, (C) whom Laura learned to (D) do experiments in class.

IV. Multiple choice. 单项选择。(30%)

1. Linda said that it was because of her interest in science _____ she chose the major.
   A. that   B. what   C. why   D. how
2. It wasn't until nearly a week later _____ the manager replied to his complaint.
   A. as   B. when   C. since   D. that
3. I guess that it was his behavior _____ attracted us most.
   A. which   B. where   C. that   D. while
4. When was _____ that the chief executive officer (CEO) left for Britain?
   A. he   B. it   C. that   D. since
5. This is _____ dictionary I am looking for.
   A. very the   B. very   C. the very   D. very a
6. It was _____ back home after the barber closed his store.
   A. until midnight that he didn't go   B. not until midnight did he go
   C. until midnight when he didn't go   D. not until midnight that he went
7. The lack of effort _____ let them fail in the past competitions.
   A. do   B. did   C. does   D. doing
8. Was it in the hall _____ we took pictures _____ the exhibition was held?
   A. where; that   B. that; where
   C. where; where   D. that; that
9. At the foot of the mountain _____ .
   A. a furniture factory lie   B. lies a furniture factory
   C. does a furniture factory lie   D. lying a furniture factory
10. Only after the fire broke out _____ that their lives were in danger.
    A. they were aware   B. they awared
    C. were they aware   D. did they aware
11. It really _____ lead many animal spicies to disappear when we exploit more and more natural resources.
    A. do   B. does   C. done   D. did
12. A person with confidence and responsibility is _____ person we need.
    A. very a   B. the very   C. very the   D. very
13. —Who are making so much noise in the reading room?
    —_____ the children.
    A. They are   B. There are   C. That is   D. It is
14. It was only when I reread her books _____ I began to appreciate them again.
    A. so   B. then   C. that   D. until

15. Hardly _____ the airport when the plane took off.
    A. had my younger sister reached   B. had my younger sister arrived
    C. my younger sister had arrived at   D. my younger sister had got to

16. When he was still in college, he wrote his first novel and it _____ turn out to be a best-seller.
    A. do   B. did   C. does   D. done

17. Was _____ that I met last year at the place of tourist interest in Yunnan?
    A. you   B. it
    C. it you   D. that yourself

18. Since body languages _____ play an important role in our daily, we pay much attention to them.
    A. do   B. does   C. doing   D. did

19. It is imagination _____ makes the world colourful, full of changes and energy.
    A. when   B. what   C. that   D. where

20. —How was _____ they discovered the entrance to the underground ancient city?
    —By chance.
    A. it which   B. he which
    C. he that   D. it that

V. Emphasize the underlined parts in the following sentences. 强调句中画线部分。（20%）

1. I saw the sea for the first time <u>in Xiamen</u>.
   _____

2. The typist did not finish typing the documents <u>until daybreak</u>.
   _____

3. <u>Our meeting</u> will be held in this room.
   _____

4. Great changes <u>took place</u> in my hometown between 2000 and 2016.
   _____

5. The telephone rang <u>when she was about to go to bed</u>.
   _____

6. He took <u>the course</u> because of his keen interest in literature.
   _____

7. The day before yesterday Mary went to work <u>by taxi</u>.
   _____

8. What he says <u>disappoints</u> his parents.
   _____

9. Our lateness <u>made</u> her serve dinner an hour later than usual.
   _____

10. Every day we <u>spend</u> half an hour reading books.
    _____

Ⅵ. Translate the following sentences into English. 将下列句子译成英语。(15%)
1. 正是这个国家政策才让这些贫穷的孩子们上了学。
2. 十年前这位法国诗人确实来过我的家乡。
3. 正是一些经济原因才迫使他放弃了自己的学业。
4. 就在这个小村里,可以轻易感受到传统文化。
5. 我们确实需要保护环境,以便我们有更好的生活。

第二十一章 虚拟语气

一、语气的概述

和时态、语态一样,语气也是谓语动词的一种形式,表明说话的目的和意图。英语中有四种语气:陈述语气、疑问语气、祈使语气和虚拟语气(Subjunctive Mood)。

陈述语气陈述一个事实或提出一个想法;疑问语气用来提出问题;祈使语气用来提出请求、邀请,给予忠告、指示,发出警告、命令等;虚拟语气用来表示说话人所说的话并不是客观存在的事实,而是一种假设、主观愿望、怀疑或推测等。如:

Beijing is the capital of China. 北京是中国的首都。(陈述语气)

Where are you from? 你来自哪里?(疑问语气)

Let's go swimming. 让我们去游泳。(祈使语气)

If only I could fly. 要是我能飞就好了。(虚拟语气)

二、虚拟语气的应用

(一) 虚拟语气在条件句中的应用

(1) 虚拟条件句

虚拟语气常用在表示条件的状语从句和表示结果的主句中,在表示与事实相反的虚拟语气时,有三种时态形式,即现在、过去和将来。虚拟条件句及其主句的谓语动词的构成形式如下表:

	条件状语从句	主句	例句
与现在事实相反	If + 主语 + 动词过去式(be 动词一律用 were)	主语 { would / should / could / might } + 动词原形	If I **were** ten years younger, I **would start** all over again. 如果我年轻十岁,我会从头再来的。
与过去事实相反	If + 主语 + had + 过去分词	主语 { would / should / could / might } + have + 过去分词	If he **had had** enough money then, he **would have bought** the house. 如果那时他有足够的钱,他会买了那所房子。

续表

	条件状语从句	主句	例句
与将来事实相反	A.谓语用动词过去式（be 动词用 were） B.谓语用 were to + 动词原形 C.谓语用 should + 动词原形	主语 {would / should / could / might} + 动词原形	If you **were to see** Mr. Johnson tomorrow, what **would you tell** him? 如果明天你见约翰逊先生的话，你会告诉他什么？

(2)混合虚拟条件句

有些条件句主句谓语和从句谓语表示的动作在时间上并不一致，这类句子称为混合虚拟条件句，这时要根据上下文的意思，主从句采用不同谓语动词形式。如：

	从句	主句	例句
从句指过去，主句指现在	If 条件句是对过去的虚拟，故用过去完成时	主句是对现在的虚拟，故用 would do 形式	If you **had taken** my advice, you **wouldn't be** in such trouble now. 如果你听了我的建议，你现在就不会有这种麻烦。
从句的时间包含现在，主句说明过去	If 条件句包含现在，故用过去时	主句是对过去的虚拟，故用 would have done 形式	If I **were** you, I **would have gone** to the theatre yesterday. 如果我是你，我昨天会去看戏的。

(3)含蓄条件虚拟结构

有些句子虽不含条件从句，但意思和条件句差不多，这种句子称为含蓄条件虚拟结构，并用虚拟语气。这些含蓄条件句中常用到 without、but for、but that、otherwise、or 和 but 等，如：

Without your help, we **could not have** succeeded.
要是没有你的帮助，我们就不会成功的。
Under such circumstances I **would probably have done** the same then.
在那样的情况下，那时我也可能做出同样的事情。

(4)省略 if 的虚拟条件句

虚拟条件句中有 had、should 和 were 时，可以将 if 去掉，然后把 had、should 和 were 提到主语之前。

If I had worked hard/ **Had I** worked hard, I would have surely succeeded.
如果我当时努力学习的话，我一定会成功的。

If it should be fine tomorrow/ **Should it** be fine tomorrow, we would go for an outing.
假如明天天气好，我们就去郊游了。

If time were to go back/ **Were time to go back**, I would work harder.
如果时光能倒流，我会加倍努力。

(二)虚拟语气在名词性从句中的应用

(1)在宾语从句中的应用

①在表示命令、建议、要求等一类动词后面所接的宾语从句中用虚拟语气,从句中的谓语动词用(should) + 动词原形,should 可省略。这类动词有:ask、advise、decide、intend、order、suggest、propose、require、demand、request、insist 和 command 等。如:

He **insisted** that **the meeting**(**should**)**be** put off. 他要求推迟那个会议。

I **advised** that **he**(**should**)**go** at once. 我建议他马上去。

注意:suggest 和 insist 不表示建议或坚持要某人做某事时,其后面的宾语从句用陈述语气。

suggest	建议	I **suggested** that **she**(**should**)**come** another day. 我建议她改天来。
	暗示,表明	The smile on his face **suggested** that he **agreed** to this plan. 他脸上的微笑表明他同意这项计划。
insist	坚决主张;坚持要求	He **insisted** that **she**(**should**)**stay** for supper. 他坚持要她留下吃晚饭。 (从句中是没有发生的事情,但是主语希望能成为事实。)
	坚持说,坚持认为	The boy **insisted** that he **hadn't broken** the window. 小男孩坚持说他没打碎窗户。(从句谓语动作发生于主句谓语动作之前,即陈述已知或已经发生过的事,用陈述语气。)

②在 wish 后面所接的宾语从句中谓语动词用虚拟语气,其形式主要有三种:

分类	形式	例句
过去虚拟	wish(that)…had done	I **wish**(that)you **had come** to the wedding. 你要是来参加了婚礼就好了。
现在虚拟	wish(that)…did	I **wish**(that)I **lived** on the seashore. 我要是住在海滨就好了。
将来虚拟	wish(that)…would do	I **wish**(that)I **would know** the answer to this question. 我要是知道这个问题的答案就好了。

(2)在主语从句中的应用

在 It is + 引起虚拟的形容词或名词 + that…结构中的主语从句的谓语动词要用虚拟语气,其形式为(should) + 动词原形,should 可省略。如:

It is **essential** that **he**(**should**)**win** the voters' hearts. 他赢得选民的心是绝对必要的。

It is **a shame** that **she**(**should**)**do** such things. 她做这种事简直是耻辱。

这类引起虚拟的形容词或名词通常有:important、necessary、natural、strange、a pity、a shame 和 no wonder 等。

(3)在表语从句和同位语从句中的应用

在 suggestion、proposal、idea、plan、order 和 advice 等名词后面的表语从句和同位语从句中也用到虚拟语气,其形式为(should) + 动词原形,should 可省略。如:

He gave **orders** that **guests（should）be** hospitably entertained.
他下命令热情款待这些客人。

His **proposal** is that **we（should）get** rid of the bad habits.
他建议我们应改掉这些不良习惯。

(4)虚拟语气在其他句型结构中的应用

①would rather、would sooner 和 would just as soon 等后面所接的从句中用虚拟语气,表示愿望,意为"宁愿""但愿"和"要是……就好了"。用法与 wish 相似,如:

I **would rather he didn't** go now. 但愿他现在不走。(现在虚拟)

I **would just as soon you had been** here yesterday.
要是你昨天在这里就好了。(过去虚拟)

②It is（high/about）time... 的句型后面所接的从句中用虚拟语气,从句中的谓语动词常用过去时,有时也用"should + 动词原形",意为"该是……的时候了",should 不能省略,如:

It is time that we **went** home. 我们该回家了。

It is time that the children **should** go to school. 孩子们该上学了。

③"If only"引起的感叹句要求用虚拟语气,表示愿望。如:

分类	形式	例句
过去虚拟	If only...had done	If only I **had written down** his phone number. 如果我记下他的号码就好了。
现在虚拟	If only... did	If only I **were** younger. 我要是年轻一些就好了。
将来虚拟	If only...would do	If only she **would listen** to me carefully. 但愿她能仔细听我讲话。

④in case、lest 和 for fear that 后面所接的从句中常用虚拟语气,从句中的谓语动词常用"should/would/might + 动词原形"。如:

He took his raincoat with him **in case** it should rain. 他带着雨衣以防下雨。

I will not make a noise **for fear that** I（should）disturb you. 我不会出声的,以免打扰你。

⑤as if 和 as though 引导的方式状语从句或表语从句,有时用虚拟语气;根据语境判断,也可以用陈述语气。如:

虚拟语气在 as if/as though 引导的方式状语从句中	1.表示与过去事实相反,谓语动词用过去完成时	He behaved **as if** nothing **had happened**. 他装作若无其事的样子。
	2.表示与现在事实相反或对现在情况有怀疑,谓语动词用过去时	The pencil seems **as though** it **were broken** when it is partly put in the water. 当把铅笔的一部分放入水中时,看上去好像断了。
	3.表示与将来事实相反	The woman looked worried, **as if** something **would happen** to her. 这个女人看上去忧心忡忡,似乎有事情要发生。
注意:在 as if/as though 句中,从句所表示的内容若为事实或可能为事实,也可用陈述语气。如:It sounds as if it is raining.听起来像是在下雨。		

(三)情态动词和虚拟语气

情态动词 + have done	例句
would + have + done 虚拟语气,表示对过去事情的假设,意思是"本来会做"	I **would have told** you the truth, but you didn't ask me. 我本来会告诉你真相,但是你没有问我
could + have + done 虚拟语气,表示对过去事情的假设,本来能够做某事而没有做。	He **could have helped** us, but he was very busy. 他本来可以帮助我们的,但是他太忙了。
can + have + done 表示对过去行为的怀疑,用于疑问句,意思是"可能做过……吗?"	They are not at home. Where **can they have gone**? 他们不在家。他们可能去什么地方呢?
can't + have + done 对过去已发生行为的否定推测,意思是"过去不可能发生过某事"	She **can't have traveled** abroad; I saw her a day ago. 她不可能去国外旅游,我一天前还见到了她。
may + have + done 表示对发生过的事情的推测,意思是"可能已经"或"也许已经",用于肯定句中	Because of the traffic jam, he **may have missed** the train. 由于交通阻塞,他可能没有赶上火车。
might + have + done 虚拟语气,表示对过去事情的推测,might 与 may 意思相同,但可能性更小	You **might have met** her if you had gone that way. 如果你走那条路的话,你也许能见到她。
must + have + done 表示对过去事情的肯定推测,译成"一定做过某事",只用于肯定句	It **must have rained** this morning, for the ground is wet. 今早一定下雨了,因为地面还是湿的。
should + have + done 意思是"本来应该做某事,而实际没做。" shouldn't + have + done 表示本来不应该做某事,而实际做了,含有指责对方或自责的含意	He **should have passed** the test, but he was too careless. 他本应该通过考试的,但是他太粗心了。 You **should not have forgotten** to water the flowers. 你本不应该忘记浇花。
ought to + have + done 表示过去应该做而实际并没有做,译成"理应做……",往往表示遗憾。与"should + have + done"用法基本一样	We **ought to have come** here fifteen minutes earlier. 我们本来应该早来十五分钟。
need + have + done 表示本来需要做某事而没有做; needn't + have + done 则表示"本来不需要做某事而做了"	The sick **need have been rescured** in time. 病人们本来需要给予及时的救助。 There was much time and she **needn't have hurried** to the airport. 还有很多时间,她本来不需要匆忙赶往机场的。

Grammar Exercises
自测训练

I. Fill in the blanks with right words. 填空。(5%)

1. Tom is very rich. You _____ (couldn't; needn't) have lent him the money.

2. I am not feeling well; I _____ (shouldn't; mustn't) have eaten so much just now.

3. Jack _____ (could; should) have arrived at 9:00 for the meeting, but he didn't show up.

4. I didn't hear the door bell ring. I _____ (must; should) have been asleep.

5. Mr. Brown _____ (might; need) have won the game easily last week, but he quit.

Ⅱ. Fill in the blanks with the proper forms of the given verbs. 用所给动词的适当形式填空。(10%)

1. If you _____ (arrive) ten minutes earlier, you could have seen them off.
2. It's time that we _____ (go) to the railway station.
3. If they _____ (not help) us, our experiment would have failed.
4. They're five minutes late. I suggested that you _____ (come) earlier tomorrow.
5. He often tells us that it is necessary that we _____ (drink) a glass of water after we get up.
6. She insisted that she _____ (send) to work in the small town.
7. If I _____ (not forget) his telephone number, I would have rung him.
8. He is busy now. If he _____ (be) free, he _____ (go) with you.
9. The manager was in his office then. If he _____ (be) here, everything _____ (settle) in a minute.
10. Noisy as it was, he went on reading as if nothing _____ (happen).

Ⅲ. Error identification. 错误辨识。(20%)

1. (A) His doctor (B) suggested that he (C) took a short leave of (D) absence.
2. If I (A) have (B) enough money, I (C) would have bought a much (D) bigger car.
3. He (A) was very (B) busy yesterday; (C) otherwise, he (D) came to the meeting.
4. The librarian (A) insists that John (B) takes no more books from the library before he (C) returns all the books he (D) has borrowed.
5. I (A) left very early (B) last night, but I (C) wish I (D) haven't left so early.
6. I (A) do not (B) have a job. I (C) would find one but I (D) had no time.
7. I (A) wish that you (B) hadn't such a bad headache because (C) I'm sure that you (D) would have enjoyed the concert.
8. He (A) insisted that (B) we all (C) would be in his office (D) at one o'clock.
9. Helen (A) couldn't go to France after all. (B) That's too bad. I'm sure she (C) would have enjoyed it if (D) she's gone.
10. It (A) was strange that we (B) were short of water in the country (C) where it (D) was always raining.

Ⅳ. Multiple choice. 单项选择。(30%)

1. I enjoyed the movie very much. I wish I _____ the book on which it was based.
   A. have read   B. had read
   C. should have read   D. are reading
2. You are late. If you _____ a few minutes earlier, you _____ him.
   A. come; would meet   B. had come; would have met
   C. come; will meet   D. had come; would meet
3. The two students talked as if they _____ friends for years.
   A. should be   B. would be   C. have been   D. had been
4. It is important that I _____ with Mr. Williams immediately.

A. speak   B. spoke   C. will speak   D. to speak

5. He looked as if he _____ ill for a long time.

   A. was   B. were   C. has been   D. had been

6. If the doctor had come earlier, the poor child would not _____.

   A. have laid there for two hours   B. have been lied there for two hours
   C. have lied there for two hours   D. have lain there for two hours

7. I wish that I _____ with you last night.

   A. went   B. could go   C. have gone   D. had gone

8. Let's say if you could go there again, how _____ feel?

   A. will you   B. did you   C. would you   D. do you

9. I can't stand him. He always talks as though he _____ everything.

   A. knew   B. knows   C. has known   D. had known

10. _____ the fog, we should have reached our school.

    A. Because of   B. In spite of   C. In case of   D. But for

11. If you had told me in advance, I _____ my cousin at the airport.

    A. had met   B. met   C. would have met   D. would meet

12. Mike can take his car apart and put it back together again. I certainly wish he _____ me how.

    A. teaches   B. will teach   C. has taught   D. would teach

13. I would have told him the answer, had it been possible, but I _____ so busy then.

    A. had been   B. were   C. was   D. would be

14. He's working hard for fear that he _____.

    A. should fall behind   B. fell behind
    C. may fall behind   D. would fallen behind

15. If it _____ another ten minutes, the game would have been called off.

    A. had rained   B. has rained   C. rains   D. rained

16. He suggested that they _____ use a trick instead of fighting.

    A. should   B. would   C. do   D. had

17. My father did not go to New York; the doctor suggested that he _____ there.

    A. not went   B. won't go   C. not go   D. not to go

18. I would have gone to the meeting if I _____ time.

    A. had had   B. have had
    C. had   D. would have had

19. Would you rather I _____ buying a new bike?

    A. decided against   B. will decide against
    C. have decided   D. shall decide against

20. You look so tired tonight. It is time you _____.

    A. go to sleep   B. went sleep
    C. go to bed   D. went to bed

虚拟语气 第二十一章

V. Fill in the blanks according to the given Chinese in the brackets. 根据括号中所给汉语补全句子。(20%)

1. Everything _____ (都会被毁掉) if Albert hadn't called the fire brigade (消防队).
2. If you hadn't gone with Tom to the party last night, you _____ (就会见到我了).
3. Suppose this ship _____ (要沉没了), do you think there would be enough life jackets for all the passengers?
4. We _____ (本来应该学习的) yesterday, but we went to the concert instead.
5. The teacher suggested that each student _____ (要制定计划) for the vacation.
6. Frankly, I'd rather you _____ (没有做任何事) about it for the time being.
7. I could not find my gloves and I _____ (一定是把它们丢了) somewhere.
8. It's high time you _____ (开始工作).
9. "If I hadn't practiced when I was younger," the musician says, "I _____ (不能) to play so well now."
10. I wish I _____ (去) to the movie with you last night.

VI. Translate the following sentences into English. 将下列句子译成英语。(15%)

1. 如果我有钱,我将做环球旅行。
2. 他们坚持把老人送进医院。
3. 我愿有一天我能够在天空飞翔。
4. 尽管他们第一次见面,他们谈起话来像老朋友似的。
5. 如果四年前他可以再有一次选择的话,他现在就是一名医生了。

第二十二章 倒 装

一、倒装的概述

语序是指各种句子成分在一个句子中的排列顺序。一般情况下,正常语序是主语位于谓语动词之前,谓语动词之后连接宾语、补语或状语。而要表示一定的句子结构的需要或强调某一句子成分时,主语位于谓语动词或助动词后,则形成了倒装语序(Inversion)。

A man with a pair of glasses came in. 一位戴着眼镜的男士走了进来。(正常语序)
In came a man with a pair of glasses. 走进来的是一位戴着眼镜的男士。(倒装语序)

二、倒装的种类

倒装可以分为两种:

倒装	完全倒装 Complete Inversion	谓语 + 主语	**There goes** the bell. 铃响了。
	部分倒装 Partial Inversion	助动词/情态动词 + 主语 + 谓语的实义动词	**Little does** he care about what I said. 他根本不关心我所说的。

(一)完全倒装

完全倒装是出于语法需要或为了强调,把谓语动词放在主语的前面。

序号	完全倒装的条件	例句
1	当表示地点的 here 和 there 位于句首时,其后用完全倒装形式。这类倒装句的谓语通常是 be、exit、appear、live、lie 和 stand 等不及物动词	**There once lived** in Greece a very wise man. 从前,在希腊曾有一位智者。 **Here is** his home. 他的家就在这里。
2	副词 away、down、in、off、out、over 和 up 等位于句首时,其后也用完全倒装语序。这类倒装句的谓语通常是表示动态的不及物动词	**Up went** the arrow into the air. 嗖的一声箭射上了天。 **From the window came** the sound of music. 从窗户里传来了音乐声。

续表

序号	完全倒装的条件	例句
3	用在直接引语中间或后面表示"某人说"这类意思的插入语	"This is the book I love most," **said** Linda. "这是我最喜欢的一本书，"琳达说。 "Please do me a favor," he said. "请帮我个忙，"他说。（主语是代词时不倒装）
4	有时为了强调，可将谓语部分的现在分词、过去分词或不定式置于句首，从而构成倒装	**Standing** beside the window **was** her husband. 站在窗子旁的是她的丈夫。 **Buried** in the desert **was** an ancient city. 一座古城被埋在这沙漠之中。
5	为了保持句子平衡或使上下文衔接紧密，有时可将状语或表语置于句首，句中主语和谓语完全倒装	**Among** these people **was** her younger sister. 她的妹妹就在这些人当中。 **By the table sat** a boy with a book in his hand. 桌子边坐着一个男孩，手里拿着一本书。
6	than 引导的比较状语从句一般为正常语序，但是主语过长时，可将谓语动词放在主语前，构成完全倒装	Roads need much fewer supplies of energy than **do** other forms of transportation. 陆运比其他运输方式消耗较少的能源。

注意：上述完全倒装的句型结构的主语必须是名词，如果主语是人称代词则不能用完全倒装。如：

Out they rushed! 他们冲了出去。

Here he comes. 他来了。

（二）部分倒装

部分倒装是指将谓语的一部分如助动词、情态动词或系动词 be 放在主语前面。如果句中的谓语没有助动词或情态动词，则需添加助动词 do、does 或 did，并将其置于主语之前。

序号	部分倒装的条件	例句
1	大多数的一般疑问句和特殊疑问句为部分倒装	**Did** you come here by bus this morning? 你今早是乘公共汽车过来的吗？ What colour **do** you like best? 你最喜欢什么颜色？
2	句首为否定或半否定的词语，如 no、not、never、seldom、little、hardly、at no time、in no way 和 not until 等	**Not until** yesterday **did** I learn anything about it. 直到昨天我才对这事情有所了解。 **Little does** he care whether we live or die. 他丝毫不在乎我们的死活。
3	so、nor 和 neither 用于句首，说明前面一句话中谓语表示的情况也适用另外一个（些）人或物时，句子要用倒装	I can speak two foreign languages. **So can** my elder brother. 我会说两门外语，我哥哥也会。 He didn't say anything. **Nor/Neither did** his wife. 他没有说话，他的妻子也没有说。

· 173 ·

续表

序号	部分倒装的条件	例句
4	由 as、however 和 though 等引导的让步状语从句中,常用部分倒装,把表语或状语提前。但是表语是名词时,这个名词不用冠词修饰	Busy **as** she was, she always found time to study. 虽然她很忙,可她总是找时间学习。 Much **though** I like it, I won't buy it. 虽然我很喜欢它,但我还是不会买它。 King **as** he is, he is unhappy. 虽然他是国王,却不快乐。
5	so… that 位于句首引起的倒装句为部分倒装句型,如果谓语动词为 be 的一般现在时或一般过去时,则为完全倒装形式	**So loudly did** he speak that everybody could hear him clearly. 他说话声音响亮,人人都听得清楚。(部分倒装) **So rough was** the sea that the ship couldn't get into the harbor. 海上波涛汹涌,使得船无法进港。(完全倒装)
6	such … that 位于句首引起的倒装句为部分倒装句型,如果谓语动词为 be 的一般现在时或一般过去时,则为完全倒装形式	**Such great progress did** he make that he was awarded the scholarship. 取得的巨大进步让他获得了奖学金。(部分倒装) **Such a smart boy is** he that all his teachers like him. 他是这么聪明,老师都喜欢他。(完全倒装)
7	if 引导的虚拟条件中有 were、had 或 should 时,把 if 省略掉后,把 were、had 或 should 放在句首	**Were** I to solve this problem, I should do it in a different way. 要是我来解决这个问题,我要用一种不同的方法。 **Had** I not helped him, he would have failed in business. 如果不是我帮了他一把,他的买卖早就垮掉了。 **Should** Joe come, I would let you know at once. 乔要是过来,我会立刻让你知道。
8	Only + 副词/副词短语/状语从句放在句首时,主句要倒装	**Only then did** I realize I made such a big mistake. 只是在那时,我才认识到我犯了一个多么大的错误。 **Only in this way can** you work it out. 只有用这种方法你才能算出这道题来。 **Only when one loses health does** he know its value. 只有当人们身体不好时才意识到健康的重要性。

注意:

1) so 用于肯定追加,neither 用于否定追加,但是当既有肯定又有否定的情况或既有系动词又有实义动词的时候,则需要用 so it is (the same) with 来连接。

He likes apples and he doesn't like bananas. **So it is (the same) with** his younger brother.
他喜欢苹果,不喜欢香蕉。他弟弟也是这样的。

His father loves footall and he is good at it. **So it is (the same) with** him.
他的父亲喜欢足球,并且擅长踢足球。他也是这样的。

2) 在倒装句中,除了上文所列否定或半否定词语,还有一些放在句首的含有否定词的介词短语,如:

by no means 绝不　　　in no time 立刻,很快　　　on no condition 无论如何也不
in no case 绝不　　　　on no account 绝不　　　　in/under no circumstances 绝不

(三)倒装特殊句型

no sooner...than... 意为"刚……就",只用于描述过去的事情,主句要用过去完成时	No sooner **had he** arrived than we wanted to leave. 他刚到我们就要离开。
hardly/scarcely...when... 意为"刚……就",主句一般用过去完成时	Hardly **had the result** been announced when the crowd applauded. 结果刚一宣布,人们就欢呼起来。 Scarcely **had I** reached the station when the train left. 我刚到车站,火车就开走了。
not only...but also... 意为"不仅……而且……",not only 放句首连接两个句子,则第一个句子倒装,第二个句子不倒装; 如果 not only 放句首连接主语,不倒装,谓语则要遵循就近一致原则	Not only **did I** make a promise, but I also kept it. 我不但许下诺言,我也遵守了诺言。 Not only I but also my younger sister **was** invited. 不但我而且我妹妹也被邀请了。
what 或 how 开头的感叹句中,表语或宾语提前	What **delicious food** it is! 多美味的食物呀! How **bright** the sunshine is! 阳光多么明亮!
the more... the more... 引导的倒装结构中,多为部分倒装结构	**The harder** she studies(状语前置),**the more books** she wants to read(宾语前置). 越努力学习,她就越想读书。

Grammar Exercises
语法训练

I. Change the following sentences into inverted ones. 将下列的句子改为倒装句。(5%)

1. The director sat in the front of the room.
   In the front of the room _____

2. He was so frightened that he did not dare to move an inch.
   So frightened _____

3. He was able to get back to work only when the war was over.
   Only when the war was over _____

4. Some bags of gold were hidden under the bed.
   Hidden under the bed _____

5. The child seldom reads newspapers.
   Seldom _____

II. Fill in the blanks with the proper forms. 用正确形式填空。(10%)

1. Only by practising a few hours every day _____ (you will) be able to master the language.
2. You don't write your term paper; neither _____ (I do).
3. We laugh at jokes, but seldom _____ (we think) about how they work.
4. I finally got the job I dreamed about. Never in all my life _____ (I feel) so happy!

5. Only when he got home _____ (he knew) what had happened to his father.
6. Hardly _____ (we reach) the railway station when the train left.
7. Much as _____ (he likes) the cell phone, he will not buy it.
8. Up _____ (the cat jumped) and caught the mouse.
9. To such an extent _____ (he was) excited that he couldn't sleep last night.
10. Not until she got off the bus _____ (she found) that her wallet had been stolen.

Ⅲ. Error identification. 错误辨识。(20%)

1. The computer (A) was used in teaching. (B) As a result, (C) not only teachers' energy was saved, but students (D) became more interested in the lessons.
2. (A) So sudden (B) the attack was that the enemy (C) had no time (D) to escape.
3. The old couple (A) have been married (B) for 50 years and never once (C) they have quarreled with (D) each other.
4. I (A) failed in the final English exam (B) last term and (C) only then I realized the (D) importance of English learning.
5. (A) Unless you (B) have right food (C) will you not be able to (D) keep fit and healthy.
6. Only (A) yesterday (B) Mary found out that (C) her watch (D) was missing.
7. (A) No sooner (B) Tom had got to his company (C) than it (D) began to rain.
8. It was (A) not until (B) did he go abroad that (C) he knew (D) it was not easy to live there.
9. Never (A) I shall (B) forget the days (C) when (D) we were together in school.
10. By no means (A) it is true (B) that (C) all English people know (D) their own language well.

Ⅳ. Multiple choice. 单项选择。(30%)

1. —Why can't I smoke here?
   —At no time _____ in the meeting-room.
   A. is smoking permitted   B. smoking is permitted
   C. smoking is it permitted   D. does smoking permit

2. Not until I began to work _____ how much time I had wasted.
   A. I realized   B. I didn't realize
   C. didn't I realize   D. did I realize

3. No sooner _____ than it rained heavily.
   A. the game began   B. has the game begun
   C. did the game begin   D. had the game begun

4. —Do you know Jim quarreled with his brother?
   —I don't know; _____.
   A. nor don't I care   B. nor do I care
   C. I don't care neither   D. I don't care also

5. Only when you have obtained sufficient data _____ come to a sound conclusion.
   A. can you   B. you can   C. would you   D. you would

倒　装　第二十二章

6. Not only _____ about the food, but he also refused to pay for it.
   A. the customer complained   B. when the customer complained
   C. did the customer complain   D. the customer did complain
7. _____ do we go for picnics.
   A. Certainly   B. Seldom   C. Sometimes   D. Once
8. Her answer is not acceptable, and _____.
   A. neither am I   B. either is mine
   C. mine is neither   D. neither is mine
9. So fast _____ that it is difficult for us to imagine its speed.
   A. light travel   B. travels the light
   C. does light travel   D. do light travel
10. _____ a little more time to think, he might have acted more sensibly.
    A. If he took   B. If he has taken
    C. Had he taken   D. Should he take
11. Beneath our feet _____ that our life depends on for food and clothing.
    A. lies the earth   B. the earth lies
    C. lie the earth   D. the earth lay
12. Here _____ you want to see.
    A. the manager comes   B. comes the manager
    C. come a manager   D. is coming a manager
13. _____ no air or water, there would be no life in the world.
    A. There are   B. Were there   C. There was   D. Is there
14. _____, I would accept the invitation and go to the party.
    A. If I had been you   B. If I was you
    C. Had I been you   D. Were I you
15. _____ the moment the bell rang.
    A. The students out ran   B. Out ran the students
    C. Ran out the students   D. Out the students ran
16. _____, his family will wait for him to have dinner together.
    A. However late he is   B. However he is late
    C. However is he late   D. However late is he
17. _____ come into the room _____ the telephone rang.
    A. He hardly; than   B. Hardly had he; when
    C. He had not; than   D. Not had he; when
18. Jack is a student and studies at No. 2 Middle School. _____.
    A. It was the same with Mike   B. So is Mike
    C. So it is with Mike   D. So does Mike
19. Many a time _____ me good advice.
    A. he gave   B. does he give   C. he has given   D. has he given

20. Only when you have finished your homework _____ go home.
    A. can you   B. would you   C. you will   D. you can

V. Fill in the blanks with the correct forms. 填写正确形式。(20%)

Why (1) _____ (I want) to go to college? Never (2) _____ (I have been) asked such a question. But many times I have asked myself. I have (3) _____ (come) up with a whole variety of reasons. The most important reason is that I want to (4) _____ (be) a better man.

Many things (5) _____ (make) human beings different from or better than or even superior to animals.

One of the most important things is education. If I fail to (6) _____ (receive) higher education, my education will not be (7) _____ (finish). As I want to be a fully (8) _____ (develop) man, I must get a well-rounded education, which good colleges and universities are supposed to (9) _____ (provide). I know one can get educated in many ways, but colleges and universities are among the best places to teach me how to educate myself. Only when I am well educated (10) _____ (I will) be a better human being and be able to be fit into society.

VI. Translate the following sentences into English. 将下列句子译成英语。(15%)

1. 她喜欢听音乐,我也喜欢。
2. 有一位老农住在那所房子里。
3. 只有当她回家时,她才知道这消息。
4. 虽然他是个孩子,可是他比其他人知道得都多。
5. 我刚到办公室,会议就开始了。

第二十三章　直接引语与间接引语

一、直接引语与间接引语的定义

①直接引语(Direct Speech)直接引用别人的原话,通常置于引号内。
They said,"We will go home by sea." 他们说:"我们乘船回家。"
②间接引语(Indirect Speech)是用自己的话来转述别人的话,并且不能用引号,间接引语大多用宾语从句表达。
They said that they would go home by sea. 他们说他们要乘船回家。

二、直接引语与间接引语之间的转变

(一)人称变化

由直接引语变间接引语时,人称变化遵循以下规则:

	变化规则	直接引语	间接引语
人称变化	如果从句中的主语是第一人称或被第一人称所修饰,从句中的人称要按照主句中主语的人称变化	She said," **I** want **you** to go with **me**." 她说:"我想让你跟我一起走。"	She said that **she** wanted **me** to go with **her**. 她说她想让我跟她一起走。
	若从句中的主语及宾语是第二人称或被第二人称所修饰,从句中的人称要跟引号外的主句的宾语一致。如果引号外的主句没有宾语,也可以用第一人称	She said to Jim,"How is **your** brother now?" 她问吉姆:"你的弟弟现在怎么样?"	She asked Jim how **his** brother was then. 她问吉姆他的弟弟那时怎么样了。
	如果从句中的主语及宾语是第三人称或被第三人称所修饰,从句中的人称一般不需要变化	My mother said," **I** will help **him** to fix **his** washing machine." 我妈妈说:"我会帮助他修理他的洗衣机。"	My mother said that **she** would help **him** to fix **his** washing machine. 我妈妈说她会帮助他修理他的洗衣机。

(二)动词变化

①在直接引语中主句谓语动词常为 said,当直接引语是陈述句时,变为间接引语时 said

不变。当直接引语中主句谓语动词为 said to sb 时,变间接引语时要变为 told sb。如:

He **said to** me,"These books are mine." 他对我说:"这些书是我的。"

→He **told** me that those books were his. 他告诉我那些书是他的。

②当直接引语是一般疑问句或特殊疑问句时,则要把 said 或 said to 变为 asked 或 asked sb.。如:

The husband **said to** his wife,"Are you ready to leave?"

丈夫对妻子说:"你准备好走了吗?"

→The husband **asked** his wife if she was ready to leave.

丈夫问妻子她是否准备好走了。

(三)时态变化

(1)直接引语中的动词为过去时

直接引语在改为间接引语时,如果主句时态是过去时,间接引语中的时态应与主句时态对应,并发生改变,变化规则如下:

	变化规则	直接引语	间接引语
时态变化	一般现在时→一般过去时	She said,"I **like** this pen." 她说:"我喜欢这支钢笔。"	She said that she **liked** that pen. 她说她喜欢那支钢笔。
	一般过去时→过去完成时	Ben said,"I **ate** a hotdog." 本说:"我吃了一个热狗。"	Ben said that he **had eaten** a hotdog. 本说他已经吃了一个热狗。
	一般将来时→过去将来时	She said,"We **will** travel abroad." 她说:"我们将要去国外旅游。"	She said that they **would** travel abroad. 她说她们将要去国外旅游。
	现在进行时→过去进行时	Mike said,"I **am reading** a book." 麦克说:"我正在读一本书。"	Mike said that he **was reading** a book. 麦克说他正在读一本书。
	现在完成时→过去完成时	He said,"I **have left** my key in your room." 他说:"我把钥匙落在你的房间了。"	He said that he **had left** his key in my room. 他说他把钥匙落在我的房间了。
	过去完成时→过去完成时(不变)	I said to him,"I **had changed** my job when I met you last time." 我跟他说:"我上次见你的时候已经换工作了。"	I said to him that I **had changed** my job when I met him last time. 我跟他说我上次见他的时候已经换工作了。
	过去进行时→过去进行时(不变)	My mother said,"I **was doing shopping** when I saw your friend in the mall." 我妈妈说:"我在商场见到你的同学的时候我正在购物。"	My mother said that she **was doing shopping** when she saw my friend in the mall. 我妈妈说她在商场见到我的朋友时她正在购物。
	can→could	She said,"I **can** finish this task alone." 她说:"我可以单独完成这份任务。"	She said that she **could** finish that task alone. 她说她可以单独完成这份任务。
	may→might	Tom said,"You **may** need to do it again." 汤姆说:"你或许需要重新做一遍。"	Tom said that I **might** need to do it again. 汤姆说我或许需要重新做一遍。
	must → must/had to	Lily said,"I **must** agree with his idea." 丽丽说:"我必须同意他的观点。"	Lily said that she **must/had to** agree with his idea. 丽丽说她必须同意他的观点。

(2)直接引语中的动词为现在时或将来时

直接引语变为间接引语时,如果主句中的谓语动词是一般现在时或一般将来时,则间接引语从句的时态保持不变。如:

He says, "I **have completed** my homework." 他说:"我已经完成了作业。"
→He says that he **has completed** his homework. 他说他已经完成了作业。
She will say, "I **will put it off** until tomorrow." 她会说:"我将推迟到明天。"
→She will say that she **will put it off** until the next day. 她会说她将推迟到明天。

(3)间接引语中时态不变

在以下几种情况下,在直接引语变为间接引语时,时态一般不变化。

①直接引语是客观真理。如:

"The earth **moves** around the sun." the teacher told me.
老师告诉我:"地球绕着太阳转。"
→The teacher told me that the earth **moves** around the sun. 老师告诉我地球绕着太阳转。

②直接引语中有具体的过去某年、某月、某日作状语,变为间接引语时,时态不变。如:

Tom said, "I **was born** on March 18, 1999." 汤姆说:"我出生在1999年3月18日。"
→Tom said that he **was born** on March 18, 1999. 汤姆说他出生在1999年3月18日。

③直接引语如果是一般现在时,表示一种反复出现或习惯性的动作,变间接引语,时态不变。如:

He said, "I **eat** an egg every morning." 他说:"我每天早上吃一个鸡蛋。"
→He said he **eats** an egg every morning. 他说他每天早上吃一个鸡蛋。

④如果直接引语中的情态动词没有过去时的形式(ought to、had better 或 used to)和已经是过去时的形式时(could、should、would 或 might),时态不再变。如:

Peter said, "You **had better** tell me the truth today." 皮特说:"你最好是今天对我说实话。"
→Peter said that I **had better** tell him the truth that day. 皮特说我最好那天对他说实话。

(四)时间状语、地点状语、指示代词和动词的变化

	直接引语	间接引语
时间状语	now 现在	then 那时;当时
	today 今天	that day 那天
	tonight 今晚	that night 那天晚上
	this week 本周	that week 那一周
	yesterday 昨天	the day before 前一天
	the day before yesterday 前天	two days before 两天前
	three days ago 三天前	three days before 三天前
	last week 上周	the last week 前一周
	tomorrow 明天	the next day 第二天
	next week 下周	the next week 第二个星期

续表

	直接引语	间接引语
指示代词	this 这	that 那
	these 这些	those 那些
地点状语	here 这儿	there 那儿
动词	come 来	go 去

(五)各种形式由直接引语变为间接引语的方法

(1)直接引语是陈述句

规则	直接引语	间接引语
间接引语为 that 引导的宾语从句(口语中 that 可以省略),主句的引述动词主要有 say、tell、repeat、explain 和 think 等	He said, "You are my hero." 他说:"你是我的英雄。"	He said (that) I was his hero. 他说我是他的英雄。

(2)直接引语是疑问句

规则	直接引语	间接引语
一般疑问句或反义疑问句变为 if (whether) 引导的宾语从句	She said to me, "**Do** you **like** coming here to read newspapers?" 她对我说:"你喜欢到这儿来读报纸吗?" She asked me, "You have been arrested by the police, **haven't you**?" 她问我:"你已经被警察逮捕过,是吧?"	She asked me **if/whether** I liked going there to read newspapers. 她问我是不是喜欢到那儿来读报纸。 She asked me **if/whether** I had been arrested by the police. 她问我是不是已经被警察逮捕过。
选择疑问句变为 whether...or... 宾语从句	I asked him, "**Will** you **stay** at school or go home tonight?" 我问他:"你今晚是待在学校还是回家?"	I asked him **whether** he **would stay** at school or go home that night. 我问他那天晚上是待在学校还是回家。
特殊疑问句变为由原来的疑问词引导的宾语从句	He asked, "**Where are you** from?" 他问:"你从哪儿来的?"	He asked me **where I was** from. 他问我从哪儿来的。

(3)直接引语是祈使句

规则	直接引语	间接引语
引述祈使句多半采用"动词+宾语+不定式"的结构。常见的引述动词有 ask、tell、beg、urge、order、warn、advise、remind 等	His father said to him, "**Don't eat** junk food." 他的父亲跟他说:"不要吃垃圾食品。"	His father told him **not to eat** junk food. 他的父亲告诉他不要吃垃圾食品。

续表

规则	直接引语	间接引语
引述表示命令的祈使句时,可以用宾语从句结构转述,从句中谓语动词通常为"be to + 不定式"或"have got to + 不定式"	"**Open** the door", he said to me. 他跟我说:"打开门。"	He told me that I **was to open** the door. He said **that I had got to open** the door. 他跟我说打开门。
引述表示建议、劝告的祈使句时,可以用"suggest + that 从句"或者"suggest + doing 动名词结构"等	"**Let's arrive** there before the door is opened." he said. 他说:"我们在开门之前到达那边。"	He **suggested that they (should) arrive** there before the door was opened. He **suggested arriving** there before the door was opened. 他建议在开门之前到达那边。
引述表示建议、提议的祈使句时,可以用"offer + 不定式"结构	"**Let me** put forward some suggestions for you." he said. 他说:"让我给你提出点建议吧。"	He **offered to** put forward some suggestions for me. 他提议给我提供点建议。

(4) 直接引语是感叹句

规则	直接引语	间接引语
间接引语为 what 或 how 引导的感叹句型,也可以用 that 引导宾语从句	She said, "**What an amazing flower** it is!" 她说:"这是多么迷人的花呀!"	She said **what an amazing flower** it was. She said **that it was** an amazing flower. 她说真是迷人的花。
根据原句意义加以改写,使之变为意义相当的陈述句	"Congradulations!" he said. 他说:"祝贺!"	He **congradulated** me. 他祝贺了我。

Grammar Exercises
语法训练

I. Fill in each blank with a right word. 用所学知识填空。(5%)

1. "I am having breakfast," he said.
   He said that _____ _____ having breakfast.
2. "I have been to Hainan Island five times," Tina said to me.
   Tina _____ me that she _____ to Hainan Island five times.
3. "I went to work with my sister," she said.
   She said that _____ _____ _____ to work with her sister.
4. "I met her the day before yesterday," he said to me.
   He told me that he _____ met her _____ before.
5. "Did you read the book fifteen days ago?" he said.
   He _____ _____ I had read the book fifteen days _____.

Ⅱ. **Change the following sentences from direct speech into indirect speech.** 请将下列直接引语变为间接引语。(10%)

1. You said to me, "I saw the film two days ago."
   _____

2. He said to his younger sister, "You may come with me."
   _____

3. The teacher said to his class, "Don't waste your time!"
   _____

4. "I'll be very busy today," said the man.
   _____

5. He said to the old woman, "Don't worry. I'll take you there."
   _____

6. The man asked me, "How many times have you been here?"
   _____

7. Mary said, "I joined the League in August 1998."
   _____

8. "Are you interested in playing the piano?" he said.
   _____

9. The teacher said, "The sun is larger than the moon."
   _____

10. The boy said to us, "I usually get up at six every day."
    _____

Ⅲ. **Error identification.** 错误辨识。(20%)

1. 直接引语 He said to me, "I've left my book in my room."
   间接引语 He (A) told me (B) that he (C) left his book in (D) his room.

2. 直接引语 She asked me, "Is this book worth reading?"
   间接引语 She asked me (A) if (B) this book (C) was (D) worth reading.

3. 直接引语 The teacher asked me, "How did you repair it?"
   间接引语 The teacher asked (A) me how (B) I (C) have (D) repaired it.

4. 直接引语 The boy said to us, "I usually go to bed at ten every day."
   间接引语 The boy (A) told us (B) that he usually (C) went to bed (D) at ten every day.

5. 直接引语 "Sound travels about 4 times faster in water than in air," the physics teacher said to them.
   间接引语 The physics teacher (A) told them (B) that sound (C) traveled (D) about 4 times faster in water than in air.

6. 直接引语 "Do not look out of the window!" this young woman said to me.
   间接引语 (A) That young woman (B) told me (C) do not (D) look out of the window.

7. 直接引语 He said, "We are still students, studying medicine."
   间接引语 He said that (A) they (B) were (C) still students, (D) studying medicine.

8. 直接引语 "Will you go to the concert with me this evening?" Mary asked me.
   间接引语 Mary asked me (A) whether I (B) would go to the concert (C) with her (D) this evening.

9. 直接引语 "What did you do here yesterday?" the old man asked my brother.
   间接引语 The old man asked my brother what (A) he (B) had done (C) there (D) yesterday.

10. 直接引语 "Listen to me. Keep quiet, children!" he said.
    间接引语 He (A) asked the children (B) listen to (C) him and (D) be quiet.

IV. Multiple choice. 单项选择。(30%)

1. Our teacher asked us _____ our dictionaries to school.
   A. bring   B. brought   C. bring   D. to bring

2. The teacher told the boy students _____ football on the grass.
   A. not play   B. not to play   C. played   D. playing

3. "You have already got well, haven't you?" she asked. →She asked _____.
   A. that I have already got well
   B. that I had already got well
   C. if I have already got well
   D. whether I had already got well

4. These pictures will show you _____.
   A. what the city looks like
   B. what does the city look like
   C. how the city looks like
   D. how does the city look like

5. Betty asked her sister _____ to the railway station to see her off.
   A. not to come   B. not to go   C. to not come   D. to not go

6. The pupil asked his teacher _____ faster than sound.
   A. that light travels
   B. that light traveled
   C. whether light travels
   D. whether light traveled

7. Mr. Li _____ Wang Ling _____ a taxi to the airport.
   A. asked; take   B. asked; taking   C. told; take   D. told; to take

8. She asked him _____.
   A. whose dictionary this is
   B. whose dictionary that was
   C. whose dictionary is this
   D. whose dictionary that is

9. Linda's mother asked her _____.
   A. that whether she had finished her homework
   B. if she has finished her homework
   C. if she had finished her homework
   D. that if she had finished her homework

10. The monitor said to me, "Have you filled in your registration form?"
    →The monitor asked me _____ in my registraion form.
    A. whether I have filled
    B. if I filled
    C. whether I had filled
    D. if I fill

11. She said to her son, "Don't play football in the street." →She _____ play football in the

street.

   A. told her son that he didn't
   B. told her son that he didn't
   C. told her son not to
   D. said to her son not to

12. He asked me _____.
    A. how would the weather be like tomorrow
    B. what the weather would be like the next day
    C. how the weather would be like tomorrow
    D. what would the weather be like the next day

13. He told us that he _____ an international meeting _____.
    A. had attended; five days before
    B. attended; five days ago
    C. would attend; since five days
    D. was attending; for five days

14. She told me that she _____ by her relatives at the bus stop.
    A. had been seen off
    B. have seen off
    C. have been seen off
    D. had seen off

15. Linda said that she _____ to Hong Kong.
    A. has never gone
    B. had never gone
    C. has never been
    D. had never been

16. She asked, "Are you a Party member or a League member?" →She asked me _____.
    A. if I was a Party member and a League member
    B. whether I was a Party member or a League member
    C. that I was a Party member or a League member
    D. whether I was a Party member and a League member

17. More and more students and teachers have begun to know _____.
    A. how important the foreign language are
    B. how the foreign language is important
    C. how important the foreign language is
    D. how important is the foreign language

18. The hostess said that it _____ time that they _____ supper.
    A. was; had   B. was; had had   C. is; have   D. is; have had

19. The boss asked his secretary _____ he had finished typing the report _____.
    A. if; or not   B. if; not   C. whether; or not   D. whether; not

20. I wonder how much _____.
    A. does he spend on his car
    B. did he spend on his car
    C. he spent on his car
    D. he spent in his car

V. Fill in the blanks with the correct forms of indirect speech in the following passage. 填写间接引语的正确形式。(20%)

My father was very strict with my study when I was a little girl. Once, he asked me if I (1) _____ (finish) my homework. My study was poor at that time and I told him that I (2) _____ (not write) my English composition and that I (3) _____ (will) finish it (4)

_____ (tomorrow). Unexpectedly, he was not angry with me that time. He told me that I (5) _____ (be punctual) and finish my homework (6) _____ (today). He suggested that I (7) _____ (go) to my friend's home and talk with her about my homework. He told me that he always (8) _____ (finish) his homework punctually when he (9) _____ (be) a little boy, so his teacher always said that what a good student he (10) _____ (be)!

Ⅵ. Translate the following sentences into English. 将下列句子译成英语。(15%)

1. 老师告诉我们月亮绕着地球转。
2. 杰克问我他在街上见到我的时候我正要去哪儿。
3. 周二的时候他跟我说他昨天去我家了。
4. 彼得说他必须去工作了。
5. 我问他那天晚上他是去看电影还是待在家里。

附 件

Test 1

I. Multiple Choice. (45%)

1. _____ Browns are naturally _____ musical family.
   A. A; a
   B. The; a
   C. The; an
   D. /; an
2. —Can I help you? —I'd like three _____.
   A. boxs of organges
   B. box of oranges
   C. boxes of organge
   D. boxes of oranges
3. She looks so pale; she _____ be ill.
   A. must
   B. have to
   C. can
   D. need
4. There is _____ wrong with my mobile phone and I can't use it.
   A. something
   B. anything
   C. nothing
   D. everything
5. The teacher came in the classroom, _____ a book _____ his right hand.
   A. with; on
   B. with; in
   C. like; in
   D. like; on
6. My _____ daughter will start school this year.
   A. seven year old
   B. seven-year-old
   C. seven years old
   D. seven-years-old
7. When he was at school, he _____ to the cinema once a week.
   A. goes
   B. went
   C. going
   D. gone
8. At eight o'clock yesterday evening, I _____ with my friend on the phone.
   A. am talking
   B. talk
   C. was talking
   D. talked
9. If it _____ fine tomorrow, we won't go skating.
   A. isn't
   B. won't be
   C. wasn't
   D. doesn't
10. Look, the new bridge _____ by the workers.
    A. is being built
    B. build
    C. builds
    D. has built
11. I felt _____ by his interest in my new invention.
    A. to encourage
    B. encouraged
    C. was encouraged
    D. encourage
12. Most people enjoy _____ letters, but few seem to be fond of writing them.
    A. receiving
    B. received
    C. being received
    D. to receive
13. _____ several times, the young scientist still kept on making his experiments.
    A. Failing
    B. Having failed
    C. Failed
    D. To have failed

14. The door is still open; I forgot _____ it.
    A. closing   B. to close   C. having closed   D. to have close
15. We don't know _____ the day after tomorrow.
    A. when does she come   B. how will she come
    C. if she comes   D. whether she will come
16. School children spend too much time on video games, which does _____ to their eyes.
    A. harm   B. harmful   C. harmless   D. harmfulness
17. The fact has worried us _____ the earth is becoming warmer and warmer these years.
    A. which   B. what   C. though   D. that
18. It _____ we had stayed together for a couple of weeks _____ I found we had a lot in common.
    A. was until; when   B. was until; that
    C. wasn't until; when   D. wasn't until; that
19. We are taught to understand _____ important education is to our future.
    A. such   B. so   C. how   D. that
20. My father, together with some of his old friends, _____ there already.
    A. will be   B. has been   C. have been   D. were
21. Only then _____ how much damage had been damaged.
    A. she realized   B. she had realized
    C. had she realized   D. did she realize
22. If I _____ hard before, I _____ a rich man now.
    A. worked; will be   B. had worked; would be
    C. have worked; are   D. were working; are being
23. _____ surprised me most was _____ such a little boy could write so many words.
    A. What; that   B. That; what   C. What; what   D. That; which
24. October 1st is the national day of China, _____ the Chinese will never forget.
    A. when   B. that   C. which   D. what
25. _____ nice time the boys had playing basketball with the school team last week!
    A. How a   B. What a   C. What   D. How
26. No one failed in the final test, _____ ?
    A. did one   B. didn't one   C. did he   D. did they
27. _____ I really don't like art, I find her works marvelous.
    A. If   B. As   C. Since   D. While
28. I have learned _____ 1 500 English words last term.
    A. no more than   B. not any more   C. no more   D. not more than
29. You had better take a book to read when you stay at the airport _____ you have to wait.
    A. even if   B. in case   C. in order that   D. as if
30. The new worker is supposed to report to the manager as soon as he _____.
    A. is going to arrive B. is arriving   C. arrives   D. will arrive

Ⅱ. **Error Identificaiton.** (20%)

31. When Peter (A) <u>was</u> a child, his mother always (B) <u>let</u> him (C) <u>have a breakfast</u> (D) <u>in bed</u>.

32. She is (A) <u>a</u> newcomer to (B) <u>the chemistry</u>, but she (C) <u>has made</u> some important (D) <u>discoveries</u>.

33. The boy (A) <u>was</u> (B) <u>made</u> (C) <u>clean</u> his room by (D) <u>his mother</u>.

34. —(A) <u>Could</u> you (B) <u>tell</u> me how I (C) <u>would improve</u> my English?
    —By doing (D) <u>more speaking</u>.

35. The (A) <u>coach</u> has (B) <u>kept</u> the players (C) <u>to run</u> for (D) <u>a whole</u> hour.

36. (A) <u>To have been</u> together for fifty years, Ross and Betty (B) <u>were regarded</u> as the (C) <u>happiest</u> couple (D) <u>of the village</u>.

37. One reason (A) <u>why</u> he didn't accept the job was (B) <u>because</u> he would (C) <u>go abroad</u> to do (D) <u>further</u> study.

38. I would rather (A) <u>to watch TV</u> (B) <u>at home</u> (C) <u>than</u> (D) <u>go to the cinema</u>.

39. Tom is (A) <u>much</u> (B) <u>shorter than</u> (C) <u>any other boys</u> in his class. In fact, he is (D) <u>the shortest</u> boy in our school.

40. I don't know (A) <u>whether</u> (B) <u>will he come</u> tomorrow. (C) <u>If he</u> (D) <u>comes</u>, I will tell you.

Ⅲ. **Cloze.** (20%)

One Friday night, a poor young man stood at the gate of the railway station, playing his violin. Many people put some money into the hat lying __41__ him.

The next day, the young man came to the gate of the railway station again, and put his hat __42__ the ground. But different from __43__ he always did in the past days, he took out a large piece of paper and it said, "Last night, a gentleman __44__ George Miller put an important thing into my hat by mistake. Please come soon, Mr. Miller."

About half an hour later, a middle-aged man ran to the young man in a hurry and said, "It's you! You __45__ come. I know you are an honest man and will certainly come here." The young man asked, "Are you Mr. Miller? Did you lose anything?" "A lottery (彩票) ticket." answered the middle-aged man. The young man then returned it to the man. Yesterday when the man knew the fact __46__ his lottery ticket was worth $500 000, he was so __47__ that he threw the ticket together with the money into the young man's hat!

Someone asked the young man, "You play the violin to make __48__. Why didn't you keep the ticket and take the prize for yourself?" The young man said, "__49__ I don't have much money, I live happily. But if I __50__ honesty, I won't be happy forever."

41. A. in front of   B. in the front of   C. on the top of   D. at the top of
42. A. over   B. at   C. in   D. on
43. A. which   B. what   C. that   D. how
44. A. name   B. named   C. was named   D. names
45. A. does   B. have done   C. do   D. did

46.	A. that	B. which	C. what	D. why
47.	A. exciting	B. excited	C. excites	D. felt excited
48.	A. yourself	B. living	C. music	D. money
49.	A. Even	B. Even if	C. If	D. In spite of
50.	A. have lost	B. lost	C. lose	D. loses

Ⅳ. Translation. (15%)

51. The harder you work, _____
    (你取得的进步就越大).

52. Not until the 19th century _____ (人们才发明了第一台计算机).

53. _____ (我们要参观的第一个地方) is the National Museum of China.

54. There is a suggestion that _____ (多喝开水有益健康).

55. At that time _____ (我没有多少朋友以至于我感到孤独).

Test 2

I. Multiple Choice. (45%)

1. The movie that we saw last week was quite interesting, _____?
   A. wasn't it   B. was it   C. didn't we   D. weren't we
2. Excuse me, sir. Could you tell me _____?
   A. where the bank nearest   B. where is the nearest bank
   C. where the nearest bank is   D. the nearest bank is where
3. Your bike is excellent _____ the color.
   A. except   B. except for   C. besides   D. beside
4. —I like watching movies, but I do not like watching TV series.
   —_____.
   A. Neither do I   B. So do I   C. So it is with me   D. Me too
5. _____, Tom jumped into the river and had a good time in it.
   A. Be a good swimmer   B. Being a good swimmer
   C. Having been good swimmer   D. To be a good swimmer
6. _____ old lady in brown is _____ university professor.
   A. An; a   B. An; /   C. The; an   D. The; a
7. The music of the film _____ by him sounds so _____.
   A. playing; exciting   B. played; excited
   C. playing; excited   D. played; exciting
8. —Oh! I came in a hurry and forgot to bring food.
   —Never mind. You can have _____.
   A. us   B. ours   C. you   D. yours
9. You won't know the value of the health _____ you lose it.
   A. until   B. after   C. when   D. because
10. What you said sounded _____, but in fact it was untrue.
    A. reason   B. reasonable   C. reasonless   D. unreason
11. _____ speaking, I didn't do it on purpose.
    A. Honestly   B. Honest   C. Honesty   D. Dishonest
12. I would have gone to the concert, if I _____ time.
    A. had   B. have had
    C. had had   D. would have had
13. Not until I began to work _____ how much time I had wasted.
    A. didn't realize   B. did I realize   C. I didn't realize   D. I realized
14. My parents don't mind what job I do _____ I am happy.
    A. even though   B. as soon as   C. as long as   D. as though
15. I don't think _____ possible to master a foreign language without much memory work.
    A. this   B. it   C. that   D. its

16. He sent me an E-mail, _____ to get further information.
    A. hoped   B. hope   C. to hope   D. hoping
17. There _____ a birthday party this Sunday.
    A. shall be   B. will have
    C. will be   D. will going to be
18. His uncle _____ the Communist Party of China (中国共产党) since 1985.
    A. was   B. has been in
    C. joined   D. has joined
19. _____ more attention, the trees could have grown better.
    A. Given   B. To give   C. Having given   D. Giving
20. —What did you do in the garden at that time?
    —I watched my father _____ his car.
    A. to repair   B. repaired   C. repairing   D. repairs
21. Through the window we can see nothing but _____ buildings.
    A. tall very many   B. very many tall
    C. very tall many   D. many very tall
22. Was it at the age of 30 _____ he decided to settle down to write?
    A. when   B. while   C. that   D. in which
23. I don't know what time it is now, because my watch _____.
    A. is repairing   B. is being repaired
    C. has repaired   D. has been repaired
24. —_____ I take the newspaper away?
    —No, you mustn't. You _____ read it only here.
    A. Must; can   B. Need; must
    C. May; can   D. Must; must
25. The Smiths _____ their breakfast when the morning post came.
    A. had   B. are having
    C. has been having   D. were having
26. The students want to know whether they _____ an English test today.
    A. had   B. has   C. will have   D. are
27. I am so tired that I can't walk _____.
    A. much far   B. any farther
    C. even far   D. very further
28. The reason _____ he was late for school was _____ he had to send his mother to a hospital.
    A. that; why   B. why; because
    C. why; that   D. that; because
29. The soldier died for saving the child, so his _____ is heavier than Mount Tai.
    A. die   B. dead   C. died   D. death

30. Canada is mainly a (an) _____ country.
    A. English-spoken   B. speak-English
    C. spoken-English   D. English-speaking

Ⅱ. Error Identification. (20%)

31. There were (A) <u>too</u> many nice things (B) <u>that</u> I didn't (C) <u>know</u> (D) <u>what to choose</u>.
32. The actress was always (A) <u>speaking highly of</u> her role (B) <u>in the play</u>, (C) <u>that</u> (D) <u>made</u> the others unhappy.
33. (A) <u>Following</u> (B) <u>the road</u> and you (C) <u>will find</u> the (D) <u>post office</u>.
34. Harry is very (A) <u>unhappy</u> and (B) <u>doesn't know</u> (C) <u>how</u> to do about (D) <u>his life</u>.
35. I have (A) <u>caught a bad cold</u> (B) <u>for</u> a week and I (C) <u>can't</u> (D) <u>get rid of it</u>.
36. You'd better (A) <u>take a raincoat</u> (B) <u>along with</u> (C) <u>you</u> in case (D) <u>of it rains</u>.
37. His (A) <u>children</u> as (B) <u>well as</u> his wife (C) <u>invited</u> to (D) <u>the party</u>.
38. Although he (A) <u>likes Chinese</u> (B) <u>food</u> very much, (C) <u>but</u> he doesn't like (D) <u>dumplings</u>.
39. My (A) <u>most</u> favorite (B) <u>sport</u> is to (C) <u>play</u> (D) <u>table tennis</u>.
40. (A) <u>In</u> Wednesday afternoon, (B) <u>some</u> students (C) <u>took part in</u> (D) <u>a speech activity</u>.

Ⅲ. Cloze. (20%)

Body language is the quiet, secret and most powerful language of all! It speaks __41__ than words. According to specialists, our bodies sent out more messages than we realize. In fact, non-verbal (非言语) communication takes up about 50% of __42__ we really mean. And body language is particularly important when we attempt to communicate across cultures. Indeed, what is called body language is so __43__ a part of us that it is actually often unnoticed. And misunderstandings occur as a result of it. For example, different societies treat the distance between people __44__. Northern Europeans usually do not like having bodily contact (接触) even with friends, and certainly not with __45__. People from Latin American countries, on the other hand, touch each other quite a lot. Therefore, it is possible that in a conversation, it may look like a Latino is following a Norwegian (挪威人) all over the room. The Latino, __46__ to express friendship, will keep moving __47__. The Norwegian, very probably seeing this as pushiness, will keep backing away — which the Latino will in return regard as __48__.

Clearly, a great deal is going on when people talk. And only a part of it is in the words themselves. And when parties are from different cultures, there's a strong possibility of misunderstanding. But __49__ the situation, the best advice is to obey the Golden Rule: treat others as you would like to __50__.

41. A. straighter   B. louder   C. harder   D. further
42. A. which   B. that   C. what   D. why
43. A. well   B. far   C. much   D. long
44. A. difference   B. differently   C. differ   D. different
45. A. strangers   B. relatives   C. neighbors   D. enemies
46. A. tried   B. trying   C. try   D. tries

47.	A. closer	B. faster	C. in	D. away
48.	A. weakness	B. carelessness	C. friendliness	D. coldness
49.	A. wherever	B. whenever	C. however	D. whatever
50.	A. treating	B. be treating	C. be treated	D. treat

IV. Translation. (15%)

51. _____ (这个小村再也不是过去的样子), since great changes have taken place there.

52. They had a dissatisfying trip and especially _____ (他们讨厌住的那个旅馆).

53. My uncle treats the little girl _____ (好像她是他的女儿).

54. _____ (表演刚开始) when the lights all went out.

55. To her, _____ (离开这个城市是忘却过去的唯一办法).

Test 3

I. Multiple Choice. (45%)

1. I could speak _____ Japanese _____ Chinese, so I had to talk with him in English.
   A. not only; but also B. either; or
   C. neither; nor D. both; and

2. This is _____ he has told me, but I am not sure whether it is true or not.
   A. what B. that C. how D. why

3. When are you going to get the roof _____?
   A. repair B. repairing C. to repair D. repaired

4. I believe that these mountains _____ with trees in a few years' time.
   A. cover B. are covered
   C. will cover D. will be covered

5. It is _____ who is waiting for you.
   A. him B. his C. he D. himself

6. When asked _____ he needed most, the businessman said that he wanted to succeed in selling all his goods.
   A. whom B. what C. which D. why

7. I used to _____ cards at night, but now I like reading at night.
   A. playing B. played
   C. be played D. play

8. —What about playing football this afternoon?
   —I would rather _____ at home than _____ football. It's too hot outside.
   A. stay; play B. stay; to play
   C. to stay; to play D. to stay; play

9. The boy _____ in the teacher's office was caught _____ in the exam.
   A. stood; to cheat B. stood; cheating
   C. standing; cheating D. standing; to cheat

10. _____ twice by the dog, the postman refused to send mails to this family.
    A. Being bitten B. Having bitten
    C. Having been bitten D. Biting

11. —Will you get there by _____ train? —No, I'll take _____ taxi.
    A. /; a B. a; the C. /; / D. the; a

12. In our city, _____ middle school students want to work as a doctor in the future.
    A. two thousands B. two thousand of
    C. thousand of D. thousands of

13. —I can't stop smoking, doctor?
    —For your health, I'm afraid you _____.
    A. may B. need C. have to D. must

· 196 ·

14. —Sonia, is this your dictionary?
    —Oh, no, it's not _____. Ask Li Lei. He is looking for _____.
    A. me; hers   B. mine; him   C. my; her   D. mine; his
15. Father's Day came _____ June 10th this year.
    A. at   B. on   C. in   D. during
16. Some of my classmates dislike doing homework and seldom _____ finish homework on time.
    A. they do   B. do they   C. they are   D. are they
17. Jin Yong is one of the greatest _____ Kung-fu writers, and he is still _____.
    A. living; alive   B. living; living   C. alive; living   D. alive; alive
18. If I knew his telephone number, I _____ him immediately.
    A. would call   B. will call   C. called   D. call
19. It was in the early morning _____ the accident happened.
    A. what   B. that   C. when   D. which
20. I _____ my key so I don't know how I can get into my house.
    A. lost   B. have lost   C. was lost   D. had lost
21. I admit I didn't understand _____.
    A. what you are talking about   B. what you were talking about
    C. what are you talking about   D. what were you talking about
22. A group of _____ are asking two _____ the way to the nearest hotel.
    A. Frenchmans; Germen   B. Germen; Frenchmen
    C. Frenchmen; Germans   D. Germans; Frenchmans
23. Everything goes right, _____?
    A. doesn't it   B. does it   C. won't it   D. don't they
24. No sooner _____ he arrived at the office than he _____ to start out on another business trip.
    A. has; asked   B. has; was asked
    C. had; asked   D. had; was asked
25. Jack enjoyed himself so much _____ he traveled in Italy last month.
    A. that   B. which   C. where   D. when
26. Is this centre _____ our coworkers visited the modern devices several days ago?
    A. the one where   B. where
    C. that   D. the one that
27. I never seem to lose any weight, _____ hard I try.
    A. even if   B. no matter how
    C. as if   D. ever since
28. —It's a long story, but you can hardly find new words in it.
    —Good! _____ it will be too hard for children.
    A. And   B. But   C. Or   D. So

29. _____ tall the boy is! He can play volleyball very well.
    A. How   B. What   C. What a   D. How a
30. I can't put up with him. He always talks as if he _____ everything.
    A. has known   B. had known   C. knew   D. knows

II. Error Identification. (20%)

31. (A) The train is leaving (B) for (C) a few minutes so we (D) must hurry.
32. The machines (A) made in China (B) are not (C) more expensive than (D) that made in Japan.
33. I (A) won't go to (B) the party (C) because I (D) haven't invited.
34. There (A) are (B) plenty of food. You can (C) have as much (D) as you like.
35. I (A) am doing my (B) homework. (C) Would you mind (D) turn down the radio?
36. Traveling (A) by car is convenient (B) unless you have (C) somewhere (D) to park.
37. (A) As they (B) walk (C) along the street, they looked (D) in to the shop windows.
38. I (A) wish I (B) knew that Gary (C) was ill. I (D) would have gone to see him.
39. You (A) can go to this hotel, (B) which is (C) more cheaper than (D) other hotels in this town.
40. Sue (A) has (B) a lot of friends, (C) many of them are (D) of great help to her in study.

II. Cloze. (20%)

Wise buying is a positive way in which you can make your money go further. The way you go about __41__ an article or a service can actually save your money or can add to the cost.

Take the __42__ example of a hairdryer. If you are buying a hairdryer, you might think that you are making the __43__ buy if you choose one __44__ look you like and which is also the cheapest __45__ price. But when you get it home, you may find that it takes twice as long as a more expensive model to dry your hair. The cost of your time could well make your hairdryer the most expensive __46__ of all. So what principles should you adopt when you go out __47__ ?

If you keep your home, your car or any valuable possession in excellent condition, you will be saving money in the long run. Before you buy a new appliance, talk to someone who owns one. If you can, use it or borrow it to check __48__ it suits your particular purpose. Before you buy __49__ expensive item, do check the price and __50__ is on sale. If possible, choose from three items or three estimates.

41. A. purchase   B. to purchase   C. purchased   D. purchasing
42. A. similar   B. simple   C. single   D. easy
43. A. good   B. better   C. best   D. well
44. A. whose   B. what   C. which   D. that
45. A. on   B. in   C. with   D. for
46. A. that   B. other   C. one   D. another
47. A. to shop   B. shops   C. shop   D. to shopping
48. A. that   B. what   C. if   D. why
49. A. the   B. a   C. ×   D. an

· 198 ·

50. A. which　　　　　B. what　　　　　C. that　　　　　D. how

IV. Translation. (15%)

51. In his opinion, _____ (成功的秘诀在于努力工作).

52. _____ (科技发展比我们预期的快得多) in terms of changes.

53. Did you remember _____ (我们共同生活和学习的那个夏天)?

54. To a certain degree, _____ (他参加还是不参加这个比赛) made no difference.

55. By the end of next May, my elder sister _____ (在这个城市四年了).

Test 4

I. Multiple Choice. (45%)

1. There were _____ many people in the street _____ the firefighters could not get close to the building.
   A. such; that B. so; that C. too; to D. not; until

2. Experiments of this kind _____ in both Russia and Italy before the First World War.
   A. had conducted
   B. had been conducted
   C. have conducted
   D. have been conducted

3. The author _____ "the Father of English Poetry", decided to write a new poem.
   A. called
   B. was calling
   C. was called
   D. had called

4. Not only _____ studying famous paintings, but he also enjoys classical music. That's why Kate likes him.
   A. Neal likes
   B. likes Neal
   C. does Neal like
   D. does Neal likes

5. It is high time that everyone here _____ something for the poor old man.
   A. does B. do C. has done D. did

6. It is _____ difficult to succeed in this field.
   A. many too B. too many C. much too D. too much

7. _____ from the top of the mountain, the tall building looks like a stick.
   A. Seeing B. Seen C. See D. Saw

8. They are considering _____ the destination from Beijing to Shanghai.
   A. changing B. change C. to changing D. to change

9. We should pay special attention to the directions when _____ the listening comprehension.
   A. doing B. to do C. being done D. having done

10. He told me that he didn't mean _____ the window, and I believed him.
    A. breaking B. having broken C. broke D. to break

11. There's _____ dictionary on _____ desk by your side.
    A. a; the B. the; the C. a; a D. the; a

12. He took several _____ of the statue.
    A. photo B. photos C. photoes D. a photo

13. —Shall I inform him of the change of the schedule right now?
    —I'm afraid you _____, in case he comes late for the meeting.
    A. will B. must C. can D. may

14. People say that our eyes are like _____ of an angel's.
    A. that B. this C. those D. these

15. The baby was born _____ 10 o'clock _____ February 15th.
    A. in; on B. in; at C. on; at D. at; on

· 200 ·

16. He won _____ place in the international competition.
    A. ninth   B. the ninth   C. nine   D. nineth
17. On the top of the page _____ in red ink.
    A. a message be written   B. was written a message
    C. were written a message   D. a message were written
18. By the time she reaches Shanghai, we _____ there for a week.
    A. have been staying   B. have stayed
    C. will stay   D. will have stayed
19. I _____ some cleaning in my room at this time yesterday.
    A. am doing   B. do
    C. was doing   D. have done
20. Mary is a careless girl, but Jack did his homework _____ than her.
    A. more careless   B. more carelessly   C. careless   D. carelessly
21. The children are too young to understand _____.
    A. what does Christmas mean   B. what Christmas does mean
    C. what mean Christmas does   D. what Christmas means
22. It is _____ he would like to turn to for help whenever he is in trouble.
    A. I that   B. my that   C. me who   D. mine whom
23. They used a special method to keep the machine _____ day and night.
    A. being work   B. works   C. to work   D. working
24. _____ over-drinking, Jim had a bad accident and ended up in hospital.
    A. Owing to   B. In addition to   C. In order to   D. So as to
25. I don't think that the farmers can work out that problem, _____?
    A. don't I   B. do I   C. can't they   D. can they
26. It was _____ she said _____ disappointed me.
    A. that; that   B. what; what   C. what; that   D. that; what
27. It is from the sun _____ we get light and heat.
    A. which   B. that   C. where   D. how
28. The pen _____ she is writing is mine.
    A. with that   B. in which   C. with which   D. in that
29. If it _____ for the snow, we _____ the mountain yesterday.
    A. did not; could have climb
    C. hadn't been; could have climbed   B. were not; would climb
    D. Had been; could climb
30. A number of people _____ a poor sense of direction.
    A. is   B. are   C. has   D. have

II. Error Identification. (20%)

31. Wu Feng,(A) <u>the man in blue</u> (B) <u>over</u> there, (C) <u>is</u> a colleague of (D) <u>my</u>.
32. (A) <u>Could</u> you (B) <u>like</u> to (C) <u>go</u> to the cinema (D) <u>with</u> me tomorrow afternoon?
33. Last Saturday she(A) <u>said</u> she (B) <u>will</u> not go to the party (C) <u>if</u> it (D) <u>rained</u>.

34. (A) Can you tell me some (B) informations (C) about the tour (D) to Beijing?
35. Everything(A) there (B) were very (C) beautiful, and we (D) had a good time.
36. (A) I don't know (B) what present he will (C) buy(D) to me on my birthday.
37. It is(A) probably that the disease (B) has(C) a genetic (D) element.
38. Finally, the thief (A) handed everything (B) which he (C) had stolen(D) to the police.
39. Taiwan is(A) an island (B) with beautiful scenery, and (C) it's the (D) most large island in China.
40. Only when Jane (A) arrived at the company (B) she realized (C) that she(D) had left the documents at home.

Ⅲ. Cloze. (20%)

Many people believe everything or almost everything they read in newspaper or hear on radio. A few years ago I read a story about a husband and wife __41__ made a terrible mistake. They had gone shopping and had taken their small baby __42__ with them. After they had finished their shopping, they returned to their car to go home. __43__ they reached their car, they put the baby in the plastic baby carrier that he rode in for safety. The couple then drove off in their car toward home. After they had driven a few miles, they glanced at the back seat to see __44__ the baby was. __45__ their surprise, the baby was not there. According to the story, the couple had put the plastic seat and the baby on the top of the car but had __46__ him inside the car. They had driven away with the baby on the top of the car.

The couple drove back towards the store but did not find the baby. They called the police, and the police said that they __47__ the baby and that the baby was fine. The baby had fallen from the top of the car but had been protected by his plastic seat. The grateful couple took their baby home, being always careful after that.

There was something wrong with the story. It was not true. Stories such as this one __48__ often reported in newspaper and on radio and television. Because they are read and heard in places that usually report the truth, many people believe them. People also believe them because, like the story __49__, they have something unusual or frightening about them. __50__ is strange is that newspaper and radio reporters also believe them.

41. A. whom   B. who   C. whose   D. what
42. A. around   B. away   C. along   D. alone
43. A. After   B. While   C. Before   D. Since
44. A. why   B. how   C. what   D. that
45. A. To   B. In   C. With   D. Without
46. A. forgot to put   B. forgotten to put
    C. forgot putting   D. forgotten putting
47. A. had   B. have had   C. have   D. had had
48. A. have   B. has   C. is   D. are
49. A. tells   B. to tell   C. tell   D. told
50. A. Why   B. How   C. What   D. That

IV. **Translation.** (15%)

51. _____ (当他写作有问题时), the writer will stop to take a break.

52. _____ (你所做的而非你所说的) left me a deep impression.

53. Although its government has put stress on the economic reform, _____ (这个国家比其他国家发展得慢).

54. We have to make efforts to _____ (防止水被污染).

55. My friend would have worked in the company, _____ (如果她多花一点时间准备面试的话).

Test 5

I. Multiple Choice. (45%)

1. Mary said that she _____ to Tibet?
   A. has never been B. has never gone
   C. had never been D. had never gone
2. It was with the help of the local guide _____ the mountain climber was rescued.
   A. who   B. that   C. when   D. how
3. He had his leg _____ in the match the day before yesterday.
   A. to break   B. breaking   C. break   D. broken
4. The secretary worked late into the night, _____ a welcome speech for the headmaster.
   A. to prepare   B. was preparing   C. preparing   D. prepared
5. _____ that we couldn't catch up with the train.
   A. So fast ran he   B. So fast did he run
   C. Such fast ran he   D. Such fast did he run
6. Nearly _____ of the earth _____ covered by sea.
   A. three fourth; is   B. three fourths; is
   C. three fourth; are   D. three fourths; are
7. _____ in diving requires not only skill and balance but also carefulness and concentration.
   A. Succeed   B. Successful   C. Successfully   D. Success
8. This garden is _____ that one.
   A. ten times as long as   B. ten times as longer as
   C. ten times longer as   D. as long as ten times
9. The police asked the children _____ cross the street _____ the traffic lights turned green.
   A. not to; until   B. not; before   C. don't; when   D. not; after
10. I really ought to go on a diet. I _____ on so much weight since I gave up jogging.
    A. put   B. am putting   C. have put   D. had put
11. I don't know if he _____ to the English corner, but I'll ask him about that when he _____ to the class.
    A. goes; will come   B. will go; will come
    C. goes; comes   D. will go; comes
12. _____ we have enough evidence, we can't win the case.
    A. Once   B. As long as   C. Unless   D. Since
13. I first met Tom 10 years ago. He _____ in a radio factory at that time.
    A. had worked   B. has been working
    C. was working   D. has worked
14. A new cinema _____ here. They hope to finish it in a few months.
    A. will be built   B. is being built

C. has been built   D. is built

15. Only by practicing a few hours every day _____ be able to master the language.
    A. you will   B. will you   C. you can   D. can you

16. You did not let me drive. If we _____ in turn, you _____ so tired.
    A. drove; didn't get   B. drove; wouldn't get
    C. had driven; wouldn't have got   D. were driving; wouldn't get

17. These red apples taste _____.
    A. to be good   B. to be well   C. well   D. good

18. He used to _____ in a small village, but now he has been used to _____ in the big city.
    A. live; living   B. live; live   C. living; living D. living; live

19. _____ the painting, he gave a sigh of relief.
    A. Finishing   B. Has finished   C. Being finished D. Having finished

20. This listening material, together with its CD-ROMs, _____ well.
    A. sells   B. sell   C. is sold   D. are sold

21. More college graduates would like to work in _____ west part of our country _____ next year.
    A. the; the   B. /; /   C. /; the   D. the; /

22. In _____ time, those mountains will be covered with trees, too.
    A. few years   B. a few years'   C. a few year   D. a few year's

23. Mr. Franklin, in addition to three salesmen, _____ to attend the meeting.
    A. are planning   B. were planning   C. have planned   D. plans

24. —Can I come this evening or tomorrow morning?
    —_____ is OK. I'm free today and tomorrow.
    A. Either   B. Neither   C. Both   D. None

25. The apple trees have lots of big apples _____ them and some birds are singing _____ the trees.
    A. in; on   B. at; in   C. on; in   D. with; through

26. When you are reading, make a note of _____ you think is of great importance.
    A. which   B. that   C. what   D. when

27. Danny left word with my secretary _____ he would call again in the afternoon.
    A. who   B. that   C. as   D. which

28. He'll never forget the people and the place _____ he has ever visited.
    A. which   B. where   C. whom   D. that

29. There _____ in this room.
    A. are too many furniture   B. is too much furniture
    C. are too much furnitures   D. is too many furnitures

30. _____ his applying for numerous jobs, he is still out of work.
    A. Despite   B. In spite   C. Although   D. Though

Ⅱ. Error Identification. (20%)

31. (A) Shortly after the accident, two (B) dozens of policemen (C) were sent to the spot to (D) keep order.

32. In order to find the (A) missed boy, villagers (B) have been doing (C) all they can (D) over the past six hours.

33. Sales of CDs (A) have greatly increased since (B) the early 1990s, when people (C) have begun to enjoy (D) the advantages of this new technology.

34. Though the city is (A) modern, (B) but there are still (C) some problems, such as air pollution and (D) crowdedness.

35. John (A) did not have time (B) to go to the concert last night, (C) because he was (D) busy to prepare for his examination.

36. He will (A) spend two hours (B) play (C) football (D) this afternoon.

37. Children (A) younger than (B) five years old (C) has emotional needs that only (D) loving parents can meet.

38. I enjoyed the movie (A) so much that I wish I (B) have read the book (C) from which it was (D) made.

39. (A) In recent years travel companies have (B) succeeded in selling us the idea (C) that the farther we go, (D) the better holiday will have.

40. The news (A) which he (B) won the table tennis match is (C) well known to almost (D) everyone in his hometown.

Ⅲ. Cloze. (20%)

Many animals use some kind of "language". They use signals and the signals have meanings. For example, when a bee has found some food, it goes back to __41__ home. It is difficult for a bee to tell the other bees __42__ the food is, but it can do a little dancing, which tells the bees how far away it is.

Some animals show what they feel by __43__ sounds. It is not difficult to know __44__ a dog is angry or not because it barks. Birds make several different sounds and __45__ has the meaning. Sometimes we humans make sounds in __46__ same way. We make sounds like "Oh" to show how we feel about something or we drop something __47__ our feet.

We humans have languages. We have words. These words have meaning of things, action, feeling or ideas. We are able to give each other some __48__ , to tell other people what we think or how we feel about something. By writing down words, we can remember what has happened or send messages to people far away.

Languages, like people, live and die. If a language is not used by people, it is called a dead language. This language cannot live and grow because __49__ speaks it.

A living language, of course, is often spoken by people today. It grows and changes with time. New words __50__ , and some old words have new meanings.

41. A. it   B. it's   C. its   D. itself

42. A. that   B. where   C. how   D. why

43. A. making	B. to make	C. make	D. made
44. A. if	B. that	C. why	D. whether
45. A. each	B. every	C. all	D. some
46. A. a	B. an	C. ×	D. the
47. A. in	B. on	C. over	D. at
48. A. informations	B. information	C. advices	D. suggestion
49. A. someone	B. anyone	C. no one	D. everyone
50. A. are created	B. create	C. are creating	D. will create

Ⅳ. **Translation.** (15%)

51. It was a pity that _____ (他没有意识到健康比财富重要).

52. A doctor _____ (是在医院工作的人).

53. _____ (如果我们充分利用时间), there would have been more than 24 hours a day.

54. My friend was _____ (对我如此生气以至于他一句话没说就走了).

55. She told that _____ (自从她出生以来就没未见过她的父亲).

Appendix

英语不规则动词表

英语动词按其过去式和过去分词的构成方式可分为规则动词(Regular Verbs)和不规则动词(Irregular Verbs)。规则动词的过去式和过去分词由词尾加-ed 构成,而不规则动词的变化因词而异。现按照其变化规律列表如下。

Group 1. AAA

动词原形 do	过去式 did	过去分词 done	词义
bet	bet	bet	打赌
bid	bid	bid	出价,投标
broadcast	broadcast	broadcast	广播,播放
burst	burst	burst	爆炸
cast	cast	cast	投,掷
cost	cost	cost	花费
cut	cut	cut	割,切
hurt	hurt	hurt	受伤
hit	hit	hit	打,撞
let	let	let	让
put	put	put	放下
read	read	read	读
rid	rid/ridded	rid/ridded	使摆脱;解除,免除
set	set	set	安排,安置
spread	spread	spread	展开,传播;涂
spit	spit/spat	spit/spat	吐痰
split	split	split	分裂;分开
shut	shut	shut	关上,闭起,停止营业

Group 2. AAB

动词原形	过去式	过去分词	词义
beat	beat	beaten	打败

Group 3. ABA

动词原形	过去式	过去分词	词义
become	became	become	变
come	came	come	来
run	ran	run	跑
overcome	overcame	overcome	克服;战胜

Group 4. ABB

(1) 原形→ought →ought[ɔːt]

动词原形	过去式	过去分词	词义
bring	brought	brought	带来
buy	bought	bought	买
fight	fought	fought	打架
think	thought	thought	思考,想
seek	sought	sought	寻找,追求,搜索

(2) 原形→aught →aught[ɔːt]

动词原形	过去式	过去分词	词义
catch	caught	caught	捉,抓
teach	taught	taught	教

(3) 原形→lt/pt/ft→lt/pt/ft

动词原形	过去式	过去分词	词义
creep	crept	crept	匍匐而行
feel	felt	felt	感到
keep	kept	kept	保持
leave	left	left	离开
sleep	slept	slept	睡觉
smell	smelt	smelt	闻
sweep	swept	swept	扫
weep	wept	wept	哭泣

(4) 在动词原形后加一个辅音字母 d、t 或 ed 构成过去式或过去分词

动词原形	过去式	过去分词	词义
burn	burnt	burnt	燃烧
deal	dealt	dealt	解决
dream	dreamed/dreamt	dreamed/dreamt	做梦
hear	heard	heard	听见
hang	hanged/hung	hanged/hung	绞死 悬挂
learn	learned/learnt	learned/learnt	学习
light	lit/lighted	lit/lighted	点燃,照亮
mean	meant	meant	意思
shine	shined/shone	shined/shone	使照耀,使发光
show	showed	showed/shown	展示,给……看
smell	smelled/smelt	smelled/smelt	闻,嗅
speed	sped/speeded	sped/speeded	加速
spell	spelled/spelt	spelled/spelt	拼写

(5) 变其中一个元音字母

动词原形	过去式	过去分词	词义
dig	dug	dug	掘(土),挖(洞、沟等)
feed	fed	fed	喂
get	got	got/gotten	得到
hold	held	held	拥有,握住,支持
lead	led	led	引导,带领,领导
meet	met	met	遇见
sit	sat	sat	坐
shoot	shot	shot	射击
spit	spit/spat	spit/spat	吐痰
stick	stuck	stuck	插进,刺入,粘住,
win	won	won	赢

(6) 把动词原形的最后一个辅音字母"d"改为"t"构成过去式或过去分词

动词原形	过去式	过去分词	词义
build	built	built	建筑
bend	bent	bent	弯曲,屈服
lend	lent	lent	借给

续表

动词原形	过去式	过去分词	词义
rebuild	rebuilt	rebuilt	改建,重建
send	sent	sent	送
spend	spent	spent	花费

(7)其他

动词原形	过去式	过去分词	词义
find	found	found	发现,找到
lay	laid	laid	下蛋,放置
pay	paid	paid	付
say	said	said	说
stand	stood	stood	站
understand	understood	understood	明白
lose	lost	lost	失去
have	had	had	有
make	made	made	制造
sell	sold	sold	卖
tell	told	told	告诉
retell	retold	retold [riːˈtəuld]	重讲,重复,复述
wind	wound	wound	缠绕;转动

Group 5. ABC

(1)原形→过去式→原形+(e)n

动词原形	过去式	过去分词	词义
bite	bit	bitten	咬
blow	blew	blown	吹
drive	drove	driven	驾驶
draw	drew	drawn	画画
eat	ate	eaten	吃
fall	fell	fallen	落下
give	gave	given	给
forgive	forgave	forgiven	原谅,饶恕
grow	grew	grown	生长
know	knew	known	知道
mistake	mistook	mistaken	弄错;误解,

续表

动词原形	过去式	过去分词	词义
overeat	overate	overeaten	(使)吃过量
prove	proved	proven	证明,证实,试验
take	took	taken	拿
throw	threw	thrown	抛,扔
ride	rode	ridden	骑
rise	rose	risen	升起
see	saw	seen	看见
shake	shook	shaken	摇动,震动
show	showed	showed/shown	展示
write	wrote	written	写

(2)原形→过去式→过去式+(e)n

动词原形	过去式	过去分词	词义
awake	awoke	awoken	唤醒;唤起;觉悟
break	broke	broken	打破
choose	chose	chosen	选择
get	got	got/gotten	得到
hide	hid	hidden	隐藏
forget	forgot	forgotten	忘记
freeze	froze	frozen	冷冻,结冰;感到严寒
speak	spoke	spoken	说
steal	stole	stolen	偷
wake	woke	waken	叫醒

(3)变单词在重读音节中的元音字母"i"分别为"a"(过去式)和"u"(过去分词),[i→a →u]

动词原形	过去式	过去分词	词义
begin	began	begun	开始
drink	drank	drunk	喝
ring	rang	rung	打电话
sing	sang	sung	唱
shrink	shrank	shrunk	收缩
sink	sank	sunk	下沉,沉没
swim	swam	swum	游泳

(4)其他

动词原形	过去式	过去分词	词义
be(am, is, are)	was/ were	been	是
bear	bore	born/borne	负担;忍受
do	did	done	做
fly	flew	flown	飞
go	went	gone	去
lie	lay	lain	躺
lie	lied	lied	说谎
strike	struck	stricken	重击
wear	wore	worn	穿

Reference Version

Key to Chapter 2

I. Fill in the blanks with what you have learnt. 填空。(5%)
1. 专有名词 2. 普通名词 3. 抽象名词 4. 不可数名词 5. 可数名词

II. Fill in the blanks with the noun's syntactic function. 填写名词的句法功能。(10%)
1. 宾语 2. 主语 3. 表语 4. 同位语 5. 连词
6. 补语 7. 定语 8. 状语 9. 表语 10. 宾语

III. Error identification. 错误辨识。(20%)
1. C 2. B 3. B 4. A 5. C
6. D 7. C 8. C 9. B 10. B

IV. Multiple choice. 单项选择。(30%)
1. C 2. D 3. B 4. B 5. D
6. A 7. C 8. A 9. D 10. C
11. B 12. A 13. C 14. D 15. A
16. D 17. C 18. A 19. B 20. B

V. Fill in the blanks with the correct forms of nouns in the following passage. 填写名词的正确形式。(20%)
1. name 2. stories 3. Carolina 4. life 5. years
6. jobs 7. money 8. prison 9. New York 10. readers'

VI. Translate the following sentences into English. 将下列句子译成英语。(15%)

1. Many people/persons come to China (in order) to learn Chinese and the country's culture.
2. Only pupils/students in primary school celebrate June 1st, the Children's Day.
3. Now the main question is how to find his lost sheep.
4. He has to borrow some money, because there is no money at home.
5. —How much are two cups of coffee? /How much do two cups of coffee cost?
   —About five dollars.

Key to Chapter 3

I. Write the corresponding Ordinal Numbers for the following Cardinal Numbers in English. 用英语写出下列基数词相应的序数词。(5%)

基数词	序数词	基数词	序数词
one	first	thirty	thirtieth

· 214 ·

续表

基数词	序数词	基数词	序数词
two	second	forty-one	forty-first
three	third	five	fifth
eight	eighth	twelve	twelfth
nine	ninth	twenty-six	twenty-sixth

Ⅱ. Write the following time expressions in English. 用英语表示下列时间。(10%)

1. 5:30 <u>five thirty/half past five</u>
2. 7:15 <u>seven fifteen/a quarter past seven</u>
3. 8:25 <u>eight twenty-five/twenty-five past eight</u>
4. 9:50 <u>nine fifty/ten to ten</u>
5. 10:45 <u>ten forty-five/fifteen to eleven</u>
6. 7:20 <u>seven twenty/twenty past seven</u>
7. 12:10 <u>twelve ten/ten past twelve</u>
8. 11:35 <u>eleven thirty-five/twenty-five to twelve</u>
9. 5:55 <u>five fifty-five/five to six</u>
10. 6:00 <u>six o'clock</u>

Ⅲ. Error identification. 错误辨识。(20%)

1. B   2. A   3. B   4. D   5. C
6. C   7. B   8. A   9. B   10. C

Ⅳ. Multiple choice. 单项选择。(30%)

1. D   2. B   3. C   4. C   5. A
6. C   7. B   8. B   9. B   10. B
11. A   12. B   13. D   14. B   15. C
16. B   17. C   18. B   19. B   20. B

Ⅴ. Fill in the blanks with the correct forms of words. 填写词的正确形式。(20%)

1. A   2. B   3. B   4. D   5. A
6. B   7. B   8. A   9. A   10. C

Ⅵ. Translate the following sentences into English. 将下列句子译成英语。(15%)

1. This is my first visit to America.
2. They won the third prize in the debating competition.
3. Four-fifths of the work has been <u>done/finished</u>.
4. The opening ceremony of the 29th Olympic Games was held on <u>the 8th of August/August (the) 8th</u>, 2008 in Beijing.
5. Shall we meet at the cinema at <u>ten to seven/six fifty</u>?

Key to Chapter 4

Ⅰ. Write the comparative and superlative forms of the words. 写出下列词的比较级和高级。(5%)

原级	比较级	最高级
happy	happier	happiest
wild	wilder	wildest
long	longer	longest
short	shorter	shortest
big	bigger	biggest

Ⅱ. Fill in the blanks with proper forms of the given words. 用所给词的适当形式填空。(10%)

1. wider; brighter　　2. fewer　　　　3. better　　　　4. best　　　　　5. largest
6. angrier　　　　　7. careful　　　　8. many　　　　　9. much　　　　10. more; less

Ⅲ. Error identification. 错误辨识。(20%)

1. C　　　　　2. C　　　　　3. C　　　　　4. B　　　　　5. C
6. B　　　　　7. B　　　　　8. C　　　　　9. B　　　　　10. D

Ⅳ. Multiple choice. 单项选择。(30%)

1. C　　　　　2. C　　　　　3. C　　　　　4. D　　　　　5. C
6. C　　　　　7. C　　　　　8. B　　　　　9. C　　　　　10. D
11. A　　　　12. A　　　　13. D　　　　14. A　　　　15. D
16. C　　　　17. B　　　　18. B　　　　19. D　　　　20. B

Ⅴ. Fill in the blanks with the correct forms of adjectives and adverbs. 填写形容词和副词的正确形式。(20%)

1. farther　　　　2. farthest　　　3. small　　　　4. beautiful　　　5. largest
6. most beautiful　7. busiest　　　8. more　　　　　9. happy　　　　10. better

Ⅵ. Translate the following sentences into English. 将下列句子译成英语。(15%)

1. This shirt is much cheaper than that one.
2. This song soon became more and more popular.
3. The more books you read, the smarter you will become.
4. Jim is one of the best students in our school.
5. My dictionary is thicker than his (dictionary).

Key to Chapter 5

Ⅰ. Fill in the blanks with "a" or "an". 用 a 或者 an 填空。(5%)

1. a　　　　　2. a　　　　　3. an　　　　　4. a　　　　　5. an
6. a　　　　　7. an　　　　　8. a　　　　　9. a　　　　　10. a

Ⅱ. Fill in the blanks with "a", "an" or "the". 用 a, an 或者 the 填空。(10%)

1. a; the　　　2. a　　　　　3. a; an　　　4. a　　　　　5. an; the
6. The; the　　7. the; the　　8. an　　　　9. the　　　　10. the

Ⅲ. Error identification. 错误辨识。(20%)

1. C　　　　　2. C　　　　　3. B　　　　　4. D　　　　　5. D
6. B　　　　　7. D　　　　　8. B　　　　　9. D　　　　　10. B

Ⅳ. Multiple choice. 单项选择。(30%)

1. B　　　　　2. A　　　　　3. B　　　　　4. D　　　　　5. D
6. B　　　　　7. A　　　　　8. B　　　　　9. B　　　　　10. C
11. D　　　　12. D　　　　13. A　　　　14. A　　　　15. B
16. C　　　　17. D　　　　18. D　　　　19. D　　　　20. B

Ⅴ. Fill in the blanks with the proper articles. 用适当的冠词填空。(20%)

1. An　　　　　2. a　　　　　3. a　　　　　4. the　　　　　5. the
6. a　　　　　7. The　　　　8. a　　　　　9. the　　　　　10. the

Ⅵ. Translate the following sentences into English. 将下列句子译成英语。(15%)

1. There is a store here. I want to buy a pen in the store.

2. That is the best film in the world.
3. We cannot see the sun at night.
4. Please pass me the eraser on the desk. /Please pass the eraser on the table to me.
5. She has a good command of several foreign languages.

Key to Chapter 6

I. Fill in the blanks with what you have learnt. 填空。(5%)
1. he   2. you   3. her   4. they   5. us

II. Fill in the blanks with the pronoun's syntactic function. 填写代词的句法功能。(10%)
1. 宾语   2. 定语   3. 主语   4. 表语   5. 宾语
6. 主语   7. 表语   8. 表语   9. 宾语   10. 同位语

III. Error identification. 错误辨识。(20%)
1. A   2. B   3. C   4. A   5. A
6. C   7. B   8. D   9. C   10. D

IV. Multiple choice. 单项选择。(30%)
1. D   2. D   3. D   4. C   5. A
6. C   7. B   8. A   9. D   10. D
11. D   12. B   13. A   14. B   15. A
16. D   17. A   18. B   19. A   20. D

V. Fill in the blanks with the correct forms of pronouns. 填写代词的正确形式。(20%)
1. His   2. He   3. his   4. mine   5. His
6. mine   7. her   8. her   9. my   10. Our

VI. Translate the following sentences into English. 将下列句子译成英语。(15%)
1. The girl who visited me last week is my sister.
2. It took him four hours to find his key. /He spent four hours (in) finding his key.
3. — Whose dog is over there? — It is mine. /It is my dog.
4. Which of you is the monitor?
5. Because it is raining, nobody wants to do the job.

Key to Chapter 7

I. Fill in the blanks with prepositions. 用介词填空。(10%)
1. for   2. from   3. at   4. about   5. to
6. like   7. as   8. into 9. with   10. after

II. Fill in the blanks with the prepositional phrases' syntactic function. 填写介词短语的句法功能。(5%)
1. 定语   2. 状语   3. 宾语补足语   4. 状语   5. 表语

III. Error identification. 错误辨识。(20%)
1. A   2. B   3. D   4. A   5. D
6. C   7. B   8. D   9. B   10. C

IV. Multiple choice. 单项选择。(30%)
1. A   2. C   3. D   4. C   5. D
6. A   7. B   8. D   9. A   10. C

11. B	12. B	13. A	14. D	15. C
16. B	17. B	18. C	19. A	20. C

V．Fill in the blanks with the correct prepositions. 填写正确的介词。（20%）

1. for	2. by	3. of	4. in	5. by
6. to	7. in	8. in	9. on	10. as

VI．Translate the following sentences into English. 将下列句子译成英语。（15%）

1. The earth goes around the sun.
2. That little girl went through the forest by herself/on her own.
3. You shouldn't be afraid of making mistakes.
4. Classmates get along well with each other.
5. These toy planes are made of bamboo.

Key to Chapter 8

I．Combine the two sentences with the conjuctions in the brackets. 用括号内连词连接句子。（5%）

1. She cooked on both Saturday and Sunday.
2. She neither did her homework nor watched TV.
3. You may either leave at once or wait till tomorrow.
4. I neither care who did this nor want to know what happened.
5. You apologize to me either face to face or by writing a letter.

II．Match the two parts of the sentences. 连线。（10%）

A. 1. E	2. C	3. D	4. B	5. A
B. 6. C	7. B	8. A	9. E	10. D

III．Error identification. 错误辨识。（20%）

1. D	2. C	3. A	4. D	5. D
6. B	7. C	8. B	9. B	10. D

IV．Multiple choice. 单项选择。（30%）

1. A	2. B	3. C	4. D	5. A
6. D	7. B	8. C	9. D	10. A
11. C	12. B	13. B	14. C	15. A
16. D	17. B	18. B	19. D	20. C

V．Fill in the blanks with proper conjunctions. 用恰当的连词填空。（20%）

1. as well as	2. either	3. but/yet/however	4. not only	5. both
6. or	7. otherwise	8. than	9. and	10. nor/neither

VI．Translate the following sentences into English. 将下列句子译成英语。（15%）

1. Put on your coat, or/otherwise you will get a cold.
2. A good company should not only offer employees good salaries but also care for their health.
3. The plan sounds almost impossible, but he decides to try.
   /The plan sounds almost impossible; however, he decides to try.
4. I will either stay at school to study or go to work in this summer vacation/holiday.
5. The result of the game was neither very good nor very bad.

Key to Chapter 9

Ⅰ. Fill in the blanks with what you have learnt. 填空。(5%)

1. could 2. might 3. must 4. will 5. shall

Ⅱ. Fill in the blanks with the verb category. 填写动词种类。(10%)

1. 情态动词 2. 及物动词 3. 系动词 4. 助动词 5. 情态动词
6. 系动词 7. 不及物动词 8. 情态动词 9. 情态动词 10. 助动词

Ⅲ. Error identification. 错误辨识。(20%)

1. C 2. B 3. D 4. B 5. B
6. B 7. A 8. A 9. D 10. A

Ⅳ. Multiple choice. 单项选择。(30%)

1. B 2. B 3. C 4. A 5. D
6. D 7. A 8. C 9. A 10. B
11. B 12. D 13. D 14. C 15. D
16. B 17. C 18. C 19. B 20. A

Ⅴ. Fill in the blanks with the correct forms of verbs. 填写动词的正确形式。(20%)

1. developing 2. lack 3. is 4. solve 5. developed
6. take 7. appears 8. continues 9. has 10. needed

Ⅵ. Translate the following sentences into English. 将下列句子译成英语。(15%)

1. To some extent/degree, I don't think that you are right.
2. We all know that the news couldn't be true.
3. How long have you been a teacher since your graduation/you graduated?
4. Would/Will you marry me if you love me?
5. Mr. Li plays football, while his wife plays the violin every day.

Key to Chapter 10

Ⅰ. Fill in each blank with one word. 填空。(5%)

1. was having 2. had seen 3. would have taken 4. would buy 5. is

Ⅱ. Fill in the blanks with the proper forms of the given verbs in the brackets. 用括号里所给动词的适当形式填空。(10%)

1. goes 2. are playing 3. was listening 4. will bring 5. has taken
6. would come 7. had left 8. lost 9. has gone 10. rains

Ⅲ. Error identification. 错误辨识。(20%)

1. C 2. A 3. B 4. C 5. D
6. A 7. C 8. A 9. C 10. A

Ⅳ. Multiple choice. 单项选择。(30%)

1. B 2. B 3. C 4. A 5. C
6. C 7. C 8. D 9. D 10. A
11. C 12. C 13. A 14. B 15. A
16. C 17. C 18. A 19. D 20. D

Ⅴ. Fill in the blanks with the correct forms of the given verbs. 填写动词的正确形式。(20%)

1. looks 2. was chosen 3. am 4. have seen 5. likes

6. said   7. will do   8. pays   9. encourages   10. watched

Ⅵ. Translate the following sentences into English. 将下列句子译成英语。(15%)
1. The football match has begun when we got there.
2. Now Mr. Li is attending a conference/meeting in New York.
3. David said that he would get married soon.
4. By the end of this term, these students will have learned English for six years.
5. It is the second time that I have been to Beijing.

Key to Chapter 11

Ⅰ. Fill in the blanks with the right forms. 用正确形式填空。(5%)
1. has been translated   2. was used up   3. is spent
4. will be interviewed   5. is reported

Ⅱ. Change the following sentences into Passive Voice. 请将下列句子变成被动语态。(10%)
1. In the old days teapots were used (by people) to make tea.
2. The longest bridge is being built (by the workers) now.
3. The TV will be turned off (by me) as soon as the football game ends.
4. He was told (by the doctor) to take the medicine three times a day.
5. A calculator cannot be used (by you) in the maths test.
6. The little girl was sad because she was laughed at (by some boys).
7. Many pictures have been taken by my friend since he got his first camera.
8. She said that the day would be remembered (by her) forever.
9. Human beings were made to have early fires on the earth (by nature).
10. Her clothes were being washed (by my sister) at seven yesterday evening.

Ⅲ. Error identification. 错误辨识。(20%)
1. B   2. C   3. B   4. A   5. B
6. D   7. B   8. C   9. B   10. D

Ⅳ. Multiple choice. 单项选择。(30%)
1. A   2. C   3. B   4. A   5. D
6. A   7. C   8. C   9. B   10. B
11. A   12. B   13. C   14. D   15. B
16. A   17. C   18. A   19. D   20. C

Ⅴ. Fill in the blanks with the correct forms of verbs. 填写动词的正确形式。(20%)
1. come   2. see   3. are asked   4. are placed   5. throw
6. went   7. were   8. was covered   9. found   10. be punished

Ⅵ. Translate the following sentences into English. 将下列句子译成英语。(15%)
1. This library had been built by the end of last year.
2. Don't worry. Your car is being repaired now.
3. It is reported that the price this year has increased by 10%.
4. The problem between you and him should be solved in time.
5. The important meeting/conference will be held/is to be held in Beijing next week.

Key to Chapter 12

I. Fill in the blanks with what you have learnt. 填空。(5%)
1. 动名词　　2. 人称　　3. ing　　4. 动词　　5. 过去分词

II. Fill in the blanks with the Non-Finite Verbs' syntactic function. 填写非谓语动词的句法功能。(10%)
1. 宾语　　2. 主语　　3. 定语　　4. 主语　　5. 定语
6. 宾补　　7. 状语　　8. 定语　　9. 表语　　10. 定语

III. Error identification. 错误辨识。(20%)
1. D　　2. A　　3. D　　4. C　　5. C
6. A　　7. B　　8. D　　9. C　　10. A

IV. Multiple choice. 单项选择。(30%)
1. A　　2. A　　3. B　　4. B　　5. A
6. A　　7. D　　8. D　　9. C　　10. A
11. C　　12. A　　13. C　　14. B　　15. C
16. B　　17. C　　18. D　　19. B　　20. D
21. C　　22. D　　23. D　　24. B　　25. D
26. B　　27. C　　28. A　　29. D　　30. D

V. Fill in the blanks with the right forms of the verbs given in brackets. 用括号里动词的正确形式填空。(20%)
1. to eat　　2. pointed　　3. cut　　4. growing　　5. being killed
6. to make　　7. growing　　8. will be　　9. are gone　　10. to live

VI. Translate the following sentences into English. 将下列句子译成英语。(15%)
1. It is a waste of money buying anything we don't need.
2. Thank you very much for helping me (to) find the lost wallet.
3. Something unexpected seemed to have happened to their family.
4. They sent me an invitation, inviting me to a birthday party.
5. Not having heard from her parents for a long time, Alice looks forward to receiving their letter.

Key to Chapter 13

I. Change the word form according to the requirement. 按照要求变词形。(5%)
1. happiness　　2. dishonest　　3. European　　4. purify　　5. movement

II. Fill in the blanks with right forms. 用正确形式填空。(10%)
1. death　　2. sadly　　3. satisfaction　　4. latest　　5. permission
6. silent　　7. freedom　　8. Honestly　　9. healthy　　10. enrich

III. Error identification. 错误辨识。(20%)
1. D　　2. C　　3. A　　4. B　　5. D
6. D　　7. B　　8. B　　9. A　　10. A

IV. Multiple choice. 单项选择。(30%)
1. C　　2. B　　3. A　　4. D　　5. A
6. C　　7. B　　8. C　　9. D　　10. B
11. D　　12. A　　13. C　　14. B　　15. A
16. A　　17. C　　18. B　　19. D　　20. D

Ⅴ. **Fill in the blanks with the correct forms of words in the following passage.** 填写正确形式。（20%）

1. decided   2. impossible   3. admission   4. finally   5. determined
6. graduated   7. education   8. serious   9. America   10. difficult

Ⅵ. **Translate the following sentences into English.** 将下列句子译成英语。（15%）

1. Although she was born in America, she is still a Chinese.
2. These studies/researches show that 0.2 percent/a fifth of one percent of women are color-blind.
3. Most of people are interested in this interesting story.
4. A few days ago haze was so serious that many children got sick/ill.
5. —The singer looks very nervous.
   —We are also looking at him nervously.

Key to Chapter 14

Ⅰ. **Turn the following sentences into negative sentences.** 将下列句子变成否定句。（5%）

1. They needn't go to work every day.
2. Mrs. Black doesn't usually take an umbrella with her when she goes out.
3. These students cannot/can't speak Japanese very well.
4. The guide won't/will not take you to the Summer Palace.
5. Jessica didn't write an email to her professor last Sunday.

Ⅱ. **Turn the following sentences into exclamatory sentences.** 将下列各句变成感叹句。（10%）

1. What an inspiring story (it is)!
2. What a hospitable housewife (she is)!
3. How exciting the news is!
4. How early his grandpa gets up every day!
5. How expensive these cars are!
6. How excellently they did in the examination!
7. How carelessly she drives her car!
8. What an exciting football game they are watching now!
9. How comfortable the weather in Kunming is!
10. What a good time we had in summer vacation!

Ⅲ. **Error identification.** 错误辨识。（20%）

1. A   2. A   3. B   4. A   5. C
6. B   7. A   8. A   9. B   10. A

Ⅳ. **Multiple choice.** 单项选择。（30%）

1. A   2. B   3. B   4. C   5. B
6. C   7. C   8. A   9. B   10. B
11. D 12. C 13. D 14. A 15. C
16. B 17. C 18. D 19. A 20. C

Ⅴ. **Cloze.** 完形填空。（20%）

1. B   2. A   3. C   4. A   5. D
6. B   7. D   8. A   9. C   10. C

Ⅵ. **Translate the following sentences into English.** 将下列句子译成英语。（15%）

1. —Must I finish this plan this month?

—No, you needn't.
2. How slowly the old woman/lady walks!
3. She speaks both Chinese and English. What a smart girl (she is)! /How smart she is!
4. The old people don't use expensive mobile phones.
5. What a long way it is from Xinjiang to Beijing! /How far it is from Xinjiang to Beijing!

Key to Chapter 15

I. Complete the following imperative sentences. 完成下列祈使句。(5%)
1. <u>Let's have</u> a rest.
2. <u>Let him</u> leave.
3. <u>Remember this significant</u> day.
4. Please <u>take the/this umbrella</u>.
5. <u>Keep off</u> the lawn. /<u>Don't step on</u> the lawn.

II. Add tag questions to the following sentences. 完成下列反义疑问句。(10%)
1. This computer doesn't work well, <u>does it</u>?
2. Nothing can stop us from pursuing our dreams, <u>can it</u>?
3. She used to live in her hometown, <u>didn't she/usedn't she</u>?
4. Rose would like to go shopping with us, <u>wouldn't she</u>?
5. Professor Smith seldom has lunch at school, <u>does he</u>?
6. Your answer is incorrect, <u>isn't it</u>?
7. Such things ought not to be allowed, <u>ought they</u>?
8. Robert has picked up a lot of English when he worked in London, <u>hasn't he</u>?
9. Those are your daughter's colour pens, <u>aren't they</u>?
10. Everyone knows the answer, <u>don't they</u>?

III. Error identification. 错误辨识。(20%)

| 1. B | 2. C | 3. B | 4. A | 5. C |
| 6. A | 7. A | 8. B | 9. D | 10. D |

IV. Multiple choice. 单项选择。(30%)

1. D	2. D	3. A	4. B	5. C
6. B	7. C	8. C	9. C	10. B
11. A	12. B	13. D	14. A	15. C
16. D	17. B	18. A	19. B	20. B

V. Cloze. 完形填空。(20%)

1. B	2. A	3. C	4. C	5. D
6. A	7. D	8. B	9. A	10. C
11. D	12. C	13. A	14. B	15. C
16. A	17. A	18. B	19. D	20. B

VI. Translate the following sentences into English. 将下列句子译成英语。(15%)
1. How do we go to the office, by bus or on foot?
2. Never stop the love for reading <u>because books are like wise teachers as well as good friends/because books are not only good friends but also wise teachers in our life</u>.
3. —What's the date today?

—June 2nd. /It's June 2nd.
4. —What day is it today?
    — It's Wednesday.
5. How important/significant (good) health/well-being (it is)! Let's exercise/keep fit together.

Key to Chapter 16

Ⅰ. Fill in the blanks with what you have learnt. 填空。(5%)
1. 单数形式　　2. 复数形式　　3. 一致　　4. 意义一致　　5. 就近一致

Ⅱ. Fill in the blanks with the correct forms. 填写正确形式。(10%)
1. is　　　　　2. are　　　　　3. are　　　　　4. has　　　　　5. was
6. am　　　　　7. are　　　　　8. is　　　　　　9. stands　　　　10. is

Ⅲ. Error identification. 错误辨识。(20%)
1. B　　　　　2. B　　　　　3. D　　　　　4. C　　　　　5. A
6. A　　　　　7. C　　　　　8. B　　　　　9. C　　　　　10. C

Ⅳ. Multiple choice. 单项选择。(30%)
1. C　　　　　2. B　　　　　3. A　　　　　4. B　　　　　5. D
6. C　　　　　7. D　　　　　8. A　　　　　9. B　　　　　10. A
11. B　　　　12. C　　　　13. D　　　　14. C　　　　15. A
16. D　　　　17. C　　　　18. B　　　　19. A　　　　20. A

Ⅴ. Fill in the blanks with the correct forms in the following passage. 在短文中填写正确形式。(20%)
1. are　　　　2. is　　　　　3. is　　　　　4. has　　　　　5. like
6. helps　　　7. gives　　　　8. is　　　　　9. are　　　　　10. comes

Ⅵ. Translate the following sentences into English. 将下列句子译成英语。(15%)
1. Reading is a necessary skill at any time.
2. What heroes have done is remembered by history and their countries.
3. Nobody but them really helps themselves (to) get out of trouble, when they are in trouble.
4. Either he or his neighbors have been invited to the Christmas party several times.
5. —What is there in the box?
    —There is just some rice(in the box).

Key to Chapter 17

Ⅰ. Fill in the blanks by choosing proper words from the brackets. 选词填空。(5%)
1. that　　　　2. how　　　　3. what　　　　4. that　　　　5. what

Ⅱ. Decide what clause the underlined part is. 判断画线部分是什么从句。(10%)
1. 宾语从句　　2. 宾语从句　　3. 主语从句　　4. 同位语从句　　5. 主语从句
6. 主语从句　　7. 主语从句　　8. 表语从句　　9. 同位语从句　　10. 表语从句

Ⅲ. Error identification. 错误辨识。(20%)
1. D　　　　　2. A　　　　　3. A　　　　　4. B　　　　　5. C
6. D　　　　　7. D　　　　　8. C　　　　　9. B　　　　　10. D

Ⅳ. Multiple choice. 单项选择。(30%)
1. C　　　　　2. C　　　　　3. B　　　　　4. A　　　　　5. B

6. B	7. D	8. B	9. D	10. A
11. A	12. C	13. A	14. C	15. A
16. B	17. A	18. A	19. B	20. C

V. Fill in the blanks with proper conjunctions. 用适当的引导词填空。（20%）

1. that/which	2. that	3. that	4. whether	5. What
6. that	7. what	8. whether	9. what	10. that

VI. Translate the following sentences into English. 将下列句子译成英语。（15%）

1. We all agreed to the plan that we should go to travel together.
2. They think that wherever they will hold the party is OK.
3. What Tom said was different from what he did.
4. It is said that our company is going to hold a big party.
5. She is always worried about whether she will lose her job.

Key to Chapter 18

Ⅰ. Use attributive clauses to connect the following sentences. 用定语从句连接句子。（5%）

1. I'm writing a letter to Mike whose mother is ill.
2. This happened in 1947 when/in which I was a baby.
3. This is the reason why/for which I didn't come here.
4. The city is Chengdu in which/where he lives.
5. The house (that/which) we bought last month is very nice.

Ⅱ. Replace the words in italics by when, where or why. 用 when, where 或 why 代替句中斜体部分单词。（10%）

1. when	2. where	3. why; when	4. when	5. where
6. where	7. when	8. where	9. when	10. why

Ⅲ. Error identification. 错误辨识。（20%）

1. D	2. A	3. B	4. B	5. A
6. A	7. C	8. C	9. D	10. C

Ⅳ. Multiple choice. 单项选择。（30%）

1. A	2. D	3. C	4. D	5. C
6. C	7. B	8. B	9. D	10. B
11. D	12. D	13. D	14. C	15. A
16. B	17. A	18. B	19. A	20. D

V. Fill in the blanks with the correct relatives. 填写正确的关系词。（20%）

1. who	2. whom	3. that	4. which/that	5. that/which; who
6. that	7. which	8. which/that	9. that	10. who

Ⅵ. Translate the following sentences into English. 将下列句子译成英语。（15%）

1. (which/that) you lost yesterday
2. (that) I have ever read
3. (which/that) my sister bought for me
4. which/that is grown/grows in the south of China
5. who gave them the report last Saturday

Key to Chapter 19

I. Choose the right word. 选择正确的词。(5%)

1. despite   2. Since   3. in order that   4. By the time   5. for fear of

II. Fill in the blanks with the words in the box. 选词填空。(10%)

1. In spite of   2. before   3. however   4. By the time   5. as though
6. even if   7. due to   8. so long as   9. in case   10. Now that

III. Error identification. 错误辨识。(20%)

1. A   2. B   3. C   4. A   5. C
6. D   7. D   8. B   9. C   10. C

IV. Multiple choice. 单项选择。(30%)

1. A   2. D   3. A   4. B   5. A
6. C   7. B   8. B   9. D   10. C
11. B   12. A   13. C   14. B   15. A
16. A   17. D   18. B   19. D   20. C

V. Choose the proper conjunction. 选择正确的连词。(20%)

1. when   2. that   3. as if   4. before   5. Even though
6. as   7. As soon as   8. lest   9. In order to   10. which

VI. Translate the following sentences into English. 将下列句子译成英语。(15%)

1. <u>Whatever/No matter what</u> happens, just stay here and keep silent.

2. The child talked to us as if he <u>was/had been an adult/a grown-up.</u>

3. Some students spend so much time on cell phones that they don't have time to study.

4. He didn't start to learn Russian until he was fifty (years old).

5. As long as we are alive, we won't give up.

Key to Chapter 20

I. Fill in the blanks with what you have learnt. 填空。(5%)

1. 被强调的部分   2. 谓语动词   3. 主语   4. does   5. 原形

II. Choose the correct forms to fill in the blanks. 选择正确形式填空。(10%)

1. that   2. did   3. that   4. do   5. was
6. can we   7. It   8. that   9. do   10. that

III. Error identification. 错误辨识。(20%)

1. A   2. C   3. D   4. B   5. A
6. C   7. A   8. B   9. B   10. C

IV. Multiple choice. 单项选择。(30%)

1. A   2. D   3. C   4. B   5. C
6. D   7. B   8. A   9. B   10. C
11. B   12. B   13. D   14. C   15. A
16. B   17. C   18. A   19. C   20. D

V. Emphasize the underlined parts in the following sentences. 强调句中画线部分。(20%)

1. It was in Xiamen that I saw the sea for the first time.

2. It was not until daybreak that the typist finished typing the documents.

3. It is our meeting that will be held in this room.
4. Great changes did take place in my hometown between 2000 and 2016.
5. It was when she was about to go to bed that the telephone rang.
   /Only when she was about to go to bed did the telephone ring.
6. It was the course that he took because of his keen interest in literature.
7. It was by taxi that Mary went to work the day before yesterday.
8. What he says does disappoint his parents.
9. Our lateness did make her serve dinner an hour later than usual.
10. Every day we do spend half an hour reading books.

Ⅵ. Translate the following sentences into English. 将下列句子译成英语。(15%)
1. It is the national policy that enables these poor children to go to school.
2. The French poet did come to my hometown ten years ago.
3. It was some economic reasons that forced him to give up his study.
4. It is in the small village that the traditional culture can be felt easily.
5. We do need to protect the environment in order that/so that we can have a better life.

Key to Chapter 21

Ⅰ. Fill in the blanks with right words. 填空。(5%)
1. needn't   2. shouldn't   3. should   4. must   5. might

Ⅱ. Fill in the blanks with the proper forms of the given verbs. 用所给动词的适当形式填空。(10%)
1. had arrived   2. should go/went   3. had not helped   4. (should) come
5. (should) drink   6. (should) be sent   7. had not forgotten   8. were; would go
9. had been; would have been settled   10. had happened

Ⅲ. Error identification. 错误辨识。(20%)
1. C   2. A   3. D   4. B   5. D
6. D   7. B   8. C   9. D   10. B

Ⅳ. Multiple choice. 单项选择。(30%)
1. B   2. B   3. D   4. A   5. D
6. D   7. D   8. C   9. A   10. D
11. C   12. D   13. C   14. A   15. A
16. A   17. C   18. A   19. A   20. D

Ⅴ. Fill in the blanks according to the given Chinese in the brackets. 根据括号中所给汉语补全句子。(20%)
1. would have been destroyed
2. would have met me
3. were to sink
4. should have studied
5. (should) make plans/a plan
6. didn't do anything
7. must have lost them
8. started to work
9. wouldn't be able

10. could have gone/had gone

Ⅵ. Translate the following sentences into English. 将下列句子译成英语。(15%)

1. If I had the money, I would travel round the world.
2. They insisted that the old man (should) be sent to hospital.
3. I wish (that) I could fly in the sky one day.
4. Although they met for the first time, they talked as if they had been old friends.
5. If he had had another choice four years ago, he would be a doctor now.

Key to Chapter 22

Ⅰ. Change the following sentences into inverted ones. 将下列的句子改为倒装句。(5%)

1. In the front of the room <u>sat the director</u>.
2. So frightened <u>was he that he did not dare to move an inch</u>.
3. Only when the war was over <u>was he able to get back to work</u>.
4. Hidden under the bed <u>were some bags of gold</u>.
5. Seldom <u>does the child read newspapers</u>.

Ⅱ. Fill in the blanks with the proper forms. 用正确形式填空。(10%)

1. will you	2. do I	3. do we think	4. do I feel	5. did he know
6. had we reached	7. he likes	8. jumped the cat	9. was he excited	10. did she find

Ⅲ. Error identification. 错误辨识。(20%)

1. C	2. B	3. C	4. C	5. C
6. B	7. B	8. B	9. A	10. A

Ⅳ. Multiple choice. 单项选择。(30%)

1. A	2. D	3. D	4. B	5. A
6. C	7. B	8. D	9. C	10. C
11. A	12. B	13. B	14. D	15. B
16. A	17. B	18. C	19. C	20. A

Ⅴ. Fill in the blanks with the correct forms. 填写正确形式。(20%)

1. do I want	2. have I been	3. come	4. be	5. make
6. receive	7. finished	8. developed	9. provide	10. will I

Ⅵ. Translate the following sentences into English. 将下列句子译成英语。(15%)

1. She likes listening to music and so do I.
2. There lived an old farmer in that house.
3. Only when she came home did he learn the news.
4. Child as he is, he knows more than others.
5. No sooner had I got to my office than the meeting began/started..

Key to Chapter 23

Ⅰ. Fill in each blank with a right word. 填空。(5%)

1. He said that <u>he</u> <u>was</u> having breakfast.
2. Tina <u>told</u> me that she <u>had</u> <u>been</u> to Hainan Island five times.
3. She said that <u>she</u> <u>had</u> <u>gone</u> to work with her sister.
4. He told me that he <u>had</u> met her <u>two</u> <u>days</u> before.

5. He asked if/whether I had read the book fifteen days before.

II. Change the following sentences from direct speech into indirect speech. 请将下列直接引语变为间接引语。(10%)

1. You told me that you had seen the film two days before.
2. He told his younger sister that she might go with him.
3. The teacher told his class not to waste their time.
4. The man said that he would be very busy that day.
5. He told the old woman not to worry and that he would take her there.
6. The man asked me how many times I had been there.
7. Mary said that she joined the League in August 1998.
8. He asked if/whether I was interested in playing the piano.
9. The teacher said that the sun is larger than the moon.
10. The boy told us that he usually gets up at six every day.

III. Error identification. 错误辨识。(20%)

1. C	2. B	3. C	4. C	5. C
6. C	7. B	8. D	9. D	10. B

IV. Multiple choice. 单项选择。(30%)

1. D	2. B	3. D	4. A	5. B
6. C	7. D	8. B	9. C	10. C
11. C	12. B	13. A	14. A	15. D
16. B	17. C	18. A	19. C	20. C

V. Fill in the blanks with the correct forms of indirect speech in the following passage. 填写间接引语的正确形式。(20%)

1. had finished   2. had not written   3. would   4. the next day
5. should be punctual   6. that day   7. (should) go   8. finished
9. was   10. was

VI. Translate the following sentences into English. 将下列句子译成英语。(15%)

1. The teacher told us the moon moves around the earth.
2. Jack asked me where I was going when he met me in the street.
3. He told me on Tuesday that he had been to my home the day before.
4. Peter said he must go to work.
5. I asked him whether he would go to cinema or stay at home that night.

Key to Test 1

I. Multiple Choice (45%)

1. B	2. D	3. A	4. A	5. B
6. B	7. B	8. C	9. A	10. A
11. B	12. A	13. B	14. B	15. D
16. A	17. D	18. D	19. C	20. B
21. D	22. B	23. A	24. C	25. B
26. D	27. D	28. A	29. B	30. C

Ⅱ. **Error Identification**（20%）

| 31. C | 32. B | 33. C | 34. C | 35. C |
| 36. A | 37. B | 38. A | 39. C | 40. B |

Ⅲ. **Cloze**（20%）

| 41. A | 42. D | 43. B | 44. B | 45. C |
| 46. A | 47. B | 48. D | 49. B | 50. C |

Ⅳ. **Translation**（15%）

51. the greater progress you will make

52. did people invent the first computer

53. The first place (that) we want to visit

54. drinking much boiled water (should) be good for health

55. I had so few friends that I felt lonely

Key to Test 2

Ⅰ. **Multiple Choice**（45%）

1. A	2. C	3. B	4. C	5. B
6. D	7. D	8. B	9. A	10. B
11. A	12. C	13. B	14. C	15. B
16. D	17. C	18. B	19. A	20. C
21. D	22. C	23. B	24. C	25. D
26. C	27. B	28. C	29. D	30. D

Ⅱ. **Error Identification**（20%）

| 31. A | 32. C | 33. A | 34. C | 35. A |
| 36. D | 37. C | 38. C | 39. A | 40. A |

Ⅲ. **Cloze**（20%）

| 41. B | 42. C | 43. C | 44. B | 45. A |
| 46. B | 47. A | 48. D | 49. D | 50. C |

Ⅳ. **Translation**（15%）

51. The small village is no longer what it used to be

52. they hated the hotel in which/where they lived

53. as if she were his daughter

54. The performance had hardly begun/Hardly had the performance begun

55. leaving the city is the only way to forget the past/the only way to forget the past is leaving the city

Key to Test 3

Ⅰ. **Multiple Choice**（45%）

1. C	2. A	3. D	4. D	5. C
6. B	7. D	8. A	9. C	10. C
11. A	12. D	13. C	14. D	15. B
16. B	17. A	18. A	19. B	20. B
21. B	22. C	23. A	24. D	25. D
26. A	27. B	28. C	29. A	30. C

Ⅱ. Error Identification (20%)
31. B   32. D   33. D   34. A   35. D
36. B   37. B   38. B   39. C   40. C

Ⅲ. Cloze (20%)
41. D   42. B   43. C   44. A   45. B
46. C   47. A   48. C   49. D   50. B

Ⅳ. Translation (15%)
51. the secret of success lies in <u>working hard/hard working</u>
52. Science and technology develop <u>far/much</u> faster than we expect
53. the summer <u>in which/when</u> we lived and studied together
54. <u>whether he took part in the match or not</u>
55. <u>will have been in/will have lived in</u> the city for four years

Key to Test 4

Ⅰ. Multiple Choice (45%)
1. B   2. B   3. A   4. C   5. D
6. C   7. B   8. A   9. A   10. D
11. A   12. B   13. B   14. C   15. D
16. B   17. B   18. D   19. C   20. B
21. D   22. C   23. D   24. A   25. D
26. C   27. B   28. C   29. C   30. D

Ⅱ. Error Identification (20%)
31. D   32. A   33. B   34. B   35. B
36. D   37. A   38. B   39. D   40. B

Ⅲ. Cloze (20%)
41. B   42. C   43. C   44. B   45. A
46. B   47. A   48. D   49. D   50. C

Ⅳ. Translation (15%)
51. When he has problems <u>in/with</u> writing
52. What you have done, instead of what you have said
53. the country develops more slowly than <u>any other country/other countries</u>
54. <u>prevent /stop/keep</u> water from being polluted
55. if she had spent much time (in) preparing her interview

Key to Test 5

Ⅰ. Multiple Choice (45%)
1. C   2. B   3. D   4. C   5. B
6. B   7. D   8. A   9. A   10. C
11. D   12. C   13. C   14. B   15. B
16. C   17. D   18. A   19. D   20. A
21. D   22. B   23. D   24. A   25. C
26. C   27. B   28. D   29. B   30. A

II. Error Identification (20%)

| 31. B | 32. A | 33. C | 34. B | 35. D |
| 36. C | 37. C | 38. B | 39. D | 40. A |

III. Cloze (20%)

| 41. C | 42. B | 43. A | 44. D | 45. A |
| 46. D | 47. B | 48. B | 49. C | 50. A |

IV. Translation (15%)

51. he does not realize/is not aware that health is more important than wealth

52. is a person who/that works in a hospital/is a person working in a hospital

53. If we had made full use of time

54. so angry with me that he left without (saying) a word

    too angry with me to say a word before leaving

55. she had never seen her father since she was born